enVision Mathematics

Volume 1 Topics 1–4

Authors

Robert Q. Berry, III
Professor of Mathematics Education, Department of Curriculum, Instruction and Special Education, University of Virginia, Charlottesville, Virginia

Zachary Champagne
Assistant in Research Florida Center for Research in Science, Technology, Engineering, and Mathematics (FCR-STEM) Jacksonville, Florida

Eric Milou
Professor of Mathematics Rowan University, Glassboro, New Jersey

Jane F. Schielack
Professor Emerita Department of Mathematics Texas A&M University, College Station, Texas

Jonathan A. Wray
Mathematics Supervisor, Howard County Public Schools, Ellicott City, Maryland

Randall I. Charles
Professor Emeritus Department of Mathematics San Jose State University San Jose, California

Francis (Skip) Fennell
Professor Emeritus of Education and Graduate and Professional Studies, McDaniel College Westminster, Maryland

SAVVAS
LEARNING COMPANY

SAVVAS
LEARNING COMPANY

ISBN-13: 978-0-13-498355-4
ISBN-10: 0-13-498355-6

3 20

CONTENTS

TOPICS

1. Use Positive Rational Numbers

2. Integers and Rational Numbers

3. Numeric and Algebraic Expressions

4. Represent and Solve Equations and Inequalities

5. Understand and Use Ratio and Rate

6. Understand and Use Percent

7. Solve Area, Surface Area, and Volume Problems

8. Display, Describe, and Summarize Data

DIGITAL RESOURCES

Go Online

INTERACTIVE STUDENT EDITION
Access online or offline

VISUAL LEARNING
Interact with visual learning animations

ACTIVITY
Use with *Solve & Discuss It, Explore It,* and *Explain It* activities and Examples

VIDEOS
Watch clips to support *3-Act Mathematical Modeling* Lessons and *enVision® STEM Projects*

PRACTICE
Practice what you've learned and get immediate feedback

TUTORIALS
Get help from *Virtual Nerd* any time you need it

MATH TOOLS
Explore math with digital tools

GAMES
Play math games to help you learn

KEY CONCEPT
Review important lesson content

GLOSSARY
Read and listen to English and Spanish definitions

ASSESSMENT
Show what you've learned

realize.
Everything you need for math anytime, anywhere.

TOPIC 1

Use Positive Rational Numbers

TOPIC 2
Integers and Rational Numbers

TOPIC 3
Numeric and Algebraic Expressions

TOPIC 4
Represent and Solve Equations and Inequalities

TOPIC 5

Understand and Use Ratio and Rate

TOPIC 6

Understand and Use Percent

TOPIC 7

Solve Area, Surface Area, and Volume Problems

TOPIC 8

Display, Describe, and Summarize Data

Math Practices and Problem Solving Handbook

 The **Math Practices and Problem Solving Handbook** is available online.

1 Make sense of problems and persevere in solving them.

2 Reason abstractly and quantitatively.

3 Construct viable arguments and critique the reasoning of others.

4 Model with mathematics.

5 Use appropriate tools strategically.

6 Attend to precision.

7 Look for and make use of structure.

8 Look for and express regularity in repeated reasoning.

A rancher is building a fence on a 200-foot stretch of field. He has 30 posts and 225 feet of fencing. He plans to place one post every 6 feet. Will he have enough posts to build the fence as planned?

6 ft
Post
Post

200 feet
stretch
of field

Total 30 posts

Can I see a pattern or structure in the problem or solution strategy?
I can see that one post is needed for every 6 feet.

How can I use the pattern or structure I see to help me solve the problem?
I can write an equation that finds the number of posts needed for 200 feet.

Other questions to consider:
- Are there attributes in common that help me?
- Can I see the expression or equation as a single object or as a composition of several objects?

Do I notice any repeated calculations or steps? Each post covers a 6-foot distance.

Are there general methods that I can use to solve the problem? I can divide the total distance to be fenced by the distance between posts.

Other questions to consider:
- What can I generalize from one problem to another?
- Can I derive an equation from a series of data points?
- How reasonable are the results that I am getting?

Math Practices

1 ▶ **Make sense of problems and persevere in solving them.**

Mathematically proficient students:

- can explain the meaning of a problem
- look for entry points to begin solving a problem
- analyze givens, constraints, relationships, and goals
- make conjectures about the solution
- plan a solution pathway
- think of similar problems, and try simpler forms of the problem
- evaluate their progress toward a solution and change pathways if necessary
- can explain similarities and differences between different representations
- check their solutions to problems.

2 ▶ **Reason abstractly and quantitatively.**

Mathematically proficient students:

- make sense of quantities and their relationships in problem situations:
  - They *decontextualize*—create a coherent representation of a problem situation using numbers, variables, and symbols; and
  - They *contextualize* – attend to the meaning of numbers, variables, and symbols in the problem situation
- know and use different properties of operations to solve problems.

3 ▶ **Construct viable arguments and critique the reasoning of others.**

Mathematically proficient students:

- use definitions and problem solutions when constructing arguments
- make conjectures about the solutions to problems
- build a logical progression of statements to support their conjectures and justify their conclusions
- analyze situations and recognize and use counterexamples
- reason inductively about data, making plausible arguments that take into account the context from which the data arose
- listen or read the arguments of others, and decide whether they make sense
- respond to the arguments of others
- compare the effectiveness of two plausible arguments
- distinguish correct logic or reasoning from flawed, and—if there is a flaw in an argument—explain what it is
- ask useful questions to clarify or improve arguments of others.

4 ▶ Model with mathematics.

Mathematically proficient students:

- can develop a representation—drawing, diagram, table, graph, expression, equation–to model a problem situation
- make assumptions and approximations to simplify a complicated situation
- identify important quantities in a practical situation and map their relationships using a range of tools
- analyze relationships mathematically to draw conclusions
- interpret mathematical results in the context of the situation and propose improvements to the model as needed.

5 ▶ Use appropriate tools strategically.

Mathematically proficient students:

- consider appropriate tools when solving a mathematical problem
- make sound decisions about when each of these tools might be helpful
- identify relevant mathematical resources, and use them to pose or solve problems
- use tools and technology to explore and deepen their understanding of concepts.

6 ▶ Attend to precision.

Mathematically proficient students:

- communicate precisely to others
- use clear definitions in discussions with others and in their own reasoning
- state the meaning of the symbols they use
- specify units of measure, and label axes to clarify their correspondence with quantities in a problem
- calculate accurately and efficiently
- express numerical answers with a degree of precision appropriate for the problem context.

7 ▶ Look for and make use of structure.

Mathematically proficient students:

- look closely at a problem situation to identify a pattern or structure
- can step back from a solution pathway and shift perspective
- can see complex representations, such as some algebraic expressions, as single objects or as being composed of several objects.

8 ▶ Look for and express regularity in repeated reasoning.

Mathematically proficient students:

- notice if calculations are repeated, and look both for general methods and for shortcuts
- maintain oversight of the process as they work to solve a problem, while also attending to the details
- continually evaluate the reasonableness of their intermediate results.

USE POSITIVE RATIONAL NUMBERS

? Topic Essential Question

How can you fluently add, subtract, multiply, and divide decimals? How can you multiply and divide fractions?

Topic Overview

Topic Vocabulary

• reciprocal

Lesson Digital Resources

INTERACTIVE STUDENT EDITION
Access online or offline.

VISUAL LEARNING ANIMATION
Interact with visual learning animations.

ACTIVITY Use with *Solve & Discuss It, Explore It*, and *Explain It* activities, and to explore Examples.

VIDEOS Watch clips to support *3-Act Mathematical Modeling Lessons* and *STEM Projects*.

Go online

Stocking UP

▶ Stocking Up

When shopping for groceries, it is useful to set a budget and stick to it. Otherwise, you may buy items you do not need and spend more money than you should. Some people avoid overspending by bringing cash to pay for their groceries. If you bring $50 in cash, you cannot spend $54. Think about this during the 3-Act Mathematical Modeling lesson.

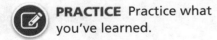 **PRACTICE** Practice what you've learned.

 KEY CONCEPT Review important lesson content.

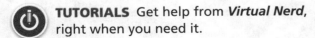 **TUTORIALS** Get help from *Virtual Nerd*, right when you need it.

 GLOSSARY Read and listen to English/Spanish definitions.

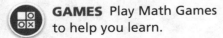 **MATH TOOLS** Explore math with digital tools.

 ASSESSMENT Show what you've learned.

 **GAMES** Play Math Games to help you learn.

enVision® STEM Project

Did You Know?

Engineering is the **application of math and science** to solve problems.

Engineers solve problems by designing and building products, materials, machinery, structures, transportation vehicles, and so many other things.

Engineers work in nearly every area from chemical and electrical engineering to biomedical and oceanographic engineering.

Engineers design equipment to **make you safer.**

Engineers find ways to **improve and enhance performance** of all kinds of products.

Engineers help **keep you healthy.**

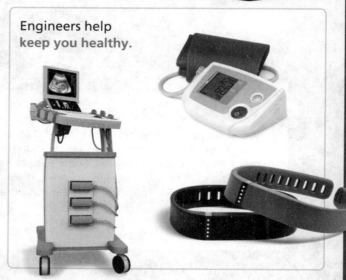

Your Task: Improve Your School

Think like an engineer! Take a walk around the inside and the outside of your school building. Make a list of specific things or areas that need improvement. Then choose one idea and do some background research to gain an understanding of factors that might impact improvement efforts. In the next topic, you and your classmates will learn about and implement the engineering design process to propose possible ways to make the improvements.

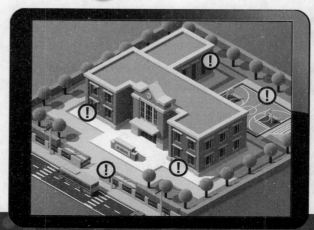

Review What You Know!

Vocabulary

Choose the best term from the box to complete each definition.

| compatible numbers |
| decimal |
| divisor |
| estimate |
| quotient |

1. Numbers that are easy to compute mentally are _____ .

2. The number used to divide is the _____ .

3. A(n) _____ is an approximate answer.

4. The result of a division problem is a(n) _____ .

Whole Number Operations

Calculate each value.

5. $4\overline{)348}$

6. $9{,}007 - 3{,}128$

7. 35×17

8. $7{,}964 + 3{,}872$

9. $22\overline{)4{,}638}$

10. 181×42

Mixed Numbers and Fractions

Write each mixed number as a fraction. Write each fraction as a mixed number.

11. $8\frac{1}{3}$

12. $5\frac{3}{5}$

13. $2\frac{5}{8}$

14. $3\frac{4}{9}$

15. $\frac{24}{7}$

16. $\frac{43}{9}$

17. $\frac{59}{8}$

18. $\frac{32}{5}$

Verbal Expressions

19. How are the expressions "$\frac{1}{4}$ of 12" and "12 divided by 4" related?

Decimals

20. What decimal does this model represent? Explain.

Language Development

Fill in the boxes with terms and phrases related to *Decimals* and *Fractions* from the given bank. Include illustrations or examples.

annex zeroes (1–1)	algorithm (1–2)
compatible numbers (1–1)	denominator (1–3)
decimal point (1–1)	mixed number (1–3)
estimate (1–1)	numerator (1–3)
hundredths (1–1)	unit fraction (1–3)
line up place value (1–1)	reciprocal (1–4)
rounding (1–1)	rewrite (1–4)
tenths (1–1)	multistep problems (1–7)

Decimals	Fractions

PROJECT 1A

What is the most challenging board game you have ever played?

PROJECT: MAKE YOUR OWN BOARD GAME

PROJECT 1B

What is your favorite party food?

PROJECT: PLAN THE MENU FOR A SCHOOL FUNDRAISER

PROJECT 1C

If you planted a garden, what would be in it?

PROJECT: DESIGN A VEGETABLE AND HERB GARDEN

PROJECT 1D

How much food does a tiger eat?

PROJECT: PRESENT A PROPOSAL FOR A TIGER EXHIBIT

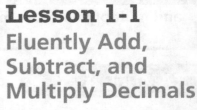
Solve & Discuss It!

ACTIVITY

Maxine is making a model windmill for a science fair. She is connecting 4 cardboard tubes together vertically. Each tube is 0.28 meter in length. What is the combined measure of the connected tubes?

Use Appropriate Tools
You can use decimal grids to calculate with decimals.

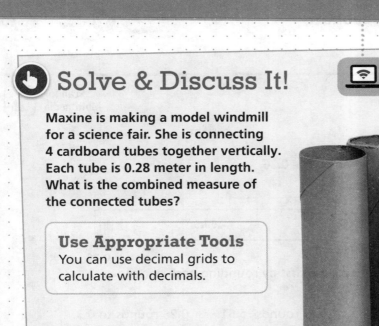

0.28 m

I can...
add, subtract, and multiply decimals.

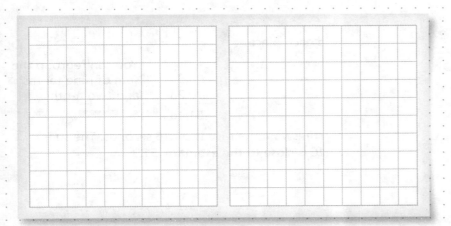

Focus on math practices

Look for Relationships Suppose that Maxine made another windmill model by connecting 4 cardboard tubes that are each 2.8 meters long. What is the combined measure of this model? What relationships do you see in the factors you used here and above? Explain how this helps you solve the problem.

EXAMPLE 1 👁 Add Decimals

Scan for Multimedia

Kim and Martin swam 50 meters. Martin took 0.26 second longer than Kim. What was Martin's time in the race?

Be Precise Why is precision important when working with decimals?

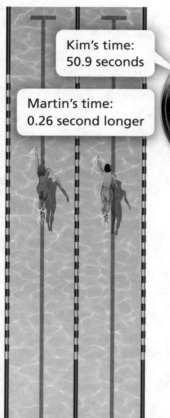

Kim's time: 50.9 seconds

Martin's time: 0.26 second longer

Find $50.9 + 0.26$.

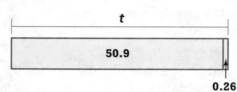

Estimate first by rounding each addend.

50.9 rounds to 51.   0.26 rounds to 0.3.

$$51 + 0.3 = 51.3$$

Find the sum.

```
  50.90
+ 0.26
```

Annex a zero so each place has a digit.

Remember to line up the place values to add.

Add each place.

```
  1
  50.90
+ 0.26
------
  51.16
```

You can regroup the sum of nine tenths and two tenths.

Martin swam the race in 51.16 seconds. The sum 51.16 is close to the estimate, 51.3.

☑ Try It!

Suppose that Martin finished the race 0.47 second after Kim. What was Martin's time in the race? Use an estimate to check that your answer is reasonable.

Convince Me! If Martin finished the race 0.267 second after Kim, you would need to add 0.267 to 50.9 to solve the problem. How is adding 0.267 to 50.9 different from adding 0.26 to 50.9?

EXAMPLE 2 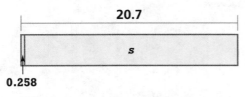 Subtract Decimals

Amy ran a race in 20.7 seconds. Katie finished the race 0.258 second before Amy. How long did it take Katie to run the race?

Find 20.7 − 0.258.

```
|←————— 20.7 —————→|
┌──────────────────┐
│        s         │
└──────────────────┘
↑
0.258
```

Estimate the difference by rounding.

$$20.7 - 0.3 = 20.4$$

0.258 rounds to 0.3.

To find the difference, line up the place values.

$$\begin{array}{r} 20.700 \\ -\ 0.258 \end{array}$$ ·········· Annex zeros as placeholders.

Subtract each place. Regroup as needed.

$$\begin{array}{r} 20.\overset{9}{\cancel{7}}\overset{6\ 10\ 10}{\cancel{0}\cancel{0}} \\ -\ 0.258 \\ \hline 20.442 \end{array}$$

Katie ran the race in 20.442 seconds. 20.442 is close to the estimate, 20.4, so the answer is reasonable.

 Try It!

Suppose that Katie finished the race 0.13 second before Amy. What was Katie's time in the race? Use an estimate to check that your answer is reasonable.

EXAMPLE 3 Multiply Decimals

What is the area of this antique map? Use the formula $A = \ell w$ to find the area of the map.

Multiply as you would with whole numbers. Then place the decimal point in the product. Annex zeros if needed. The number of decimal places in the product is the sum of the number of decimal places in the factors.

$$\begin{array}{r} 3.25 \\ \times\ 2.5 \\ \hline 1625 \\ +\ 6500 \\ \hline 8.125 \end{array}$$

3.25 ·········· 2 decimal places (hundredths)
× 2.5 ·········· 1 decimal place (tenths)

8.125 ·········· 3 decimal places (tenths times hundredths equals thousandths)

The area of the antique map is 8.125 ft².

2.5 ft

3.25 ft

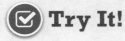 Try It!

How do you determine where to place the decimal point in the product?

0.43 ·········· [ ] decimal place(s)

× 0.2 ·········· [ ] decimal place(s)

0.086 ·········· [ ] decimal place(s)

Annex zeros if needed.

To add decimals, line up place values and add. Regroup as needed.

$$\begin{array}{r} 5\overset{1}{0}.90 \\ +\ 0.26 \\ \hline 51.16 \end{array}$$

To subtract decimals, line up place values and subtract. Regroup as needed.

$$\begin{array}{r} \overset{9}{6}\cancel{1}\overset{10}{0}\overset{10}{0} \\ 20.7\cancel{0}\cancel{0} \\ -\ 0.258 \\ \hline 20.442 \end{array}$$

To multiply decimals, multiply as you would with whole numbers. Then use the number of decimal places in the factors to place the decimal point in the product.

$$\begin{array}{r} 1.35 \\ \times\ 4.6 \\ \hline 810 \\ +\ 5400 \\ \hline 6.210 \end{array}$$

Do You Understand?

1. **? Essential Question** How can you add, subtract, and multiply with decimals?

2. **Generalize** How is adding and subtracting decimals similar to and different from adding and subtracting whole numbers?

3. What can you do if a decimal product has final zeros to the right of the decimal point?

4. **Critique Reasoning** Diego says that the product of 0.51 × 2.427 will have five decimal places. Is Diego correct? Explain.

Do You Know How?

In **5–10**, find each sum or difference.

5. 5.9 + 2.7

6. 4.01 − 2.95

7. 6.8 − 1.45

8. 9.62 − 0.3

9. 2.57 + 7.706

10. 15 − 6.108

In **11–16**, place the decimal point in the correct location in the product.

11. 4 × 0.94 = 376

12. 5 × 0.487 = 2435

13. 3.4 × 6.8 = 2312

14. 3.9 × 0.08 = 312

15. 0.9 × 0.22 = 198

16. 9 × 1.2 = 108

In **17 and 18**, find each product.

17. 5.3 × 2.7

18. 8 × 4.09

Practice & Problem Solving

 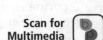

In 19–27, find each sum or difference.

19. 2.17 − 0.8

20. 4.3 + 4.16

21. 46.91 − 28.7

22. 4.815 + 2.17

23. 5.1 − 0.48

24. 27 + 0.185

25. 9.501 − 9.45

26. 14 + 9.8

27. 12.65 + 14.24

In 28–33, find each product.

28. 7 × 0.5

29. 12 × 0.08

30. 24 × 0.17

31. 0.4 × 0.17

32. 1.9 × 0.46

33. 3.42 × 5.15

34. Write an equation that illustrates the following:
A number with two decimal places multiplied by
a number with one decimal place. The product
has only two nonzero digits.

35. The Bright-O Shampoo Factory includes
1.078 ounces of vanilla oil in a 6.35-ounce
bottle of shampoo. How much of the bottle
of shampoo is **NOT** vanilla oil?

In 36–38, use the graph to solve.

36. The fastest speed a table tennis ball has been
hit is about 13.07 times as fast as the speed for
the fastest swimming. What is the speed for the
table tennis ball?

37. Look for Relationships How fast would
1.5 times the fastest rowing speed be? Before
you solve, tell the number of decimal places in
your answer.

38. Which activity has a recorded speed about
7 times as fast as the fastest rowing speed?

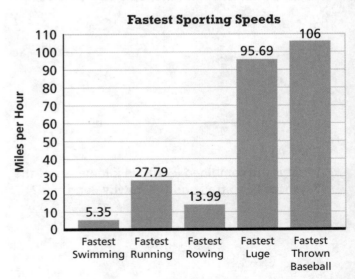

Fastest Sporting Speeds

39. Matthew bought a jersey, a pennant, and a hat. He paid with a $50 bill and some money he borrowed from his friend. If Matthew got $6.01 in change from the cashier, how much did he borrow from his friend to pay for all the items?

Sports Shop
New York, NY 10019

11:01AM 001 JAN01 2017

Jersey   39.99
Pennant   10.25
Hat   13.75
Total:
Cash:
Change: 6.01

THANK YOU FOR SHOPPING
AT THE SPORTS SHOP

40. Anna's running time for a race was 23.1 seconds. Another runner's time was 5.86 seconds faster. Find the other runner's time.

41. Higher Order Thinking Explain why 0.25 × 0.4 has only one decimal place in the product.

42. The wings of some hummingbirds beat 52 times per second when hovering. If a hummingbird hovers for 35.5 seconds, how many times do its wings beat?

43. The students at Walden Middle School are selling tins of popcorn to raise money for new uniforms. They sold 42 tins in the first week. How much money did they make in the first week?

POPCORN $9.25 each

Assessment Practice

44. Use the information in the table to solve each problem.

Trails in Everglades National Park

Trail	Length (kilometers)
Bayshore Loop	3.2
Coastal Prairie	12.1
Rowdy Bend	4.2
Snake Bight	2.6

PART A

What is the combined length in kilometers of the Bayshore Loop trail and the Rowdy Bend trail?

PART B

How many kilometers longer is the Coastal Prairie trail than the Snake Bight trail?

Solve & Discuss It!

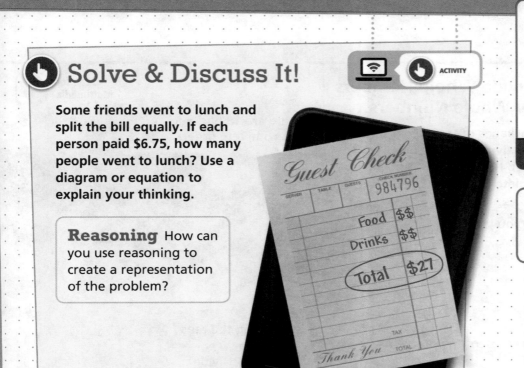

ACTIVITY

Some friends went to lunch and split the bill equally. If each person paid $6.75, how many people went to lunch? Use a diagram or equation to explain your thinking.

Reasoning How can you use reasoning to create a representation of the problem?

I can...
divide whole numbers and decimals.

Focus on math practices

Reasoning Suppose $7.00 was added to the bill for a dessert that everyone shared. How much more does each person have to pay?

VISUAL LEARNING ASSESS

EXAMPLE 1 ◉ **Divide Whole Numbers by Whole Numbers**

A tortilla bakery makes 863 packages of tortillas to sell to restaurants. Each restaurant receives the same number of packages as a complete order. How many restaurants can receive a complete order?

> There are 18 packages in a complete order.

Scan for Multimedia

Use Structure How can you use structure to divide 863 by 18?

Find $863 \div 18 = n$.

A bar diagram can be used to represent the problem.

packages of tortillas | 863

packages per box | 18 — n → n, completely filled boxes

Use compatible numbers to estimate $863 \div 18$.

$$900 \div 20 = 45$$

The quotient of $863 \div 18$ is about 45, so the first digit of the quotient will be in the tens place.

> Start by dividing the tens.

```
      4
18)863      Step 1   Divide
   -72      Step 2   Multiply
    14      Step 3   Subtract
            Step 4   Compare
```

Next, bring down the ones. Repeat the steps as needed to complete the division.

```
      47 R17
18)863
   -72↓
    143
   -126
     17
```

> The answer is reasonable since 47 is close to the estimate, 45.

The bakery can sell complete orders to 47 restaurants.

☑ **Try It!**

Workers at an electronics company pack 2,610 smart phones in boxes. Each box holds 9 smart phones. How many boxes do they fill?

```
9) 2, 6  1  0
 - 1  8

       8  1
    -

          0
    -
          0
          0
```

Convince Me! Why is the first digit of the quotient in the Try It! not in the same place as the first digit of the quotient in Example 1?

How can you write a decimal quotient when dividing whole numbers?

Find $180 \div 8$.

Estimate. Because $180 \div 10 = 18$, start dividing in the tens place.

Divide the tens and ones.

```
        22
   8)180
    −16
      20
    −16
       4
```

Write the remainder as a decimal. Place the decimal point and annex a 0 in the tenths place.

Then complete the division.

```
      22.5
  8)180.0
   −16
     20
   −16
      40
    −40
       0
```

EXAMPLE **3** **Divide Decimals**

Use the division algorithm to divide with decimals.

A. Find $\$809.40 \div 12$.

$\$809.40$

| n | n | n | n | n | n | n | n | n | n | n | n |

Use compatible numbers to estimate, and then divide to solve.

809.40 is close to 840, and $840 \div 12 = 70$.

> Place the decimal point in the quotient above the decimal point in the dividend.

```
      67.45
  12)809.40
    −72
      89
     −84
       54
      −48
        60
       −60
         0
```

> The quotient 67.45 is close to the estimate of 70, so the answer is reasonable.

$\$809.40 \div 12 = \$67.45$

B. Find $\$4.20 \div \$1.40$.

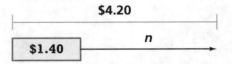

$\$4.20$

$\$1.40$ ——— n ——→

Multiply both the divisor and the dividend by the same power of 10 that will make the divisor a whole number.

Multiply 1.40 and 4.20 by 10^2 or 100.

```
              3
1.40)4.20   140)420
                −420
                   0
```

> Divide. Place a decimal point in the quotient if needed.

$\$4.20 \div \$1.40 = 3$

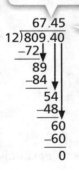 **Try It!**

Divide.

a. $65 \div 8$ **b.** $14.4 \div 8$ **c.** $128.8 \div 1.4$

To divide by a decimal, rewrite the decimal so that you are dividing by a whole number. Multiply both the divisor and the dividend by the same power of 10. Then divide as you would with whole numbers.

$$35.2 \div 0.16$$

$$\begin{array}{r} 100 \\ \times\, 35.2 \\ \hline 200 \\ 5000 \\ +\,30000 \\ \hline 3,520.0 \end{array}$$

$$\begin{array}{r} 100 \\ \times\, 0.16 \\ \hline 600 \\ +\,1000 \\ \hline 16.00 \end{array}$$

$$\begin{array}{r} 220 \\ 16\overline{)3,520} \\ -\,32 \\ \hline 32 \\ -\,32 \\ \hline 0 \end{array}$$

Do You Understand?

1. **? Essential Question** How can you divide whole numbers and decimals?

2. When dividing with decimals, why is it necessary to multiply both the divisor and the dividend by the same power of 10?

3. **Use Structure** Explain how you can decide where to place the first digit of the quotient for 6,139 ÷ 153.

4. **Use Structure** How do you know where to place the decimal point in the quotient when dividing a decimal by a whole number?

Do You Know How?

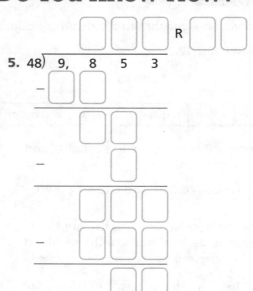

5. $48\overline{)\,9,\ 8\ 5\ 3}$

In 6 and 7, divide. Record remainders.

6. 2,789 ÷ 36

7. $18\overline{)153}$

In 8 and 9, divide. Write remainders as decimals.

8. $4\overline{)139}$

9. 215 ÷ 2

In 10 and 11, divide.

10. $5\overline{)34.75}$

11. 215.25 ÷ 5

In 12 and 13, divide. Annex zeros if needed to write remainders as decimals.

12. 5.3 ÷ 0.2

13. $0.4\overline{)8.9}$

Name: _____

Practice & Problem Solving

Scan for
Multimedia

Leveled Practice In **14** and **15**, divide.

14. 62) 5, 8 4 1

15. 4) 3 5 0 .

In 16–19, divide. Record remainders.

16. 2,593 ÷ 21

17. 19)6,927

18. 9)2,483

19. 968 ÷ 38

In 20–23, divide. Write remainders as decimals.

20. 5)56

21. 232 ÷ 40

22. 44 ÷ 10

23. 4)2,626

In 24–27, divide.

24. 6)$54.18

25. 187.2 ÷ 8

26. 7)6.3

27. 137.5 ÷ 5

In 28–31, divide. Annex zeros if needed to write remainders as decimals.

28. 6.4 ÷ 0.8

29. 0.6)0.2430

30. 52.056 ÷ 7.23

31. 0.745)9.089

---

32. Ants are one of the Thorny Devil lizard's favorite foods. It can eat 45 ants per minute. How long would it take this lizard to eat 1,080 ants? Express your answer in minutes.

1-2 Fluently Divide Whole Numbers and Decimals   **19**

33. Critique Reasoning Henrieta divided 0.80 by 20 as shown. Is her work correct? If not, explain why and give a correct response.

$$
\begin{array}{r}
0.40 \\
20\overline{)0.80} \\
-80 \\
\hline
0
\end{array}
$$

34. Which brand of fruit snacks costs less per pound? How much less?

Fruit Snacks

Brand A	Brand B
15 lb	25 lb
$16.20	$22.25

35. Be Precise How many times as much does each item cost in 2010 as in 1960?

Item	1960 Cost	2010 Cost
Movie Ticket	$0.75	$9.75
Regular Popcorn	$0.25	$4.10
Regular Drink	$0.35	$3.08

Movie Ticket _____

Regular Popcorn _____

Regular Drink _____

36. Higher Order Thinking Kendra has 5.5 pounds of popcorn and wants to package it equally in 50 bags. How can she use place-value reasoning to find the amount of popcorn to put in each bag?

37. You and a friend are paid $38.25 for doing yard work. You worked 2.5 hours and your friend worked 2 hours. You split the money according to the amount of time each of you worked. How much is your share of the money? Explain.

Assessment Practice

38. What is the value of the expression 1,248 ÷ 25?

Ⓐ 49

Ⓑ 49 R 9

Ⓒ 49.9

Ⓓ 49 R 23

39. Which expression has the same solution as 3,157 ÷ 41?

Ⓐ 1,852 ÷ 24

Ⓑ 1,928 ÷ 25

Ⓒ 2,079 ÷ 27

Ⓓ 2,184 ÷ 28

Solve & Discuss It!

ACTIVITY

The art teacher gave each student half of a sheet of paper. Then she asked the students to color one fourth of their pieces of paper. What part of the original sheet did the students color?

Model with Math How can you use a picture to represent the problem?

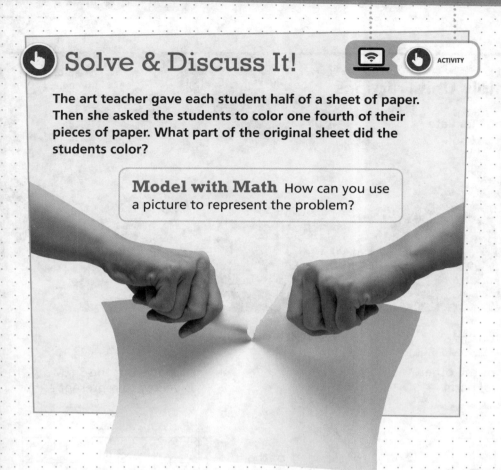

Lesson 1-3
Multiply Fractions

Go Online

I can...
use models and equations to multiply fractions and mixed numbers.

Focus on math practices

Reasoning Should your answer be less than or greater than 1? Explain.

VISUAL LEARNING   ASSESS

EXAMPLE 1 **Multiply Unit Fractions**

Scan for Multimedia

There was $\frac{1}{4}$ of a pan of lasagna left. Tom ate $\frac{1}{3}$ of this amount. What fraction of a whole pan of lasagna did Tom eat?

To find a part of a whole, multiply to solve the problem.

Find $\frac{1}{3} \times \frac{1}{4}$.

ONE WAY Divide one whole into fourths.

Divide $\frac{1}{4}$ into 3 equal parts.

Divide each of the other $\frac{1}{4}$s into 3 equal parts.

12 parts make one whole, so one part is $\frac{1}{12}$.

$$\frac{1}{3} \times \frac{1}{4} = \frac{1 \times 1}{3 \times 4} = \frac{1}{12}$$

Tom ate $\frac{1}{12}$ of a whole pan of lasagna.

ANOTHER WAY

Shade 1 of the 3 rows yellow to represent $\frac{1}{3}$.

Shade 1 of the 4 columns red to represent $\frac{1}{4}$.

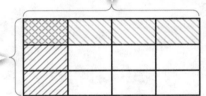

The orange overlap shows the product $\frac{1}{3} \times \frac{1}{4}$.

1 out of 12 parts are shaded orange.

$$\frac{1}{3} \times \frac{1}{4} = \frac{1 \times 1}{3 \times 4} = \frac{1}{12}$$

Tom ate $\frac{1}{12}$ of a whole pan of lasagna.

Try It!

Find $\frac{1}{4} \times \frac{1}{5}$ using the area model. Explain.

$\frac{1}{4}$ .... 1 of ☐ rows

$\frac{1}{5}$ .... 1 of ☐ columns

Convince Me! Why is the product of $\frac{1}{4} \times \frac{1}{5}$ less than each factor?

EXAMPLE **2** **Multiply Fractions**

  ACTIVITY   ASSESS

Find $\frac{2}{3} \times \frac{3}{4}$ using a number line.

$\frac{1}{3}$ means 1 of 3 equal parts, so $\frac{1}{3}$ of $\frac{3}{4}$ is $\frac{1}{4}$.

$\frac{2}{3}$ means 2 of 3 equal parts, so $\frac{2}{3}$ of $\frac{3}{4}$ is 2 times $\frac{1}{4}$.

$\frac{2}{3} \times \frac{3}{4} = \frac{6}{12}$ or $\frac{1}{2}$

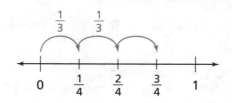

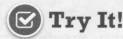 Try It!

Find $\frac{3}{4} \times \frac{4}{6}$ using the number line. Explain.

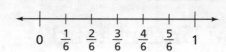

 EXAMPLE **3** **Multiply Mixed Numbers**

Find $7\frac{1}{2} \times 2\frac{3}{4}$.

Estimate first. $7\frac{1}{2}$ times $2\frac{3}{4}$ is about 8 times 3.
So, the answer should be about 24.

ONE WAY You can use an area model to find the partial products. Then add to find the final product.

	← 7 →	← $\frac{1}{2}$ →
2	$2 \times 7 = 14$	$2 \times \frac{1}{2} = 1$
$\frac{3}{4}$	$\frac{3}{4} \times 7 = \frac{21}{4}$ or $5\frac{1}{4}$	$\frac{3}{4} \times \frac{1}{2} = \frac{3}{8}$

$14 + 1 + 5\frac{1}{4} + \frac{3}{8} =$

$14 + 1 + 5\frac{2}{8} + \frac{3}{8} = 20\frac{5}{8}$

$5\frac{1}{4}$ is renamed $5\frac{2}{8}$.

ANOTHER WAY You can use an equation to find the product. Rename the mixed numbers and then multiply.

$$7\frac{1}{2} \times 2\frac{3}{4} = \frac{15}{2} \times \frac{11}{4}$$

$$= \frac{165}{8}$$

$$= 20\frac{5}{8}$$

Because $20\frac{5}{8}$ is close to the estimate of 24, the answer is reasonable.

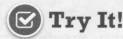 Try It!

A clothing factory makes T-shirts. If each machine makes $3\frac{1}{3}$ T-shirts per hour, how many T-shirts does one machine make in $4\frac{1}{2}$ hours? Write and solve an equation.

You can find the product of fractions or mixed numbers.

Multiply the numerators.

Multiply the denominators.

$$\frac{2}{5} \times \frac{3}{4} = \frac{2 \times 3}{5 \times 4} = \frac{6}{20} \text{ or } \frac{3}{10}$$

$$3\frac{1}{3} \times 1\frac{1}{2} = \frac{10}{3} \times \frac{3}{2} = \frac{10 \times 3}{3 \times 2} = \frac{30}{6} \text{ or } 5$$

Rename mixed numbers as fractions.

Do You Understand?

1. **? Essential Question** How can you multiply fractions and mixed numbers?

2. **Reasoning** Is the product of $\frac{3}{6} \times \frac{5}{4}$ equal to the product of $\frac{3}{4} \times \frac{5}{6}$? Explain.

3. **Construct Arguments** Why is adding $\frac{3}{9}$ and $\frac{6}{9}$ different from multiplying the two fractions?

4. Tina has $\frac{1}{2}$ of a pan of cornbread left from a dinner party. She eats $\frac{1}{2}$ of the leftover part the next night. How much of the whole pan does Tina eat? Write and solve an equation.

5. **Construct Arguments** Explain how you would multiply $5 \times 2\frac{1}{2}$.

6. In Example 1, find the fraction of a whole pan of lasagna that Tom ate if he started with $\frac{7}{8}$ of a pan.

Do You Know How?

7. Find $\frac{5}{6} \times \frac{1}{2}$. Use the model to help solve.

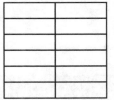

8. Find $\frac{3}{4} \times \frac{4}{9}$.

In 9–16, find each product.

9. $\frac{2}{3} \times \frac{1}{2}$

10. $\frac{5}{9} \times \frac{1}{9}$

11. $\frac{7}{10} \times \frac{3}{4}$

12. $\frac{1}{3} \times \frac{1}{4}$

13. $\frac{5}{6} \times \frac{3}{7}$

14. $\frac{3}{5} \times \frac{11}{12}$

15. $\frac{4}{10} \times \frac{2}{5}$

16. $\frac{3}{4} \times \frac{2}{9}$

In 17 and 18, estimate the product. Then complete the multiplication.

17. $2\frac{3}{4} \times 8 = \frac{\boxed{}}{4} \times \frac{8}{1} = \boxed{}$

18. $4\frac{1}{2} \times 1\frac{1}{4} = \frac{\boxed{}}{2} \times \frac{\boxed{}}{4} = \boxed{}$

Practice & Problem Solving

In 19 and 20, find each product. Shade the model to help solve.

19. $\frac{1}{3} \times \frac{5}{6}$

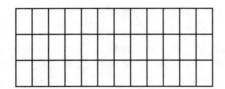

20. $\frac{2}{3} \times \frac{1}{12}$

In 21–28, find each product.

21. $\frac{7}{8} \times \frac{1}{2}$

22. $\frac{2}{5} \times \frac{1}{12}$

23. $\frac{5}{7} \times \frac{7}{9}$

24. $\frac{1}{2} \times \frac{3}{4}$

25. $\frac{1}{4} \times \frac{7}{8}$

26. $\frac{5}{6} \times \frac{9}{10}$

27. $\frac{1}{4} \times \frac{1}{8}$

28. $\frac{1}{3} \times \frac{3}{7}$

In 29–36, estimate the product. Then find each product.

29. $2\frac{1}{6} \times 4\frac{1}{2}$

30. $\frac{3}{4} \times 8\frac{1}{2}$

31. $1\frac{1}{8} \times 3\frac{1}{3}$

32. $3\frac{1}{5} \times \frac{2}{3}$

33. $3\frac{1}{4} \times 6$

34. $5\frac{1}{3} \times 3$

35. $2\frac{3}{8} \times 4$

36. $4\frac{1}{8} \times 5\frac{1}{2}$

In 37 and 38, use the diagram at the right.

37. Linda walked $\frac{3}{4}$ of the length of the Tremont Trail before stopping for a rest. How far had Linda walked on the trail?

Tremont Trail
$3\frac{1}{2}$ miles

Seton Trail
$1\frac{1}{4}$ miles

Wildflower Trail
$2\frac{3}{8}$ miles

38. The city plans to extend the Wildflower Trail to make it $2\frac{1}{2}$ times its current length in the next 5 years. How long will the Wildflower Trail be at the end of 5 years?

39. The world's smallest gecko is $\frac{3}{4}$ inch long. An adult male Western Banded Gecko is $7\frac{1}{3}$ times as long. How long is an adult male Western Banded Gecko?

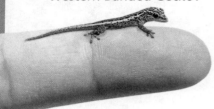

40. Higher Order Thinking In Ms. Barclay's classroom, $\frac{2}{5}$ of the students play chess. Of the students who play chess, $\frac{5}{6}$ also play sudoku. If there are 30 students in Ms. Barclay's class, how many play chess and sudoku?

41. The Boca Grande Causeway in Florida is about $1\frac{4}{9}$ times as long as the Golden Gate Bridge in San Francisco. The Golden Gate Bridge is about 9,000 feet long. About how long is the Boca Grande Causeway?

42. If $\frac{7}{8}$ is multiplied by $\frac{4}{5}$, will the product be greater than either of the two factors? Explain.

43. Be Precise To amend the U.S. Constitution, $\frac{3}{4}$ of the 50 states must approve the amendment. If 35 states approve an amendment, will the Constitution be amended?

44. A scientist had $\frac{3}{4}$ of a bottle of a solution. She used $\frac{1}{6}$ of the solution in an experiment. How much of the bottle did she use?

45. In the voting for City Council Precinct 5, only $\frac{1}{2}$ of all eligible voters cast votes. What fraction of all eligible voters voted for Shelley? Morgan? Who received the most votes?

Candidate	Fraction of Votes Received
Shelley	$\frac{3}{10}$
Morgan	$\frac{5}{8}$

☑ Assessment Practice

46. Which of these equations is equivalent to $1\frac{1}{2} \times 3\frac{1}{5} = 4\frac{1}{2}$?

Ⓐ $4\frac{1}{2} \div 3\frac{1}{5} = 1\frac{1}{2}$

Ⓑ $1\frac{1}{2} \div 4\frac{1}{2} = 3\frac{1}{5}$

Ⓒ $1\frac{1}{2} \div 3\frac{1}{5} = 4\frac{1}{2}$

Ⓓ $3\frac{1}{5} \div 4\frac{1}{2} = 1\frac{1}{2}$

47. Which of these equations is equivalent to $\frac{3}{4} \times 8\frac{1}{5} = 6\frac{3}{20}$? Select all that apply.

☐ $\frac{3}{4} \div 8\frac{1}{5} = 6\frac{3}{20}$

☐ $6\frac{3}{20} \div \frac{3}{4} = 8\frac{1}{5}$

☐ $6\frac{3}{20} \div 8\frac{1}{5} = \frac{3}{4}$

☐ $\frac{3}{4} \div 6\frac{3}{20} = 8\frac{1}{5}$

☐ $8\frac{1}{5} \div 6\frac{3}{20} = \frac{3}{4}$

1. **Vocabulary** How can you use a *compatible number* to estimate a quotient when dividing a decimal by a whole number? *Lesson 1-2*

2. Keaton is building a rectangular tabletop and wants to put a metal border around the edge. The length of the tabletop is 1.83 meters and the width is 0.74 meter. Use the formula $P = 2\ell + 2w$ to find the perimeter of the tabletop. *Lesson 1-1*

3. Norbert's Nursery is having a sale. Flats of flowers are priced as marked, including tax. Jake buys 2 flats of petunias, 3 flats of daisies, and 1 flat of begonias. If he pays with a $50 bill, how much change should Jake receive? *Lesson 1-1*

Norbert's Nursery

Flower	Price per Flat
Petunia	$5.25
Daisy	$7.65
Begonia	$8.40

4. Marguerite is selling space in an advertisement book for a community fund-raising event. Each $\frac{1}{4}$ page in the book costs $15.50. What is the cost for $\frac{3}{4}$ page? *Lesson 1-1*

   Ⓐ $62.00 Ⓑ $46.50

   Ⓒ $20.67 Ⓓ $11.63

5. What is the value of $170 \div (4 \times 5)$? *Lesson 1-2*

6. Lucia walks $2\frac{3}{4}$ miles on Monday. On Monday, she walks $1\frac{1}{2}$ times farther than on Tuesday. Which equation can be used to find how far Lucia walks on Tuesday? *Lesson 1-3*

   Ⓐ $2\frac{3}{4} \times 1\frac{1}{2} = 4\frac{1}{8}$ Ⓑ $2\frac{3}{4} + 1\frac{1}{2} = 4\frac{1}{4}$

   Ⓒ $2\frac{3}{4} \div 1\frac{1}{2} = 1\frac{5}{6}$ Ⓓ $1\frac{1}{2} \div 2\frac{3}{4} = \frac{6}{11}$

How well did you do on the mid-topic checkpoint? Fill in the stars.

MID-TOPIC
PERFORMANCE TASK

Nyan Robotics Team received their challenge for the year and has to buy parts to build their robot for competitions.

Parts List

Part	Cost per Part
Beam	$5.95
Channel	$8.50
Motor controller	$99.75
Motor mount	$17.55
Gear	$12.15
Sprocket	$3.00
Wheel	$18.90
Axle	$4.35

PART A

Team members Eric and Natalia secure a grant for $75.00 to buy beams and channels. If the team needs 3 beams and 6 channels, will the grant cover the cost? If so, how much of the grant will remain?

PART B

Team members Corinne, Kevin, and Tomas decide to share the cost of 2 motor controllers and 4 wheels equally. How much does each member need to contribute?

PART C

Nyan Robotics has a budget of $99 to buy sprockets, axles, and gears. If they spend $\frac{2}{3}$ of the budget on sprockets, how much money from the budget remains to buy axles and gears?

3-ACT MATH ▷ ▷ ▷

Stocking UP

Go Online

3-Act Mathematical Modeling: Stocking Up

ACT 1

1. After watching the video, what is the first question that comes to mind?

2. Write the Main Question you will answer.

3. **Construct Arguments** Predict an answer to this Main Question. Explain your prediction.

4. On the number line below, write a number that is too small to be the answer. Write a number that is too large.

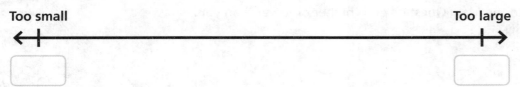

Too small   Too large

5. Plot your prediction on the same number line.

6. What information in this situation would be helpful to know? How would you use that information?

7. Use Appropriate Tools What tools can you use to solve the problem? Explain how you would use them strategically.

8. Model with Math Represent the situation using mathematics. Use your representation to answer the Main Question.

9. What is your answer to the Main Question? Is it higher or lower than your prediction? Explain why.

10. Write the answer you saw in the video.

11. Reasoning Does your answer match the answer in the video? If not, what are some reasons that would explain the difference?

12. Make Sense and Persevere Would you change your model now that you know the answer? Explain.

Reflect

13. Model with Math Explain how you used a mathematical model to represent the situation. How did the model help you answer the Main Question?

14. Reasoning How did you represent the situation using symbols? How did you use those symbols to solve the problem?

SEQUEL

15. Model with Math The store purchases boxes of pasta for $0.82 and cans of sauce for $1.62. How much profit does the store make from this purchase?

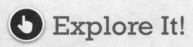 Explore It!

Students are competing in a 4-kilometer relay race. There are 10 runners.

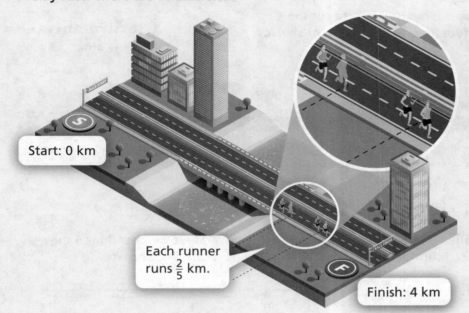

Start: 0 km

Each runner runs $\frac{2}{5}$ km.

Finish: 4 km

Lesson 1-4
Understand Division with Fractions

Go Online

I can...
use models and equations to represent fraction division.

A. Use the number line to represent the data for the race.

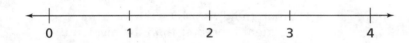

0   1   2   3   4

B. Use multiplication or division to describe your work on the number line.

Focus on math practices

Model with Math Describe what a number line would look like if there were 10 runners each running $\frac{1}{2}$ kilometer in a 5-kilometer race.

33

VISUAL
LEARNING   ASSESS

EXAMPLE 1 👁 **Divide Whole Numbers by Fractions**

Scan for
Multimedia

Mr. Roberts has a board that is 3 feet long. He plans to cut the
board into pieces that are each $\frac{3}{4}$ foot long to build a set of shelves.
How many shelves can he make?

Use Structure How
many $\frac{3}{4}$s are in 3?

0 ft   1 ft   2 ft   3 ft

ONE WAY Write 3 as a fraction with a denominator
of 4, $\frac{12}{4}$. Think of division as repeated subtraction.

$\frac{12}{4}$ ft

Board ├────────────────────┤

Each shelf │ $\frac{3}{4}$ ft │ ──── *s* shelves ──────→

$\begin{array}{c} \frac{12}{4} \\ -\frac{3}{4} \\ \hline \frac{9}{4} \end{array}$ $\begin{array}{c} \frac{9}{4} \\ -\frac{3}{4} \\ \hline \frac{6}{4} \end{array}$ $\begin{array}{c} \frac{6}{4} \\ -\frac{3}{4} \\ \hline \frac{3}{4} \end{array}$ $\begin{array}{c} \frac{3}{4} \\ -\frac{3}{4} \\ \hline 0 \end{array}$

Mr. Roberts can make 4 shelves.

ANOTHER WAY Use a number line to show
3 feet. Divide it into $\frac{3}{4}$-foot parts.

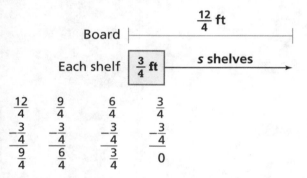

0   1   2   3

So, $3 \div \frac{3}{4} = 4$.

When the divisor is less than 1, the
quotient is greater than the dividend.

Mr. Roberts can make 4 shelves.

☑ **Try It!**

A board is 6 feet long. How many $\frac{2}{3}$-foot-long pieces can be cut from
the board? Use the number line to show your work.

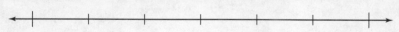

Convince Me! Why is the number of pieces that can be cut
from the board greater than the number of feet in the length of
the board?

EXAMPLE 2 Divide Fractions by Whole Numbers

How much cake will each person get if 3 friends decide to share half a cake equally? Find $\frac{1}{2} \div 3$.

Draw a picture to show $\frac{1}{2}$.

$$\frac{1}{2}$$

$\frac{1}{2}$

Divide $\frac{1}{2}$ into 3 equal parts.

$$\frac{1}{2} \div 3$$

Each part is $\frac{1}{6}$ of the whole.

$$\frac{1}{2} \div 3 = \frac{1}{6}$$

Each person will get $\frac{1}{6}$ of the cake.

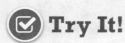 Try It!

Make a diagram to find $\frac{2}{3} \div 4$.

EXAMPLE 3 Use Relationships to Divide Whole Numbers by Fractions

You can use what you know about dividing fractions to find and use a pattern. Look at the division and multiplication sentences at the right. Find and use a pattern to solve $4 \div \frac{2}{3}$.

The pattern shows that when you divide by a fraction, you get the same result as when you multiply by its reciprocal.

$8 \div \frac{4}{1} = 2$	$8 \times \frac{1}{4} = 2$
$5 \div \frac{1}{2} = 10$	$5 \times \frac{2}{1} = 10$
$3 \div \frac{3}{4} = 4$	$3 \times \frac{4}{3} = 4$

$4 \div \frac{2}{3} = 4 \times \frac{3}{2}$

Rewrite the problem as a multiplication problem using the reciprocal of the divisor.

$$= \frac{4}{1} \times \frac{3}{2}$$

$$= \frac{12}{2} \text{ or } 6$$

Two numbers whose product is 1 are called **reciprocals** of each other. If a nonzero number is named as a fraction $\frac{a}{b}$, then its reciprocal is $\frac{b}{a}$.

 Try It!

Use the pattern in the table above to find $8 \div \frac{3}{4}$.

$$8 \div \frac{3}{4} = 8 \times \boxed{} = \boxed{}$$

To divide a whole number by a fraction:

> Write the whole number as a fraction.

$$14 \div \frac{4}{7} = \frac{14}{1} \div \frac{4}{7}$$

$$\frac{14}{1} \times \frac{7}{4} = \frac{98}{4} \text{ or } 24\frac{1}{2}$$

> Multiply the whole number by the reciprocal of the divisor.

To divide a fraction by a whole number:

> Write the whole number as a fraction.

$$\frac{4}{7} \div 14 = \frac{4}{7} \div \frac{14}{1}$$

$$\frac{4}{7} \times \frac{1}{14} = \frac{4}{98} \text{ or } \frac{2}{49}$$

> Multiply the fraction by the reciprocal of the whole number.

Do You Understand?

1. **? Essential Question** How can you represent division of fractions?

2. **Reasoning** Draw a diagram to represent $8 \div \frac{2}{3}$. Then write an equation to show the solution.

3. **Reasoning** Is $4 \div \frac{3}{2}$ the same as $4 \div \frac{2}{3}$? Explain.

4. How can you write any nonzero whole number as a fraction?

5. **Look for Relationships** How does the quotient compare to the dividend when the divisor is a fraction less than 1?

6. What division equation is represented by the diagram?

Do You Know How?

In **7–14**, find each reciprocal.

7. $\frac{3}{5}$

8. $\frac{1}{6}$

9. 9

10. $\frac{7}{4}$

11. $\frac{5}{8}$

12. 16

13. $\frac{7}{12}$

14. $\frac{11}{5}$

In **15–22**, find each quotient.

15. $6 \div \frac{2}{3}$

16. $12 \div \frac{3}{8}$

17. $\frac{1}{4} \div 3$

18. $\frac{2}{5} \div 2$

19. $2 \div \frac{1}{2}$

20. $3 \div \frac{1}{4}$

21. $9 \div \frac{3}{5}$

22. $5 \div \frac{2}{7}$

Practice & Problem Solving

Leveled Practice In **23** and **24**, complete each division sentence.

23. $6 \div \boxed{} = 12$

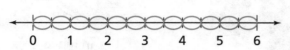

The number line shows 6 wholes.

24. $\frac{2}{3} \div \boxed{} = \frac{2}{9}$

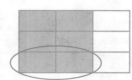

In **25** and **26**, find each quotient. Draw a diagram to help.

25. $\frac{3}{5} \div 3$

26. $2 \div \frac{2}{5}$

In **27–30**, find each reciprocal.

27. $\frac{3}{10}$

28. 6

29. $\frac{1}{15}$

30. 3

In **31–38**, find each quotient.

31. $36 \div \frac{3}{4}$

32. $2 \div \frac{3}{8}$

33. $18 \div \frac{2}{3}$

34. $9 \div \frac{4}{5}$

35. $\frac{1}{6} \div 2$

36. $\frac{2}{3} \div 3$

37. $\frac{3}{5} \div 2$

38. $\frac{1}{4} \div 4$

39. A worker is pouring 3 quarts of liquid into $\frac{3}{8}$-quart containers. How many of the containers can she fill? Write and solve a division equation.

3 quarts

$\frac{3}{8}$ quart

In 40–43, use the given information.

A tortoise can move 600 ft in $\frac{2}{3}$ h.

A snail can move 120 ft in $\frac{3}{4}$ h.

A sloth can move 250 ft in $\frac{5}{8}$ h.

40. Higher Order Thinking Without doing any calculations, how can you use the information given to tell which animal moves the fastest?

41. Reasoning The quotient $250 \div \frac{5}{8}$ tells about how far a sloth may move in one hour. How far can a sloth go in 90 minutes? Justify your reasoning.

42. The quotient $600 \div \frac{2}{3}$ tells about how far a tortoise may move in one hour. Find that distance.

43. Write and solve an equation to find how far a snail can go in one hour.

44. A waitress pours $\frac{3}{4}$ gallon of orange juice equally into 5 pitchers. What fraction of a gallon of orange juice is in each pitcher? Use the rectangle to represent the problem. Then write an equation to show the solution.

The rectangle represents 1 whole gallon. Draw lines to represent $\frac{3}{4}$ gallon first. Then divide that into 5 equal parts.

✅ Assessment Practice

45. Select all the math statements that have the same quotient.

- ☐ $12 \div \frac{2}{3}$
- ☐ $\frac{2}{3} \div \frac{1}{27}$
- ☐ $16 \div \frac{4}{5}$
- ☐ $12 \div \frac{3}{2}$
- ☐ $24 \div \frac{4}{3}$

46. Select all the math statements that are true.

- ☐ $\frac{1}{3} \div 3$ is $\frac{1}{3} \div \frac{3}{1} = \frac{1}{3} \times \frac{1}{3}$
- ☐ $\frac{4}{5} \div 5$ is $\frac{4}{5} \div \frac{5}{1} = \frac{4}{5} \times \frac{1}{5}$
- ☐ $\frac{7}{8} \div 8$ is $\frac{7}{8} \div \frac{1}{8} = \frac{7}{8} \times \frac{8}{1}$
- ☐ $\frac{2}{3} \div 6$ is $\frac{2}{3} \div \frac{6}{1} = \frac{2}{3} \times \frac{1}{6}$
- ☐ $\frac{4}{9} \div 4$ is $\frac{4}{9} \div \frac{1}{4} = \frac{4}{9} \times \frac{4}{1}$

Solve & Discuss It!

  ACTIVITY

A granola bar was cut into 6 equal pieces. Someone ate part of the granola bar so that $\frac{2}{3}$ of the original bar remains. How many $\frac{1}{6}$ parts are left? Use the picture to draw a model to represent and find $\frac{2}{3} \div \frac{1}{6}$.

$\frac{2}{3}$

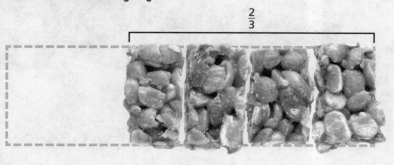

Model with Math You can model with math by dividing a whole into equal parts.

I can...
divide a fraction by another fraction.

Focus on math practices

Use Structure How can you use multiplication to check your answer?

VISUAL LEARNING ASSESS

EXAMPLE 1 👁 **Use an Area Model to Divide Fractions**

Scan for Multimedia

Simon buys $\frac{1}{2}$ yard of material to make footbags. How many footbags can Simon make? Find $\frac{1}{2} \div \frac{1}{6}$.

Simon uses $\frac{1}{6}$ yard of material for each footbag that he makes.

Model with Math How can you use an area model to represent the division?

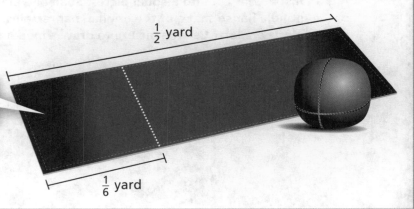

$\frac{1}{2}$ yard

$\frac{1}{6}$ yard

STEP 1 Draw an area model to show the dividend, $\frac{1}{2}$.

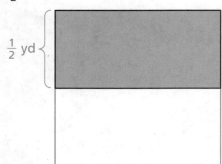

$\frac{1}{2}$ yd

Then find how many $\frac{1}{6}$s are in $\frac{1}{2}$.

STEP 2 Divide the same area model into $\frac{1}{6}$s to show the divisor.

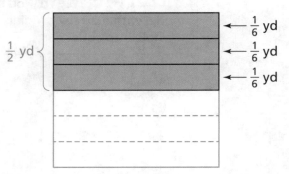

$\frac{1}{2}$ yd

← $\frac{1}{6}$ yd
← $\frac{1}{6}$ yd
← $\frac{1}{6}$ yd

There are three $\frac{1}{6}$s in $\frac{1}{2}$.

So, $\frac{1}{2} \div \frac{1}{6} = 3$.

Simon can make 3 footbags.

✓ Try It!

Use the number line below to represent $\frac{1}{6} \times 3 = \frac{1}{2}$. Then write an equivalent division sentence.

0   1

Convince Me! How are the dividend, divisor, and quotient represented on the number line?

EXAMPLE 2 Use Another Area Model to Divide Fractions

How much of a $\frac{3}{4}$-cup serving is in $\frac{2}{3}$ cup of yogurt?

STEP 1 Find $\frac{2}{3} \div \frac{3}{4}$. Show $\frac{2}{3}$ and $\frac{3}{4}$.

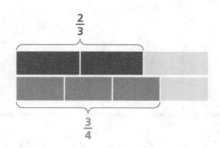

STEP 2 Multiply the denominators to find the common unit of twelfths to compare $\frac{2}{3}$ and $\frac{3}{4}$.

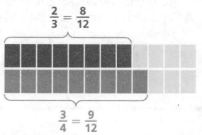

$\frac{2}{3}$ is divided into 8 equal parts, while $\frac{3}{4}$ is divided into 9 equal parts.

So, $\frac{2}{3}$ cup is $\frac{8}{9}$ of a $\frac{3}{4}$-cup serving.

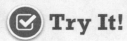 Try It!

Find $\frac{1}{4} \div \frac{3}{8}$. Draw an area model.

EXAMPLE 3 Divide Fractions

Andrew has $\frac{3}{4}$ gallon of orange juice. He wants to pour it into $\frac{1}{6}$-gallon containers. How many containers can Andrew fill?

Find $\frac{3}{4} \div \frac{1}{6}$. To divide by a fraction, rewrite the problem as a multiplication problem using the reciprocal of the divisor.

$\frac{3}{4} \div \frac{1}{6} = \frac{3}{4} \times \frac{6}{1}$ ← $\frac{6}{1}$ is the reciprocal of $\frac{1}{6}$.

$= \frac{18}{4}$ or $4\frac{1}{2}$

Andrew can fill $4\frac{1}{2}$ containers.

$\frac{3}{4}$ gallon

$\frac{1}{6}$ gallon

Try It!

How wide is a rectangular strip of land with a length of $\frac{3}{4}$ mile and an area of $\frac{1}{2}$ square mile? Use the area formula: $A = \ell \times w$.

$\frac{1}{2} = \frac{3}{4}w \rightarrow \frac{1}{2} \div \boxed{} = w \rightarrow \frac{1}{2} \times \boxed{} = w \rightarrow w = \boxed{}$

The strip of land is $\boxed{}$ mile wide.

$\frac{3}{4}$ mi $A = \frac{1}{2}$ mi²

w

KEY CONCEPT

To divide a fraction by a fraction, rewrite the division equation as a multiplication equation.

To divide by a fraction, multiply by the reciprocal of the divisor.

$$\frac{4}{5} \div \frac{3}{10} = \frac{4}{5} \times \frac{10}{3} = \frac{40}{15} \text{ or } 2\frac{2}{3}$$

Do You Understand?

1. **? Essential Question** How can you divide a fraction by a fraction?

2. **Critique Reasoning** To find the quotient of $\frac{2}{5} \div \frac{8}{5}$, Corey rewrites the problem as $\frac{5}{2} \times \frac{8}{5}$. Explain Corey's mistake and how to correct it.

3. **Reasoning** Is the quotient of $\frac{3}{5} \div \frac{6}{7}$ greater than or less than $\frac{3}{5}$? Explain.

4. How is dividing a whole number by a fraction different from dividing a fraction by a fraction?

Do You Know How?

In 5–7, write a division sentence to represent each model.

5.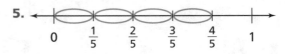

6.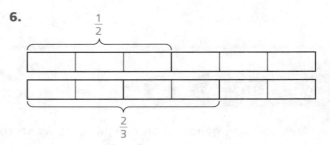

7.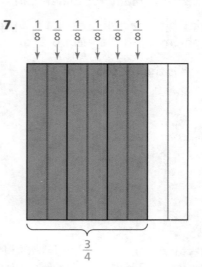

In 8–11, find each quotient.

8. $\frac{3}{4} \div \frac{2}{3}$

9. $\frac{3}{12} \div \frac{1}{8}$

10. $\frac{1}{2} \div \frac{4}{5}$

11. $\frac{7}{10} \div \frac{2}{5}$

Practice & Problem Solving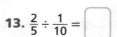

In 12 and 13, complete each division sentence using the models provided.

12. $\frac{1}{3} \div \frac{1}{12} = \boxed{}$

0            $\frac{1}{3}$

13. $\frac{2}{5} \div \frac{1}{10} = \boxed{}$ $\frac{1}{10}$ $\frac{1}{10}$ $\frac{1}{10}$ $\frac{1}{10}$

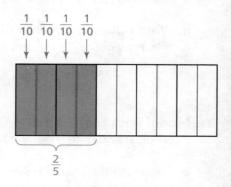

$\frac{2}{5}$

In 14–25, find each quotient.

14. $\frac{2}{3} \div \frac{1}{3}$

15. $\frac{1}{2} \div \frac{1}{16}$

16. $\frac{1}{4} \div \frac{1}{12}$

17. $\frac{6}{7} \div \frac{3}{7}$

18. $\frac{5}{14} \div \frac{4}{7}$

19. $\frac{5}{8} \div \frac{1}{2}$

20. $\frac{7}{12} \div \frac{3}{4}$

21. $\frac{2}{7} \div \frac{1}{2}$

22. $\frac{4}{9} \div \frac{2}{3}$

23. $\frac{7}{12} \div \frac{1}{8}$

24. $\frac{3}{10} \div \frac{3}{5}$

25. $\frac{2}{5} \div \frac{1}{8}$

26. Be Precise A large bag contains $\frac{12}{15}$ pound of granola. How many $\frac{1}{3}$-pound bags can be filled with this amount of granola? How much granola is left over?

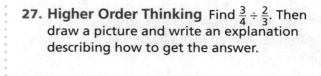

GRANOLA $\frac{1}{3}$ pound $\frac{12}{15}$ lb

27. Higher Order Thinking Find $\frac{3}{4} \div \frac{2}{3}$. Then draw a picture and write an explanation describing how to get the answer.

28. The area of a rectangular painting is $\frac{1}{6}$ square yard. The width is $\frac{2}{3}$ yard. What is the length of the painting? Use the formula $A = \ell \times w$.

29. Solve for n in the equation $\frac{13}{16} \div \frac{1}{6} = n$.

30. Model with Math A cafeteria uses $\frac{1}{6}$ pound of coffee to fill a large coffee dispenser. The cafeteria has $\frac{2}{3}$ pound of coffee to use.

$\frac{2}{3}$

a. Complete the model at the right to find how many coffee dispensers the cafeteria can fill.

b. Write a division sentence that describes the model and tells how many dispensers can be filled.

31. Model with Math A full load for a small truck to haul is $\frac{2}{3}$ ton of gravel. The truck is hauling $\frac{1}{2}$ ton of gravel.

$\frac{1}{2}$ ton gravel

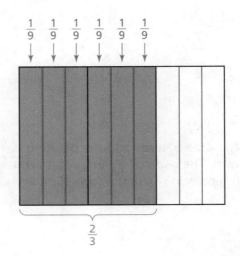

a. Complete the model below to find how much of a full load the truck is hauling.

b. Write a division sentence that describes the model and tells how much of a full load the truck is hauling.

$\frac{1}{2}$

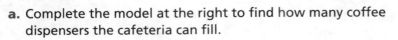
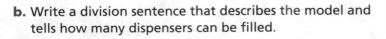

$\frac{2}{3}$

32. Use Structure How many $\frac{1}{4}$-inch pieces can be cut from a piece of metal $\frac{5}{8}$ inch long?

33. Write a problem that could be solved by finding $\frac{5}{8} \div \frac{2}{5}$.

34. Which division sentence is shown by the model at the right?

$\frac{1}{9}$ $\frac{1}{9}$ $\frac{1}{9}$ $\frac{1}{9}$ $\frac{1}{9}$ $\frac{1}{9}$

Ⓐ $\frac{2}{3} \div \frac{1}{9} = 6$

Ⓑ $\frac{1}{9} \div \frac{2}{3} = \frac{1}{6}$

Ⓒ $6 \div \frac{1}{9} = 54$

Ⓓ $6 \div \frac{2}{3} = 9$

$\frac{2}{3}$

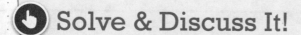 Solve & Discuss It!  ACTIVITY

A jeweler has a $5\frac{1}{2}$-inch strip of silver wire that she is cutting into $1\frac{3}{8}$-inch pieces. How many pieces can she make?

I can...
divide with mixed numbers.

$5\frac{1}{2}$ inches

Generalize How can you use what you know about solving problems with fractions to find how many pieces the jeweler can make?

Focus on math practices

Generalize Explain how to use estimation to check whether your answer is reasonable.

EXAMPLE 1 **Divide a Mixed Number by a Mixed Number**

Scan for Multimedia

Damon has $37\frac{1}{2}$ inches of space on his car bumper that he wants to use for bumper stickers. How many short bumper stickers can Damon fit side by side on his car bumper?

GO GREEN GO Long = 15 inches

I ♥ ROBOTS 🤖 Medium = $10\frac{3}{4}$ inches

MADE IN USA Short = $6\frac{1}{4}$ inches

$37\frac{1}{2}$ inches

STEP 1 Estimate $37\frac{1}{2} \div 6\frac{1}{4}$.

$37\frac{1}{2}$ in.

Bumper space |————————————|

Short sticker | $6\frac{1}{4}$ in. | — *n* stickers →

$37\frac{1}{2} \div 6\frac{1}{4}$
↓   ↓
$36 \div 6 = 6$ ← Use compatible numbers to estimate the quotient.

So, $37\frac{1}{2} \div 6\frac{1}{4} \approx 6$.

STEP 2 Find $37\frac{1}{2} \div 6\frac{1}{4}$. Write each mixed number as a fraction.

$$37\frac{1}{2} \div 6\frac{1}{4} = \frac{75}{2} \div \frac{25}{4}$$
$$= \frac{75}{2} \times \frac{4}{25}$$
$$= \frac{300}{50} \text{ or } 6$$

Use the reciprocal of $\frac{25}{4}$ to write a multiplication problem.

Because 6 is the estimate, the quotient is reasonable. Damon can fit 6 short bumper stickers on his car bumper.

☑ Try It!

How many medium bumper stickers can Damon fit side by side on his car bumper? Find $37\frac{1}{2} \div 10\frac{3}{4}$.

Convince Me! Why do you multiply $\frac{75}{2}$ by $\frac{4}{43}$ to divide $37\frac{1}{2}$ by $10\frac{3}{4}$?

$$37\frac{1}{2} \div 10\frac{3}{4} = \frac{75}{2} \div \boxed{}$$
$$= \frac{75}{2} \times \boxed{}$$
$$= \boxed{}$$

Damon can fit $\boxed{}$ medium bumper stickers on his car bumper.

EXAMPLE 2 ▶ Divide a Whole Number by a Mixed Number

Kayla drives her new car to work every day. It uses $1\frac{3}{5}$ gallons of gas for each round trip. How many round trips to work can Kayla drive on a full tank of gas?

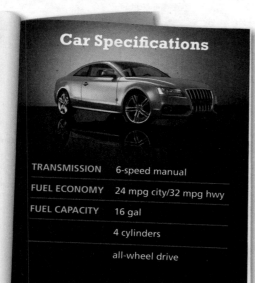

Car Specifications

TRANSMISSION	6-speed manual
FUEL ECONOMY	24 mpg city/32 mpg hwy
FUEL CAPACITY	16 gal
	4 cylinders
	all-wheel drive

STEP 1

Estimate using compatible numbers.

$$16 \div 1\frac{3}{5} \rightarrow 16 \div 2 = 8$$

So, $16 \div 1\frac{3}{5} \approx 8$.

STEP 2

$16 \div 1\frac{3}{5} = \frac{16}{1} \div \frac{8}{5}$ — Write the whole number and mixed number as fractions.

$= \frac{16}{1} \times \frac{5}{8}$ — Multiply by the reciprocal of the divisor.

$= \frac{80}{8}$ or 10

The estimate, 8, is close to the quotient, 10. The answer is reasonable. Kayla can drive 10 round trips to work on a full tank of gas.

EXAMPLE 3 ▶ Divide a Mixed Number by a Whole Number

Lillian hikes the trail in 4 hours. She hikes the same number of miles per hour. How many miles did Lillian hike each hour?

STEP 1

Estimate using compatible numbers.

$$15\frac{5}{6} \div 4 \rightarrow 16 \div 4 = 4$$

So, $15\frac{5}{6} \div 4 \approx 4$.

Trail Length

$15\frac{5}{6}$ Miles

STEP 2

$15\frac{5}{6} \div 4 = \frac{95}{6} \div \frac{4}{1}$ — Write the mixed number and whole number as fractions.

$= \frac{95}{6} \times \frac{1}{4}$ — Multiply by the reciprocal of the divisor.

$= \frac{95}{24}$ or $3\frac{23}{24}$

The estimate, 4, is close to the quotient, $3\frac{23}{24}$. The answer is reasonable. Lillian hikes $3\frac{23}{24}$ miles each hour.

 Try It!

Divide.

a. $20 \div 2\frac{2}{3}$

b. $12\frac{1}{2} \div 6$

To divide with mixed numbers, write mixed numbers and any whole numbers as fractions.

Use the reciprocal of the divisor to rewrite the problem as a multiplication problem.

$$5\frac{1}{3} \div 1\frac{1}{3} = \frac{16}{3} \div \frac{4}{3} = \frac{16}{3} \times \frac{3}{4} = \frac{48}{12} \text{ or } 4$$

Finally, multiply and use the estimate to check whether the answer is reasonable.

Use compatible numbers to estimate.

$$\downarrow \quad \downarrow$$
$$5 \div 1 = 5$$

Do You Understand?

1. **Essential Question** How can you divide with mixed numbers?

2. **Generalize** When dividing mixed numbers, why is it important to estimate the quotient first?

3. **Reasoning** In Example 1, how many long bumper stickers can Damon fit side by side on his car bumper? Will there be uncovered space? Explain.

4. What is the difference between dividing fractions less than 1 and dividing mixed numbers?

Do You Know How?

In 5–13, find each quotient.

5. $2\frac{5}{8} \div 2\frac{1}{4} = \frac{21}{8} \div \boxed{}$

$$= \frac{21}{8} \times \boxed{}$$

$$= \boxed{}$$

6. $3 \div 4\frac{1}{2}$

7. $18 \div 3\frac{2}{3}$

8. $1\frac{2}{5} \div 7$

9. $5 \div 6\frac{2}{5}$

10. $8\frac{1}{5} \div 3\frac{3}{4}$

11. $2\frac{1}{2} \div 4\frac{1}{10}$

12. $2\frac{2}{3} \div 6$

13. $6\frac{5}{9} \div 1\frac{7}{9}$

Practice & Problem Solving

Scan for
Multimedia

Leveled Practice In **14–25**, find each quotient.

14. $10 \div 2\frac{1}{4} = \frac{10}{1} \div \boxed{}$

$\quad = \frac{10}{1} \times \boxed{}$

$\quad = \boxed{}$

15. $9\frac{1}{3} \div 6 = \frac{28}{3} \div \boxed{}$

$\quad = \frac{28}{3} \times \boxed{}$

$\quad = \boxed{}$

16. $1\frac{3}{8} \div 4\frac{1}{8} = \frac{11}{8} \div \boxed{}$

$\quad = \frac{11}{8} \times \boxed{}$

$\quad = \boxed{}$

17. $2\frac{2}{3} \div 8 = \frac{8}{3} \div \boxed{}$

$\quad = \boxed{} \times \boxed{}$

$\quad = \boxed{}$

18. $4\frac{1}{3} \div 3\frac{1}{4} = \frac{13}{3} \div \boxed{}$

$\quad = \boxed{} \times \boxed{}$

$\quad = \boxed{}$

19. $1 \div 8\frac{5}{9} = \frac{1}{1} \div \boxed{}$

$\quad = \boxed{} \times \boxed{}$

$\quad = \boxed{}$

20. $3\frac{5}{6} \div 9\frac{5}{6}$

21. $16 \div 2\frac{2}{3}$

22. $2\frac{5}{8} \div 13$

23. $3\frac{6}{7} \div 6\frac{3}{4}$

24. $2\frac{1}{3} \div 1\frac{1}{3}$

25. $3\frac{3}{4} \div 1\frac{1}{2}$

26. Beth is making a rope ladder. Each step of the ladder is $2\frac{1}{3}$ feet wide. Beth has a rope that is 21 feet long. How many steps can she make from the rope?

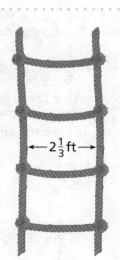

←$2\frac{1}{3}$ ft→

27. The area of this rectangle is $257\frac{1}{4}$ in.² . Find side length w.

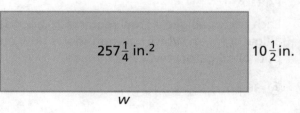

$257\frac{1}{4}$ in.² $10\frac{1}{2}$ in.

w

In 28 and 29, use the picture.

28. The larger room is twice as long as the smaller room. How long is the larger room?

29. If the length of the smaller room is divided into 4 equal parts, how long is each part?

$20\frac{4}{5}$ feet   ?

30. **Make Sense and Persevere** Luis has 3 pounds of ground turkey to make turkey burgers. He uses $\frac{3}{8}$ pound per burger to make 6 burgers. How many $\frac{1}{4}$-pound burgers can Luis make with the remaining turkey?

31. **Higher Order Thinking** If $9 \times \frac{n}{5} = 9 \div \frac{n}{5}$, then what does n equal? Explain.

32. Margaret uses $1\frac{3}{4}$ teaspoons of key lime zest to make 12 key lime cupcakes. She wants to make 30 cupcakes. How much key lime zest will Margaret use?

33. **Use Structure** A gem store in Fort Lauderdale received a shipment of $1\frac{1}{2}$ pounds of moonstone crystals. If these moonstone crystals were separated into 6 equal bags, how much would each bag weigh?

34. The owner of an aquatic store used $17\frac{1}{2}$ gallons of water to fill aquariums. He put $5\frac{5}{6}$ gallons of water in each aquarium. How many aquariums did he fill?

35. Write an explanation to a friend about how you would estimate $17\frac{1}{5} \div 3\frac{4}{5}$.

✓ Assessment Practice

36. A restaurant has $15\frac{1}{5}$ pounds of alligator meat to make tasty alligator dishes.

PART A

Each pot of alligator stew requires $2\frac{3}{8}$ pounds of alligator meat. Which solution shows how many pots of alligator stew can be made?

Ⓐ 36 pots; $15\frac{1}{5} \times 2\frac{3}{8}$

Ⓑ $\frac{5}{32}$ pot; $2\frac{3}{8} \div 15\frac{1}{5}$

Ⓒ 7 pots; $15\frac{1}{5} \div 2\frac{3}{8}$

Ⓓ 6 pots; $15\frac{1}{5} \div 2\frac{3}{8}$

PART B

The restaurant could make a smaller pot of alligator stew that uses $1\frac{3}{5}$ pounds of alligator meat. How many more smaller pots of alligator stew can be made than the larger pots?

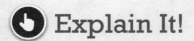

Explain It!

Jenna feeds her cat twice a day. She gives her cat $\frac{3}{4}$ can of cat food each time. Jenna is having a friend take care of her cat for 5 days. To prepare, she bought 8 cans of cat food. Did Jenna buy enough cat food?

ACTIVITY

I can... solve multistep problems with fractions and decimals.

A. What do you need to know before you can answer the question?

B. How can you determine which operations to use to solve the problem?

Focus on math practices

Reasoning To find out whether she has enough cat food, Jenna multiplies, divides, and compares. Explain how Jenna may have solved the problem.

? Essential Question How can you solve problems with rational numbers?

Scan for Multimedia

EXAMPLE 1 **Solve Multistep Problems with Fractions**

A farmer is building a small horse-riding arena. The fencing around the arena is built using three rows of wood planks. The farmer decided to use wood planks that are $8\frac{1}{2}$ feet long, so he ordered 130 of these wood planks from a local lumberyard. Did he order enough wood planks to build the arena?

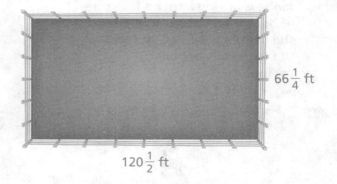

$66\frac{1}{4}$ ft

$120\frac{1}{2}$ ft

Find the perimeter of the arena.

$$P = 2 \times 120\frac{1}{2} + 2 \times 66\frac{1}{4}$$

$$= 241 + 132\frac{1}{2}$$

$$= 373\frac{1}{2} \text{ ft}$$

The farmer needs enough wood planks for 3 times the perimeter.

$$3 \times 373\frac{1}{2} = 1,120\frac{1}{2} \text{ ft}$$

Divide to find how many $8\frac{1}{2}$-foot-long planks are needed.

$$1,120\frac{1}{2} \div 8\frac{1}{2} = \frac{2,241}{2} \div \frac{17}{2}$$

$$= \frac{2,241}{2} \times \frac{2}{17}$$

$$= \frac{4,482}{34} \text{ or } 131\frac{14}{17}$$

The farmer needs at least 132 wood planks to build the fencing. He did not order enough wood planks.

✅ **Try It!**

The farmer decided that he ordered enough planks for an arena that measured $115\frac{1}{4}$ ft by $63\frac{1}{2}$ ft. Is he correct? Explain.

Convince Me! What questions do you need to answer to solve the Try It!?

EXAMPLE **2**

Solve Multistep Problems with Decimals

A 26.2-mile marathon is being planned. Water stations and medic tents must be placed along the route.

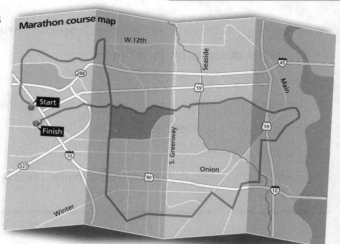

Marathon course map

A. Water stations are being set every 2.62 miles along the marathon route and at the start line. How many water stations are needed?

> Divide 26.2 by 2.62 to find the number of water stations along the route.

$$26.2 \div 2.62 = 10$$

$$10 + 1 = 11$$

> Add 1 to include the water station at the start line.

A total of 11 water stations are needed for the marathon.

B. There are 5 medic tents equally spaced along the marathon route, including one at the starting line and one at the finish line. Where should the other 3 medic tents be placed?

Be Precise You can be precise by calculating accurately when you solve problems.

> Divide 26.2 by 4 to find the location for the first medic tent after the one at the starting line.

$$26.2 \div 4 = 6.55$$

$$6.55 \times 2 = 13.1 \qquad 6.55 \times 3 = 19.65$$

> Double the distance to find the location of the third tent.

> Triple the distance to find the location of the fourth tent.

The fifth tent is at the finish line.

The medic tents are placed at the starting line, at 6.55 miles, at 13.1 miles, at 19.65 miles, and at the finish line.

 Try It!

The number of runners who finish the marathon is 320. Runners donate $2.50 for each mile they run. How much money is donated? Explain.

$$26.2 \times \boxed{} = \boxed{} \text{ miles}$$

$$\boxed{} \times \$2.50 = \boxed{}$$

When solving multistep problems with fractions or decimals:

- decide the steps to use to solve the problem.
- choose the correct operations.
- identify the information you need from the problem.
- correctly use the information.
- calculate accurately.
- interpret solutions and check that the answer is reasonable.

Do You Understand?

1. **? Essential Question** How can you solve problems with rational numbers?

2. **Be Precise** Meghan has $5\frac{1}{4}$ yards of fabric. She plans to use $\frac{2}{3}$ of the fabric to make 4 identical backpacks. To find how much fabric she will use to make the backpacks, Meghan multiplies $5\frac{1}{4}$ by $\frac{2}{3}$. What else does Meghan need to do to find how much fabric she needs for each backpack?

3. **Critique Reasoning** Each side of a square patio is 10.5 feet. The patio is made up of 1.5-foot by 1.5-foot square stones. What is the number of stones in the patio? Look at the solution below. Does it include all the steps needed to solve the problem? Explain.

   $10.5 \times 10.5 = 110.25$

   $110.25 \div 1.5 = 73.5$

Do You Know How?

4. Devon records 4 hours of reality shows on her DVR. She records comedy shows for $\frac{3}{8}$ of that amount of time. Devon watches all the reality and comedy shows in half-hour sittings.

   a. Find the number of hours of comedy shows that Devon records.

   b. Find the total number of hours of reality and comedy shows that Devon records.

   c. Find the number of half-hour sittings needed to watch all the shows.

5. An auto mechanic earns $498.75 in 35 hours during the week. His pay is $2.50 more per hour on weekends. If he works 6 hours on the weekend in addition to 35 hours during the week, how much does he earn?

   a. What questions do you need to answer to solve the problem?

   b. How much does the auto mechanic earn? Explain.

Practice & Problem Solving

Scan for
Multimedia

In 6–8, use the picture at the right.

6. You buy 3.17 pounds of apples, 1.25 pounds of pears, and 2.56 pounds of oranges. What is your total bill rounded to the nearest cent?

Oranges
$1.09 lb

Apples
$0.99 lb

Pears
$1.19 lb

7. A student pays for 8.9 pounds of apples with a $10 bill. How much change does the student receive?

   a. What do you do first to solve the problem?

   b. What do you do next?

8. A customer pays $3.27 for oranges and $4.76 for pears. How many pounds of fruit does the customer buy?

   a. What do you do first to solve the problem?

   b. What do you do next?

9. **Critique Reasoning** Students put $2\frac{1}{4}$ pounds of trail mix into bags that each weigh $\frac{3}{8}$ pound. They bring $\frac{2}{3}$ of the bags of trail mix on a hiking trip. Can you determine how many bags of trail mix are left by completing just one step? Explain.

10. Three fifths of the T-shirts in a T-shirt shop are blue. Five eighths of those T-shirts are on sale. One third of the blue T-shirts that are on sale are size medium. What fraction of the shop's T-shirts are blue T-shirts that are on sale and are size medium? Explain.

In 11 and 12, use the diagram.

A community garden is made up of three gardens: a vegetable garden, an herb garden, and a flower garden.

11. The area of the vegetable garden is 0.4 of the area of the community garden. What is the area of the vegetable garden?

Community Garden

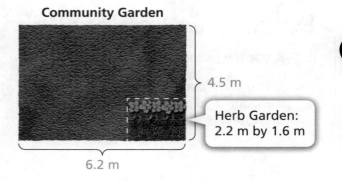

4.5 m

Herb Garden: 2.2 m by 1.6 m

6.2 m

12. The area of the flower garden is 9.7 square meters greater than the herb garden. What is the area of the flower garden?

13. **Reasoning** At the end of a party, $\frac{3}{4}$ cup of smoked fish dip is left. Jim divides $\frac{4}{5}$ of the leftover smoked fish dip equally between 2 friends. How much dip does each friend get?

14. Students are planning a 3-day hiking trip in the Everglades. The hike covers a distance of 18.5 kilometers. The students hike 0.28 of the total distance the first day. If they split the remaining distance equally between the second and third days, how far will they hike on day 3?

15. **Higher Order Thinking** Kelly buys three containers of potato salad at the deli. She brings $\frac{4}{5}$ of the potato salad to a picnic. How many pounds of potato salad does Kelly bring to the picnic? Describe two different ways to solve the problem.

POTATO SALAD WEIGHT 1.03 lb

POTATO SALAD WEIGHT 1.12 lb

POTATO SALAD WEIGHT 1.6 lb

✓ Assessment Practice

16. Students make $84\frac{1}{2}$ ounces of liquid soap for a craft fair. They put the soap in $6\frac{1}{2}$-ounce bottles and sell each bottle for $5.50. Which expression shows how much students earn if they sell all the bottles of liquid soap?

   Ⓐ $71.50; $\left(84\frac{1}{2} \div 6\frac{1}{2}\right) \times 5.50$

   Ⓑ $92.18; $\left(84\frac{1}{2} \div 5.50\right) \times 6$

   Ⓒ $18.50; $\left(84\frac{1}{2} \div 6\frac{1}{2}\right) + 5.50$

   Ⓓ $99.86; $\left(84\frac{1}{2} \times 6\frac{1}{2}\right) \div 5.50$

17. Claire mowed 5 lawns last week. She mowed each lawn in $\frac{7}{12}$ hour. She mowed the same lawns this week in $\frac{5}{12}$ hour each using her new lawn mower. How many times longer was Claire's time to mow all the lawns last week than this week?

? Topic Essential Question

How can you fluently add, subtract, multiply, and divide decimals?
How can you multiply and divide fractions?

Vocabulary Review

Complete each definition and then provide an example of each vocabulary word.

Vocabulary	reciprocal	dividend	fraction	product

Definition	Example
1. The answer to a multiplication problem is called a _____.	
2. The _____ is the quantity to be divided.	
3. To write a division expression as multiplication, you multiply by the _____ of the divisor.	

Use Vocabulary in Writing

Explain how to use multiplication to find the value of $\frac{1}{3} \div \frac{9}{5}$. Use the words *multiplication*, *divisor*, *quotient*, and *reciprocal* in your explanation.

Concepts and Skills Review

Fluently Add, Subtract, and Multiply Decimals

Quick Review

To add or subtract decimals, line up the decimal points so that place-value positions correspond. Add or subtract as you would with whole numbers, and place the decimal point in the answer. To multiply decimals, multiply as you would with whole numbers, then place the decimal point in the product by starting at the right and counting the number of places equal to the sum of the number of decimal places in each factor.

Example

Add, subtract, or multiply.

```
  22.6        22.6          22.6    1 decimal place
+ 12.4      − 12.4        × 12.4    1 decimal place
───────     ───────      ───────
  35.0        10.2           904
                            4520
                        + 22600
                        ───────
                         280.24    2 decimal places
```

Practice

Add, subtract, or multiply.

1. $91.2 + 89.9$

2. $902.3 − 8.8$

3. 5×98.2

4. 4×0.21

5. $62.99 − 10.83$

6. $423.22 + 98.30$

7. 4.4×6

8. 7×21.6

9. $24.52 − 9.6$

10. $369.45 + 32.42$

11. 12.5×163.2

12. 16×52.3

13. $121.3 + 435.7$

14. $201.7 − 104.6$

Fluently Divide Whole Numbers and Decimals

Quick Review

To divide decimals, multiply the divisor and the dividend by the same power of 10 so that the divisor is a whole number. Then use an algorithm for whole-number division.

Example

Find $2.75 \div 0.05$.

```
      55.
   ┌──────
5 )  275.
   − 25
   ──────
      25
    − 25
   ──────
       0
```

Multiply the divisor and the dividend by the same power of 10 to divide with whole numbers.

Place the decimal point in the quotient and divide.

Practice

Divide.

1. $9.6 \div 1.6$

2. $48.4 \div 0.4$

3. $13.2 \div 0.006$

4. $10.8 \div 0.09$

5. $45 \div 4.5$

6. $1{,}008 \div 1.8$

7. $1.26 \div 0.2$

8. $2.24 \div 3.2$

9. $35.75 \div 55$

10. $120.4 \div 602$

11. $330 \div 5.5$

12. $1.08 \div 0.027$

Quick Review

Multiply the numerators to find the numerator of the product. Multiply the denominators to find the denominator of the product.

Example

Find $\frac{2}{3} \times \frac{5}{6}$.

For $\frac{5}{6}$, shade 5 columns.

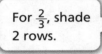

For $\frac{2}{3}$, shade 2 rows.

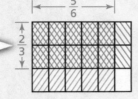

10 of the 18 rectangles are in the overlap area. So, $\frac{2}{3} \times \frac{5}{6} = \frac{10}{18}$ or $\frac{5}{9}$.

Practice

Find each product.

1. $\frac{2}{3} \times \frac{3}{8}$ 2. $\frac{1}{4} \times \frac{3}{5}$

3. $\frac{1}{6} \times \frac{1}{8}$ 4. $\frac{4}{7} \times \frac{4}{7}$

5. $\frac{6}{7} \times \frac{1}{2}$ 6. $\frac{3}{8} \times \frac{8}{3}$

7. $\frac{2}{3} \times \frac{1}{3}$ 8. $\frac{7}{8} \times \frac{3}{2}$

9. $2\frac{1}{3} \times 4\frac{1}{5}$ 10. $4\frac{1}{2} \times 6\frac{2}{3}$

11. $3\frac{3}{5} \times 2\frac{5}{7}$ 12. $14\frac{2}{7} \times 4\frac{3}{10}$

Quick Review

To divide by a fraction, use the reciprocal of the divisor to rewrite the problem as a multiplication problem.

Example

Find $4 \div \frac{4}{5}$.

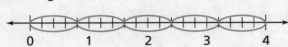

$4 \div \frac{4}{5} = 4 \times \frac{5}{4}$

Use the reciprocal of the divisor.

$\frac{4}{1} \times \frac{5}{4} = \frac{20}{4}$ or 5

Find $\frac{3}{4} \div \frac{1}{8}$.

$\frac{3}{4} \div \frac{1}{8} = \frac{3}{4} \times \frac{8}{1}$

Rewrite the problem as a multiplication problem.

$\frac{3}{4} \times \frac{8}{1} = \frac{24}{4}$ or 6

Practice

Find each quotient.

1. $7 \div \frac{1}{2}$ 2. $6 \div \frac{2}{5}$

3. $2 \div \frac{1}{8}$ 4. $8 \div \frac{4}{9}$

5. $\frac{1}{2} \div \frac{1}{4}$ 6. $\frac{8}{10} \div \frac{1}{5}$

7. $\frac{5}{6} \div \frac{3}{8}$ 8. $\frac{1}{3} \div \frac{1}{2}$

9. $5 \div \frac{5}{16}$ 10. $\frac{7}{12} \div \frac{3}{4}$

11. $20 \div \frac{5}{6}$ 12. $16 \div \frac{1}{4}$

13. $\frac{4}{5} \div \frac{1}{8}$ 14. $5 \div \frac{1}{10}$

15. $\frac{7}{11} \div \frac{1}{11}$ 16. $4 \div \frac{2}{8}$

Quick Review

To divide by a mixed number, rename each mixed number as a fraction. Then use the reciprocal of the divisor to rewrite the problem as a multiplication problem.

Example

$6\frac{1}{2} \div 1\frac{1}{6} = \frac{13}{2} \div \frac{7}{6}$ — Rename the mixed numbers as fractions.

$\frac{13}{2} \div \frac{7}{6} = \frac{13}{2} \times \frac{6}{7}$ — Write the problem as a multiplication problem using the reciprocal of the divisor.

$\frac{13}{2} \times \frac{6}{7} = \frac{78}{14}$ or $5\frac{4}{7}$ — Multiply. Rename the fraction quotient as a mixed number.

Practice

Find each quotient.

1. $6\frac{3}{8} \div 4\frac{1}{4}$ **2.** $9 \div 2\frac{2}{7}$

3. $3\frac{3}{5} \div 1\frac{1}{5}$ **4.** $5\frac{1}{2} \div 3\frac{3}{8}$

5. $3\frac{2}{5} \div 1\frac{1}{5}$ **6.** $12\frac{1}{6} \div 3$

7. $12 \div 1\frac{1}{2}$ **8.** $3\frac{1}{2} \div 2\frac{1}{4}$

9. $8 \div 1\frac{1}{4}$ **10.** $10\frac{1}{2} \div 1\frac{3}{4}$

11. $3\frac{3}{4} \div 2\frac{1}{2}$ **12.** $60 \div 3\frac{1}{3}$

Quick Review

When solving multistep problems:

- decide the steps to solve the problem.
- choose the correct operations.
- identify the information you need from the problem.
- correctly use the information.
- calculate accurately.
- check if the answer is reasonable.

Example

Jane's garden is 3.4 meters by 6.5 meters. If fencing costs $2.25 per meter, how much will it cost to enclose Jane's garden?

Step 1: Find how much fence is needed.
3.4 + 3.4 + 6.5 + 6.5 = 19.8 meters

Step 2: Multiply to find the cost.
19.8 × 2.25 = $44.55

Step 3: Estimate to check.
3 + 3 + 7 + 7 = 20 meters
20 × 2.00 = $40.00
$40 is close to $44.55, so the answer is reasonable.

Practice

Daisy has one cucumber that is 3 inches long and another cucumber that is 5 inches long. She cuts the cucumbers into $\frac{3}{8}$-inch-thick slices and adds them to a salad. How many $\frac{3}{8}$-inch-thick slices does Daisy have?

1. Write division expressions to represent the first steps in the problem.

2. Solve. Then explain your answer.

Pathfinder

Shade a path from START to FINISH. Follow the solutions in which the digit in the hundredths place is greater than the digit in the tenths place. You can only move up, down, right, or left.

I can...
multiply and divide decimals.

START

22.04 × 9	7.2⟌42.12	53.08 × 2.4	0.18 × 1.5	7⟌0.28
25⟌28	3.71 × 0.6	2.5⟌23.35	9⟌0.954	0.9 × 0.27
12.4 × 14.6	1.3⟌2.314	86.35 × 7	0.4⟌1.06	6⟌72.72
1.2⟌0.9	1.05 × 1.05	2.4⟌8.7	7.2 × 0.06	75⟌18
86.3 × 0.4	16⟌0.04	8⟌4.4	5.2 × 3.8	22.3 × 1.8

FINISH

TOPIC 2

INTEGERS AND RATIONAL NUMBERS

? Topic Essential Question

What are integers and rational numbers? How are points graphed on a coordinate plane?

Topic Overview

Topic Vocabulary

- absolute value
- coordinate plane
- integers
- opposites
- ordered pair
- origin
- quadrants
- rational number
- x- and y-axes

Go online

Lesson Digital Resources

INTERACTIVE STUDENT EDITION
Access online or offline.

VISUAL LEARNING ANIMATION
Interact with visual learning animations.

ACTIVITY Use with *Solve & Discuss It, Explore It*, and *Explain It* activities, and to explore Examples.

VIDEOS Watch clips to support *3-Act Mathematical Modeling Lessons* and *STEM Projects*.

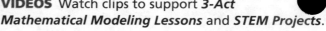

3-ACT MATH

The ULTIMATE THROW

 The Ultimate Throw

Have you ever played ultimate? It's a team sport played with a flying disc. The goal is to score the most points by passing the disc to your opponent's end zone. Ultimate is played by millions of people across the globe, from casual games to professional leagues.

There are many ways to throw a flying disc. It takes a lot of practice to learn each type of throw. If you want the disc to travel a specific path and distance, you need to try different throws with different amounts of spin and power. Think about this during the 3-Act Mathematical Modeling lesson.

PRACTICE Practice what you've learned.

TUTORIALS Get help from *Virtual Nerd*, right when you need it.

MATH TOOLS Explore math with digital tools.

GAMES Play Math Games to help you learn.

KEY CONCEPT Review important lesson content.

GLOSSARY Read and listen to English/Spanish definitions.

ASSESSMENT Show what you've learned.

Did You Know?

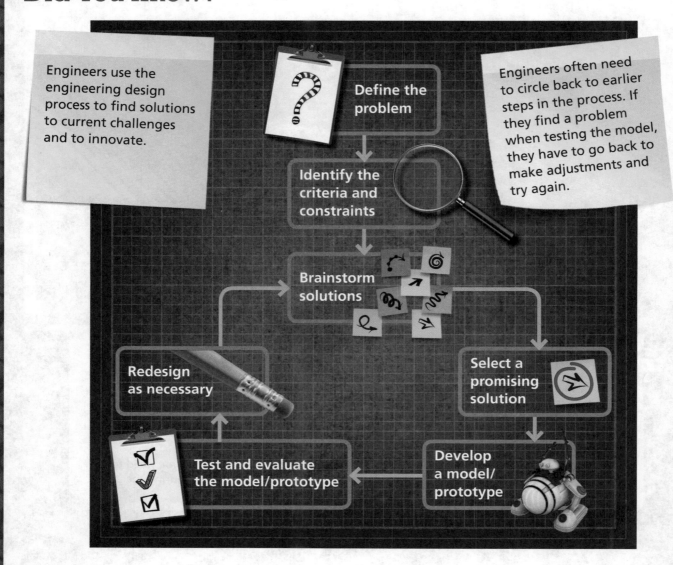

Engineers use the engineering design process to find solutions to current challenges and to innovate.

Engineers often need to circle back to earlier steps in the process. If they find a problem when testing the model, they have to go back to make adjustments and try again.

Define the problem

Identify the criteria and constraints

Brainstorm solutions

Redesign as necessary

Select a promising solution

Test and evaluate the model/prototype

Develop a model/prototype

Your Task: Improve Your School

Now that you have defined the problem, or improvement needed, you and your classmates will apply the engineering design process to propose solutions.

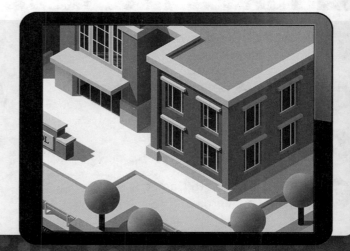

Review What You Know!

Vocabulary

Choose the best term from the box to complete each definition.

decimal
denominator
fraction
numerator

1. A _____ names part of a whole, part of a set, or a location on a number line.

2. The number above the fraction bar that represents the part

   of the whole is the _____.

3. The number below the fraction bar that represents the total

   number of equal parts in one whole is the _____.

Fractions and Decimals

Write each fraction as a decimal.

4. $\frac{2}{5}$

5. $\frac{3}{4}$

6. $\frac{10}{4}$

7. $\frac{12}{5}$

8. $\frac{3}{5}$

9. $\frac{15}{3}$

Division with Decimals

Divide.

10. $1.25 \div 0.5$

11. $13 \div 0.65$

12. $12.2 \div 0.4$

Ordered Pairs

Write the ordered pair for each point shown on the graph.

13. *J*

14. *K*

15. *L*

16. *M*

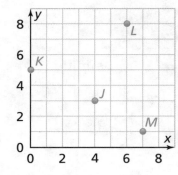

Plot each point on the coordinate plane.

17. *A*(6, 2)

18. *B*(1, 3)

19. *C*(5, 7)

20. *D*(3, 4)

Explain

21. Les said that the quotient of $3.9 \div 0.75$ is 0.52. Explain how you know Les is incorrect without completing the division.

Language Development

Use the graphic organizer to help you understand new vocabulary terms.

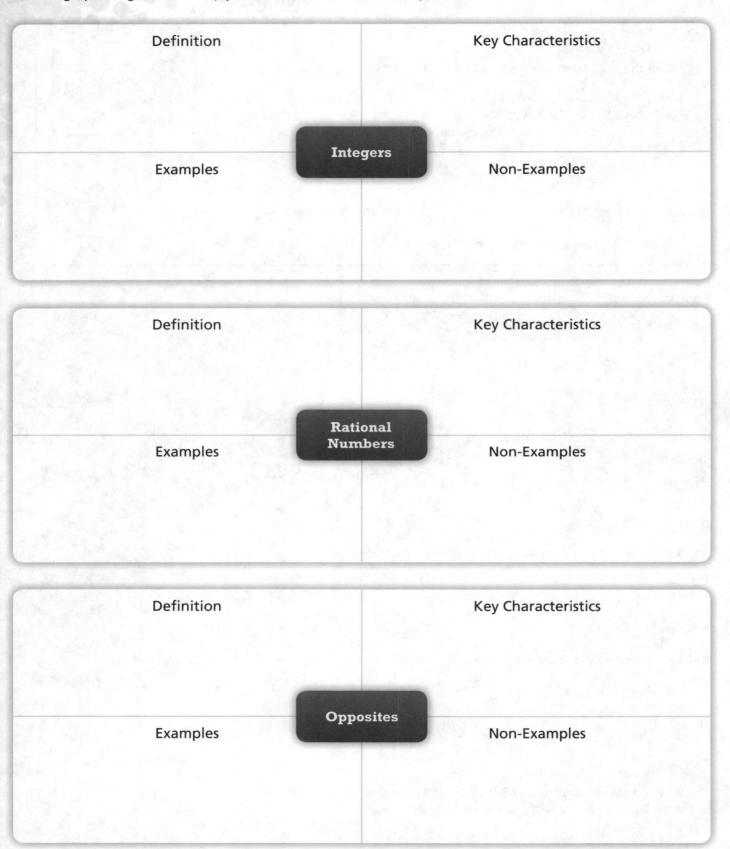

Definition	Key Characteristics
Integers	
Examples	Non-Examples

Definition	Key Characteristics
Rational Numbers	
Examples	Non-Examples

Definition	Key Characteristics
Opposites	
Examples	Non-Examples

PROJECT
2A

What places would you like to visit in the United States?

PROJECT: MAKE A TRAVEL BROCHURE

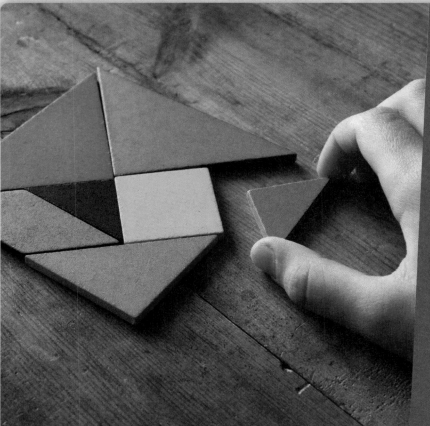

PROJECT
2B

If you were to solve a puzzle, what type would you choose?

PROJECT: DESIGN A CONNECT-THE-DOTS PUZZLE

PROJECT 2C

What are some exercises for staying fit and having fun?

PROJECT: RECORD AN EXERCISE VIDEO

PROJECT 2D

If you were going to make a commercial, what type of product would you feature?

PROJECT: WRITE YOUR OWN COMMERCIAL

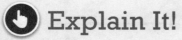 Explain It!

 ACTIVITY

Sal recorded the outdoor temperature as −4°F at 7:30 A.M.
At noon, it was 22°F. Sal said the temperature changed by
18°F because 22 − 4 = 18.

I can...
use positive and negative
integers.

A. Critique Reasoning Is Sal right or wrong? Explain.

B. Construct Arguments What was the total temperature change from
7:30 A.M. until noon? Use the thermometer to help justify your solution.

Focus on math practices

Reasoning 0°C is the temperature at which water freezes. Which is colder,
10°C or −10°C? Explain.

EXAMPLE 1 **Define Integers and Opposites**

Scan for Multimedia

The counting numbers, their opposites, and 0 are **integers**. Numbers that are located on opposite sides of 0 and are the same distance from 0 on a number line are **opposites**. What integer is the opposite of 6? What is the opposite of −6?

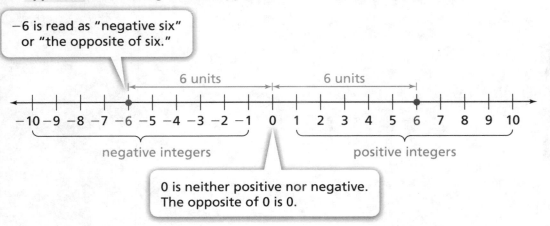

−6 is read as "negative six" or "the opposite of six."

6 units   6 units

negative integers   positive integers

0 is neither positive nor negative. The opposite of 0 is 0.

A thermometer is like a vertical number line that uses integers to show temperatures measured in degrees.

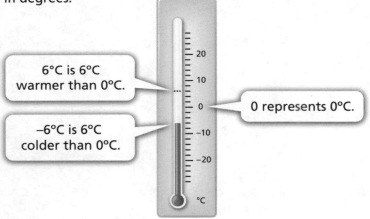

6°C is 6°C warmer than 0°C.

0 represents 0°C.

−6°C is 6°C colder than 0°C.

−6 is the opposite of 6.

The opposite of the opposite of a number is the number itself.

For example, the opposite of 6 is −6, and the opposite of −6 is 6.

Use Structure To represent the opposite of −6, write −(−6).

☑ Try It!

Label the integers on the number line.

The opposite of 4 is [ ].   The opposite of −4 is [ ].

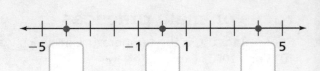

−5   −1   1   5

Convince Me! How do you know that two numbers are opposites?

EXAMPLE 2 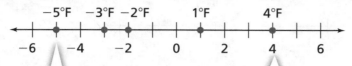 Compare and Order Integers

Riley recorded the temperatures for five days in January. Which day was the coldest day of Riley's data? Which was the warmest day? Write the temperatures from least to greatest.

Day	Monday	Tuesday	Wednesday	Thursday	Friday
Temperature (°F)	−5°F	−2°F	4°F	−3°F	1°F

−5°F is the integer farthest to the left on the number line, so Monday was the coldest day.

4°F is the integer farthest to the right on the number line, so Wednesday was the warmest day.

The temperatures from least to greatest are: −5°F, −3°F, −2°F, 1°F, 4°F.

Try It!

Which number is greater, −4 or −2? Explain.

EXAMPLE 3 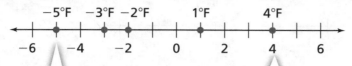 Use Integers to Represent Quantities

Integers describe many real-world situations including altitude, elevation, depth, temperature, and electrical charges. Zero represents a specific value in each situation. Which integer represents sea level? The airplane? The whale?

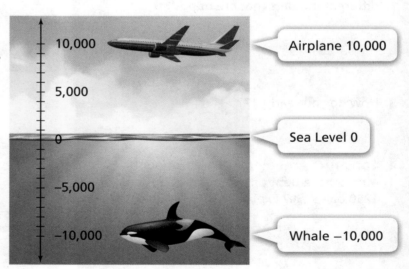

Airplane 10,000

Sea Level 0

Whale −10,000

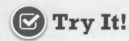 Try It!

Which integer represents each situation?

a. A $10 debt   b. Six degrees below zero   c. Deposit of $25

Integers are all of the counting numbers, their opposites, and 0.
Opposites are integers that are the same distance from 0 and on opposite sides of 0 on a number line.

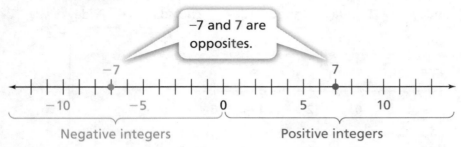

−7 and 7 are opposites.

−7   7

Negative integers   Positive integers

Do You Understand?

1. **Essential Question** What are integers and how are they used to represent real-world quantities?

2. **Reasoning** What do you know about two different integers that are opposites?

3. How do you read −17?

4. **Construct Arguments** Which amount represents a debt of two hundred fifty dollars, $250 or −$250? Explain.

5. **Generalize** When comparing two negative integers, how can you determine which integer is the greater number?

Do You Know How?

In **6–17**, write the opposite of each integer.

6. 1

7. −1

8. −11

9. 30

10. 0

11. −16

12. −(−8)

13. 28

14. −(−65)

15. 98

16. 100

17. −33

In **18–20**, write the integers in order from least to greatest.

18. 2, −3, 0, −4

19. 4, 12, −12, −11

20. −5, 6, −7, −8

Practice & Problem Solving

Scan for
Multimedia

In 21–24, use the pictures at the right.

21. Generalize Which integer represents sea level? Explain.

Ruppell's Griffons fly up to 37,000 feet above sea level.

22. Use a negative integer to represent the depth to which a dolphin may swim.

A migrating bird flies up to 5,000 feet above sea level.

23. Which of these animals can travel at the greatest distance from sea level?

24. Order the elevations of the animals as integers from least to greatest.

A dolphin can swim to 150 feet below sea level.

A sperm whale can swim to 3,000 feet below sea level.

In 25–30, plot each point on the number line below.

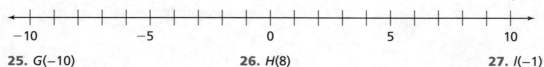

25. $G(-10)$ **26.** $H(8)$ **27.** $I(-1)$

28. $J(9)$ **29.** $K(6)$ **30.** $L(-3)$

In 31–36, write the integer value that each point represents. Then use the number line to help write its opposite.

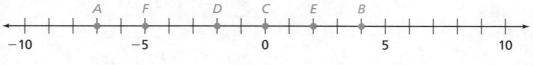

31. A **32.** B **33.** C

34. D **35.** E **36.** F

37. Write the opposite of each integer.

    A. 5   **B.** −13   **C.** −(−22)

    D. −31   **E.** −50   **F.** −(−66)

38. Compare the integers and write the integer with the greater value.

    A. −5, 1   **B.** −6, −7   **C.** −9, 8

    D. −12, −(−10)   **E.** −(−9), 11   **F.** −(−4), 3

39. The display at the right shows the daily low temperatures for several consecutive days in a New England city. Write the temperatures in order from least to greatest. On which day was it the coldest?

MON	TUE	WED	THU
4°	−5°	−7°	7°

40. In a bank account, a paid-out expense is called a *debit*, and a deposit is called a *credit*. Would you use positive or negative integers to represent credits? Debits? Explain.

41. Higher Order Thinking Atoms have negatively charged particles called *electrons* and positively charged particles called *protons*. If an atom loses an electron, it has a positive electric charge. If it gains an electron, it has a negative electric charge. Which integer would represent the electric charge of an atom that has an equal number of electrons and protons?

☑ Assessment Practice

42. Marco goes on a recreational scuba diving expedition. What is a possible diving depth for his expedition?

    Ⓐ 0 meters

    Ⓑ 40 meters

    Ⓒ 400 meters

    Ⓓ −40 meters

43. Fill in the bubbles to match each integer with its opposite.

	8	−19	−24	−(−24)
−24	Ⓐ	Ⓑ	Ⓒ	Ⓓ
19	Ⓔ	Ⓕ	Ⓖ	Ⓗ
24	Ⓘ	Ⓙ	Ⓚ	Ⓛ
−8	Ⓜ	Ⓝ	Ⓞ	Ⓟ

Lesson 2-2
Represent
Rational Numbers
on the Number
Line

Go Online

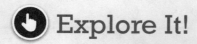 **Explore It!**

 ACTIVITY

The locations of four animals relative to sea level are shown.

Seagull $\frac{3}{4}$ yard

Dolphin $-\frac{1}{4}$ yard

Shark −0.5 yard

Sea Turtle −1 yard

I can...
represent rational numbers using
a number line.

A. What can you say about the animals
and their positions relative to sea level?

B. How can you use a number line
to represent the locations of the
animals?

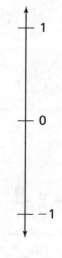

Focus on math practices

Generalize How is representing the locations of negative fractions and
decimals like representing the locations of positive fractions and decimals?
How is it different?

Scan for
Multimedia

EXAMPLE 1 **Understand Rational Numbers**

Any number that can be written as the quotient of two integers is called a **rational number**. A rational number can be written in the form $\frac{a}{b}$ or $-\frac{a}{b}$, where a and b are integers and $b \neq 0$. A rational number can be a whole number, fraction, or decimal.

How can you find and position $-\frac{4}{3}$ and -1.5 on a number line?

Generalize You can plot numbers on horizontal or vertical number lines.

$-\frac{8}{9}$ and $\frac{3}{5}$ are rational numbers in the form $\frac{a}{b}$ or $-\frac{a}{b}$.

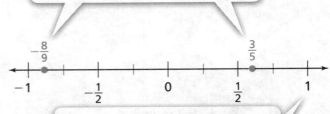

1 is a rational number because it can be written as $\frac{1}{1}$.

ONE WAY Use a horizontal number line to plot $-\frac{4}{3}$.

You can write $-\frac{4}{3}$ as a mixed number.

$$-\frac{4}{3} = -1\frac{1}{3}$$

Divide the units on the number line into thirds and find one and one-third to the left of 0.

ANOTHER WAY Use a vertical number line to plot -1.5.

You can write -1.5 as a mixed number.

$$-1.5 = -1\frac{5}{10} \text{ or } -1\frac{1}{2}$$

Divide the units on the number line into halves and find one and one-half below 0.

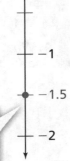

☑ Try It!

How can you find and position $-\frac{5}{4}$ and -1.75 on the number lines? Write $-\frac{5}{4}$ and -1.75 as mixed numbers, then plot the points on the number lines.

$$-\frac{5}{4} = \boxed{} \qquad -1.75 = \boxed{}$$

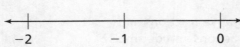

Convince Me! Why is it helpful to rename $-\frac{5}{4}$ and -1.75 as mixed numbers when plotting these points on number lines?

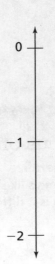

EXAMPLE **2** Compare and Order Rational Numbers

 ACTIVITY ASSESS

Haru was asked to compare and order three rational numbers. Show how he can use <, >, or = to compare $\frac{2}{3}$, 1.75, and −0.75. Then order these numbers from least to greatest.

Look for Relationships
Remember, $\frac{a}{b} = a \div b$, so $\frac{2}{3}$ means $2 \div 3 = 0.66...$ You can use this decimal form of $\frac{2}{3}$ to plot this number on a number line.

−0.75 is a negative number, so it will be farthest to the left on the number line.

1.75 is between 1 and 2.

$\frac{2}{3} = 0.66...$

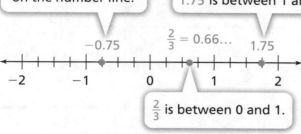

$\frac{2}{3}$ is between 0 and 1.

So, $-0.75 < \frac{2}{3} < 1.75$, and their order from least to greatest is -0.75, $\frac{2}{3}$, 1.75.

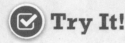 Try It!

If $\frac{1}{4}$ is ordered within the list of numbers in the example above, between which two numbers would it be placed?

EXAMPLE **3** Interpret Rational Numbers in Real-World Contexts

Sam and Rashida are scuba diving. Their locations are shown relative to sea level.

Use <, >, or = to compare the two depths and explain their relationship.

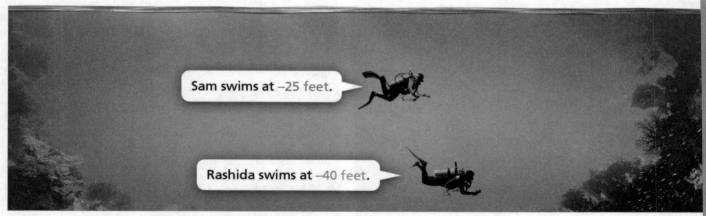

Sam swims at −25 feet.

Rashida swims at −40 feet.

$-40 < -25$. Rashida is at a greater depth than Sam.

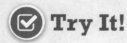 Try It!

At 10:00 P.M. one winter night, the temperature was −3°C. At midnight, the temperature was −7°C. Use <, >, or = to compare the two temperatures and explain their relationship.

A **rational number** can be expressed as a fraction in the form $\frac{a}{b}$ or $-\frac{a}{b}$, where a and b are integers and b is not 0.

The number farthest to the left is the least number.

The number farthest to the right is the greatest number.

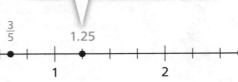

The numbers, in order from least to greatest, are: -1.75, $\frac{3}{5}$, 1.25.

Do You Understand?

1. **? Essential Question** How can you plot, compare, and order rational numbers using a number line?

2. **Generalize** Why are whole numbers rational numbers? Use 15 as an example.

3. **Vocabulary** Why are integers rational numbers? Give an example.

4. **Reasoning** Explain how the inequality $-4°C > -9°C$ describes how the temperatures are related.

Do You Know How?

In **5–7**, write the number positioned at each point.

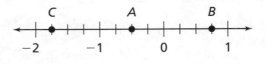

5. A   **6.** B   **7.** C

In **8–11**, plot the points on the number line below.

8. P at $-1\frac{1}{4}$ **9.** Q at 0.25

10. R at -0.75 **11.** S at $-\frac{1}{4}$

In **12–14**, use the number line to help order the numbers from least to greatest.

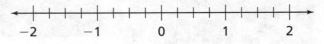

12. 1.25, $-\frac{3}{2}$, -1.25, $1\frac{1}{2}$

13. -0.5, $\frac{1}{2}$, -0.75, $\frac{3}{4}$

14. -1.5, -0.75, -1, 2

Practice & Problem Solving

In 15–20, write the number positioned at each point.

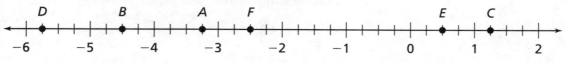

15. *A*

16. *B*

17. *C*

18. *D*

19. *E*

20. *F*

21. **Plot the numbers on the number line below.**

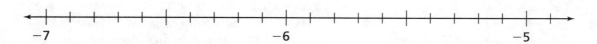

A. $-5\frac{1}{2}$

B. -6.3

C. -5.8

D. $-6\frac{7}{10}$

E. -4.9

F. $-6\frac{9}{10}$

22. Use <, >, or = to compare.

A. $\frac{1}{10}$ ◯ 0.09

B. -1.44 ◯ $-1\frac{1}{4}$

C. $-\frac{2}{3}$ ◯ -0.8

D. 0.5 ◯ $\frac{2}{4}$

E. $-2\frac{3}{4}$ ◯ -2.25

F. $-\frac{3}{5}$ ◯ -0.35

23. Order the numbers from least to greatest.

A. $-6, 8, -9, 13$

B. $-\frac{4}{5}, -\frac{1}{2}, 0.25, -0.2$

C. $4.75, -2\frac{1}{2}, -\frac{8}{3}, \frac{9}{2}$

D. $4, -3, -8, -1$

E. $-\frac{1}{4}, 0.5, \frac{3}{4}, -\frac{1}{2}$

F. $-\frac{4}{5}, -\frac{5}{4}, -\frac{3}{2}, 1.5$

24. Make Sense and Persevere What is the least number of points you must plot to have examples of all four sets of numbers, including at least one positive integer and one negative integer? Explain.

> **Rational Numbers**
> numbers that can be expressed as a quotient of two integers $\frac{a}{b}$ ($b \neq 0$)
>
> > **Integers**
> > whole numbers and their opposites
> >
> > > **Whole Numbers**
> > > zero and natural numbers
> > >
> > > > **Natural Numbers**
> > > > the set of counting numbers
> > > > 1, 2, 3, 4, 5, ...

25. Reasoning Suppose you plot the locations of the animals on a number line. Which animal would be represented by the point farthest from 0 on the number line? Explain.

Animal	Possible Locations Relative to Ocean's Surface
Bloodbelly comb jelly	-0.8 km
Deep sea anglerfish	$-\frac{2}{3}$ km
Fanfin anglerfish	$-2\frac{1}{4}$ km
Gulper eel	-1.1 km
Pacific blackdragon	$-\frac{3}{10}$ km
Slender snipe eel	-0.6 km

26. Which animal is closest to a depth of -0.7 km?

27. The change in the value of a stock is represented by the rational number -5.90. Describe, in words, what this means.

28. Construct Arguments A classmate ordered these numbers from greatest to least. Is he correct? Construct an argument to justify your answer.

$$4.4, \ 4.2, \ -4.42, \ -4.24$$

29. Make Sense and Persevere Order -3.25, $-3\frac{1}{8}$, $-3\frac{3}{4}$, and -3.1 from least to greatest. Explain.

30. Higher Order Thinking Suppose $\frac{a}{b}$, $\frac{c}{d}$, and $\frac{e}{f}$ represent three rational numbers. If $\frac{a}{b}$ is less than $\frac{c}{d}$, and $\frac{c}{d}$ is less than $\frac{e}{f}$, compare $\frac{a}{b}$ and $\frac{e}{f}$. Explain.

✅ Assessment Practice

31. Which could be a value for n?

$$n \quad -\frac{1}{5} \qquad \frac{2}{5} \qquad 0.9$$

Ⓐ $-\frac{1}{2}$

Ⓑ $-\frac{1}{3}$

Ⓒ $-\frac{1}{4}$

Ⓓ $-\frac{1}{6}$

32. Which inequality does NOT represent the correct position of two numbers on a number line?

Ⓐ $4\frac{1}{2} > \frac{25}{4}$

Ⓑ $-4\frac{1}{2} > -\frac{25}{5}$

Ⓒ $-6 < -5$

Ⓓ $-\frac{1}{2} < \frac{1}{2}$

👆 Solve & Discuss It! 📶 👆 ACTIVITY

A portion of a bank account statement is shown below. How would you interpret the value of the ending balance? Explain.

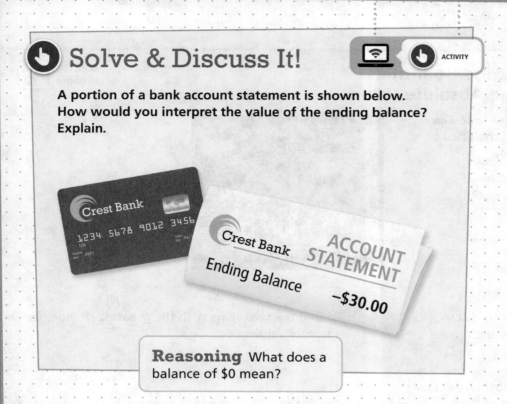

Crest Bank
1234 5678 9012 3456

Crest Bank   ACCOUNT
                    STATEMENT
Ending Balance
                    −$30.00

Reasoning What does a balance of $0 mean?

I can...
find and interpret absolute value.

Focus on math practices

Reasoning What is an example of a bank account balance that represents an amount owed greater than $40?

81

VISUAL LEARNING   ASSESS

EXAMPLE 1  Describe Quantities Using Absolute Value

Scan for Multimedia

Stock prices rise and fall during the year. The table shows the overall change in the price of a company's stock from year to year.

During which two years was the overall change in the stock price the greatest?

Year	Change in Price ($)
2015	11
2014	19
2013	−34
2012	6

The **absolute value** of a number is its distance from 0 on the number line. Distance is always positive.

> The absolute value of −5 is written as |−5|.

> The absolute value of 5 is written |5|.

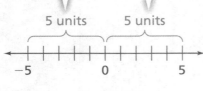

5 units   5 units

|−5| = 5 |5| = 5

> **Look for Relationships** Opposite numbers have the same absolute values because they are the same distance from zero.

To find the two years with the greatest change, use absolute values.

−34   0 6 11 19

The absolute values of the changes in the company's stock price each year are shown below.

2015: |11| = 11
2014: |19| = 19 ·········· 2nd greatest change
2013: |−34| = 34 ·········· greatest change
2012: |6| = 6

So, the two years in which the change in stock price was the greatest were 2013 and 2014.

☑ Try It!

The students in a science class recorded the change in the water level of a local river. During which week did the water level change by the greatest amount?

Use absolute values to represent the change in the water level.

Week	1	2	3
Change in Water Level (in.)	$-7\frac{1}{2}$	2.2	−4.38

The water level changed by the greatest amount in Week ☐.

Convince Me! Can a lesser number represent a greater change in water level than a greater number? Explain.

Week 1: $\left|-7\frac{1}{2}\right| =$ ☐ in.

Week 2: |2.2| = ☐ in.

Week 3: |−4.38| = ☐ in.

EXAMPLE 2 Find Absolute Value

Find each absolute value.

A. |−4| B. |0| C. |3|

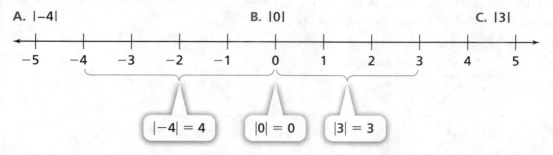

|−4| = 4 |0| = 0 |3| = 3

EXAMPLE 3 Interpret Absolute Value

Negative numbers sometimes represent debts. Yasmin is a business owner. The table shows three account balances that represent her gallery's debts.

A. Which account has the least balance?

B. Which account has the greatest debt?

Yasmin's Gallery

9:24 AM 76%

Account	Balance
A	−$35.42
B	−$50.99
C	−$12.75

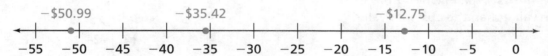

−$50.99   −$35.42   −$12.75

Because −50.99 is farther to the left on the number line than either −35.42 or −12.75, −50.99 is the least number, or the least balance.

The absolute value of each balance describes the size of each debt, or amount of money owed.

Account A	Account B	Account C
|−35.42| = 35.42	|−50.99| = 50.99	|−12.75| = 12.75

$50.99 is the greatest amount of money owed. Account B has the greatest debt.

✓ Try It!

A bank has two customers with overdrawn accounts. Which balance is the greater number? Which balance is the lesser amount owed?

Account	Balance
V. Wong	−$19.45

Account	Balance
J. Olson	−$23.76

The **absolute value** of a number is its distance from 0 on a number line.
Distance is always positive. The absolute value of any number, *n*, is written |*n*|.

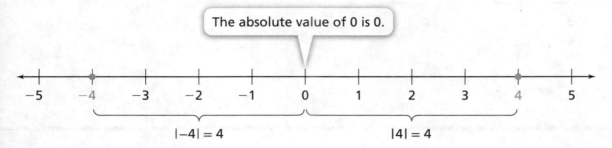

The absolute value of 0 is 0.

|−4| = 4 |4| = 4

−4 and 4 are opposites as they are the same distance from 0.

Do You Understand?

1. **? Essential Question** How are absolute values used to describe quantities?

2. **Construct Arguments** Explain why −7 has a greater absolute value than the absolute value of 6.

3. **Reasoning** Give an example of a balance that has a greater integer value than a balance of −$12, but represents a debt of less than $5.

4. Of the three elevations, −2 feet, −12 feet, and 30 feet, which represents the least number? Which represents the farthest distance from sea level?

Do You Know How?

In 5–14, find each absolute value.

5. $|-9|$

6. $\left|5\frac{3}{4}\right|$

7. $|-5.5|$

8. $|82.5|$

9. $\left|-14\frac{1}{3}\right|$

10. $|-7.75|$

11. $|-19|$

12. $\left|-2\frac{1}{2}\right|$

13. $|24|$

14. $|35.4|$

In 15–17, use the absolute value of each account balance to determine which account has the greater overdrawn amount.

15. Account A: −$5.42
    Account B: −$35.76

16. Account A: −$6.47
    Account B: −$2.56

17. Account A: −$32.56
    Account B: −$29.12

Name: _____

Practice & Problem Solving

Scan for Multimedia

In 18–33, find each absolute value.

18. $|-46|$

19. $|0.7|$

20. $\left|-\frac{2}{3}\right|$

21. $|-7.35|$

22. $\left|-4\frac{3}{4}\right|$

23. $|-54.5|$

24. $\left|27\frac{1}{4}\right|$

25. $|-13.35|$

26. $|14|$

27. $|-11.5|$

28. $|-6.3|$

29. $|3.75|$

30. $|-8.5|$

31. $|15|$

32. $\left|-6\frac{3}{4}\right|$

33. $|-5.3|$

In 34–37, order the numbers from least to greatest.

34. $|-12|, \left|11\frac{3}{4}\right|, |-20.5|, |2|$

35. $|10|, |-3|, |0|, |-5.25|$

36. $|-6|, |-4|, |11|, |0|$

37. $|4|, |-3|, |-18|, |-3.18|$

Alberto and Rebecca toss horseshoes at a stake. Whoever's horseshoe is closer to the stake wins a point.

38. Reasoning What integer best describes the location of Alberto's horseshoe in relation to the stake? What integer best describes the location of Rebecca's horseshoe?

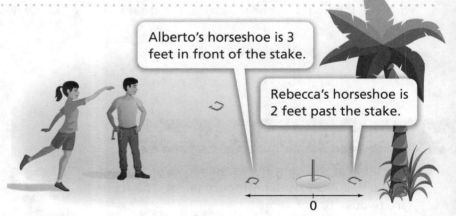

Alberto's horseshoe is 3 feet in front of the stake.

Rebecca's horseshoe is 2 feet past the stake.

39. Critique Reasoning Alberto says that −3 is less than 2, so he wins a point. Is Alberto correct? Explain.

40. Model with Math Find the distance from Alberto's horseshoe to Rebecca's horseshoe. Explain.

41. Higher Order Thinking Let a = any rational number. Is the absolute value of a different if a is a positive number or a negative number? Explain.

42. Construct Arguments Samuel and Leticia are playing a game. After the first round of the game, Samuel's score was −19, and Leticia's score was 21. The score with the greater absolute value wins each round. Who won the first round? Explain.

43. Use Structure Ana and Chuyen are exploring underwater sea life while on a helmet diving adventure. Ana's location is −30 feet below sea level, and Chuyen's location is −12 feet below sea level. Which girl is located farther from sea level?

44. Marie's account balance is −$45.62. Tom's account balance is −$42.55. Which balance represents the greater number? Which balance represents the lesser amount owed?

45. In New York, the Federal Reserve gold vault is located at a depth of |−80| feet below ground. The treasure at Oak Island is believed to be at a depth of |−134| feet. Which is farther below ground, the gold vault or the Oak Island treasure?

46. Two scuba divers are swimming below sea level. The locations of the divers can be represented by −30 feet and −42 feet. Which measure represents the location that is closest to sea level?

☑ Assessment Practice

47. The table at the right shows the scores at the end of the first round of a golf tournament. The scores are relative to par.

Golfer	Kate	Sam	Lisa	Carlos
Score	−6	5	2	−3

PART A

Par is represented as 0. Using absolute value, show the distance each score is from par.

PART B

The golfer with the least score wins the round. Who won the first round of the tournament? Explain.

1. Vocabulary Describe the relative locations of the rational numbers $-\left(-\frac{a}{b}\right)$ and $\frac{a}{b}$ on a number line. *Lessons 2-1 and 2-2*

2. Marc deposited $175 in a new bank account. After buying some furniture, he was overdrawn by $55. Select all the true statements about Marc's account. *Lesson 2-1*

☐ To start, Marc had a negative balance.

☐ In this situation, 0 represents an empty bank account.

☐ When Marc was overdrawn, he had a negative balance.

☐ After buying furniture, Marc had a positive balance.

☐ The lowest balance in the account was −$55.

3. What number is represented on the number line? Give your answer as a decimal and as a fraction. *Lesson 2-2*

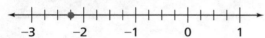

4. The absolute value of a number is 52. Select all the integers that this number could be. *Lesson 2-3*

☐ −52   ☐ −25   ☐ 25   ☐ $-\frac{1}{52}$ ☐ 52

5. The table shows the location of four treasure chests relative to sea level. How can you use the number line to find the treasure chest that is farthest from sea level? *Lesson 2-2*

Treasure Chest	Location Relative to Sea Level
A	0.75 foot
B	$-\frac{5}{4}$ feet
C	−0.5 foot
D	1 foot

6. Three customers have accounts owing money. The table shows the account balances that represent what the customers owe. Which customer owes the least amount of money? *Lesson 2-3*

Customer	Balance
M. Milo	−$85.50
B. Barker	−$42.75
S. Stampas	−$43.25

How well did you do on the mid-topic checkpoint? Fill in the stars.

MID-TOPIC PERFORMANCE TASK

Warren and Natasha started a dog-walking business. During their first week, they paid $10 to make their business cards and $6 for a 4.5-pound box of doggie treats. Warren walked a dog for 15 minutes, and Natasha walked a dog for 30 minutes.

PART A

Which integers represent the dollar amounts either spent or earned during the first week Warren and Natasha were in business? Select all that apply.

☐ $5   ☐ −$5   ☐ $10   ☐ −$10   ☐ −$6

Number of Minutes	Cost for One Dog
15	$5
30	$10
60	$20

PART B

At the end of each week, Warren records the weight in pounds of doggie treats eaten as a negative rational number. Plot the numbers of pounds eaten each week on the number line. Order the numbers from most pounds eaten to fewest pounds eaten.

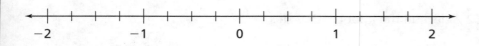

Week	Pound(s) Eaten
1	$-\frac{3}{2}$
2	$-\frac{2}{3}$
3	−0.5
4	$-\frac{5}{4}$

PART C

Find the absolute value for the number of pounds of doggie treats eaten each week. Which two weeks had the greatest number of pounds eaten?

Solve & Discuss It!  ACTIVITY

Point *B* has the same *x*-coordinate as point *A*, but its *y*-coordinate is the opposite of the *y*-coordinate of point *A*. Plot point *B* and write its coordinates.

Make Sense and Persevere
How can you use what you know about integers and graphing points on a coordinate plane to plot point *B*?

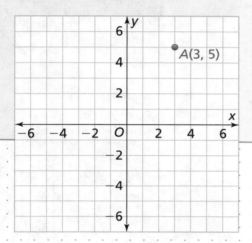

I can...
graph points with rational coordinates on a coordinate plane.

Focus on math practices
Generalize Two points have the same *x*-coordinate but opposite *y*-coordinates. Across which axis do they form mirror images of each other?

? **Essential Question** How can you graph a point with rational coordinates on a coordinate plane?

  VISUAL LEARNING ASSESS

EXAMPLE 1 **Graph Points with Integer Coordinates**

A coordinate plane is a grid containing two number lines that intersect in a right angle at 0. The number lines, called the *x*-axis and *y*-axis, divide the plane into four quadrants. How can you graph and label points on a coordinate plane?

> **Use Structure** How can you extend what you know about grids to the coordinate plane?

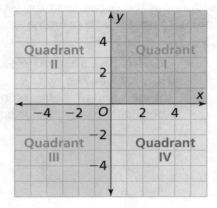

An **ordered pair** (x, y) of numbers gives the coordinates that locate a point relative to each axis. Graph the points $Q(2, -3)$, $R(-1, 1)$, and $S(0, 2)$ on a coordinate plane.

To graph any point with coordinates (x, y):

- Start at the **origin**, $(0, 0)$.

- Use the *x*-coordinate of the point to move right (if positive) or left (if negative) along the *x*-axis.

- Then use the *y*-coordinate of the point to move up (if positive) or down (if negative) following the *y*-axis.

- Draw a point on the coordinate plane and label the point.

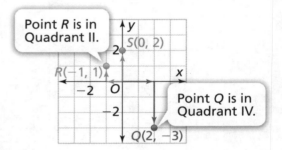

☑ **Try It!**

Graph point $P(-2, -3)$ on the coordinate plane shown.

Start at the origin (☐ , ☐).

The *x*-coordinate is negative, so move ☐ units to the left.

Then use the *y*-coordinate to move ☐ units down.

Draw and label the point.

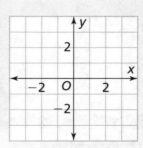

Convince Me! How do the signs of the coordinates relate to the quadrant in which a point is located? Explain for each of the four quadrants.

EXAMPLE 2 **Locate and Identify Points with Rational Coordinates**

A grid map of Washington, D.C., is shown at the right. What are the coordinates of the location of the Jefferson Memorial?

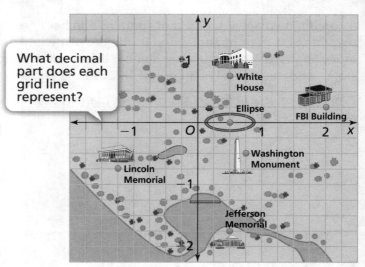

What decimal part does each grid line represent?

Find the Jefferson Memorial on the map.

• Follow the grid lines directly to the *x*-axis to find the *x*-coordinate, 0.5.

• Follow the grid lines directly to the *y*-axis to find the *y*-coordinate, −1.75.

The coordinates of the location of the Jefferson Memorial are (0.5, −1.75).

> **Model with Math** You can use decimals or fractions to represent rational number coordinates. Because $0.5 = \frac{1}{2}$ and $-1.75 = -1\frac{3}{4}$, the coordinates can also be written as $\left(\frac{1}{2}, -1\frac{3}{4}\right)$.

 Try It!

What landmark is located on the map at $\left(2, \frac{1}{4}\right)$?

EXAMPLE 3 **Reflect Points Across the Axes**

How are points *N*(−3, 2), *P*(3, −2), and *Q*(−3, −2) related to point *M*(3, 2)?

Point *N*(−3, 2) and point *M*(3, 2) differ only in the sign of the *x*-coordinate. They are reflections of each other across the *y*-axis.

Point *P*(3, −2) and point *M*(3, 2) differ only in the sign of the *y*-coordinate. They are reflections of each other across the *x*-axis.

Point *Q*(−3, −2) and point *M*(3, 2) differ in the signs of the *x*-coordinate and *y*-coordinate. They are reflections of each other across *both* axes.

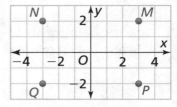

> **Be Precise** A *reflection* is a mirror image across a line.

 Try It!

The coordinates of point *A* are (−3, 5). What are the coordinates of point *B*, which is a reflection of point *A* across the *x*-axis?

A **coordinate plane** is a grid that contains number lines that intersect at right angles and divide the plane into four **quadrants**. The horizontal number line is called the **x-axis,** and the vertical number line is called the **y-axis.**

The location of a point on a coordinate plane is written as an **ordered pair** (x, y).

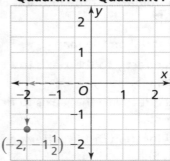

Quadrant II   Quadrant I

Quadrant III Quadrant IV

$\left(-2, -1\frac{1}{2}\right)$

Do You Understand?

1. **? Essential Question** How can you graph a point with rational coordinates on a coordinate plane?

2. What is the *y*-coordinate of any point that lies on the *x*-axis?

3. **Look for Relationships** How are the points (4, 5) and (−4, 5) related?

4. **Construct Arguments** On a larger map, the coordinates for the location of another Washington, D.C. landmark are (8, −10). In which quadrant of the map is this landmark located? Explain.

Do You Know How?

In **5–7,** graph and label each point on the coordinate plane.

5. *A*(−4, 1)

6. *B*(4, 3)

7. *C*(0, −2)

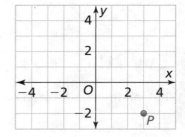

8. What ordered pair gives the coordinates of point *P* above?

In **9** and **10,** use the map in Example 2 and write the ordered pair of each location.

9. White House   10. Lincoln Memorial

In **11** and **12,** use the map in Example 2 and write the landmark located at each ordered pair.

11. (0.5, 0)   12. $\left(\frac{3}{4}, -\frac{1}{2}\right)$

Practice & Problem Solving

Scan for
Multimedia

In 13–20, graph and label each point.

13. $A(1, -1)$

14. $B(4, 3)$

15. $C(-4, 3)$

16. $D(5, -2)$

17. $E(-2.5, 1.5)$

18. $F(2, 1.5)$

19. $G\left(-2, -1\frac{1}{2}\right)$

20. $H\left(1\frac{1}{2}, -1\right)$

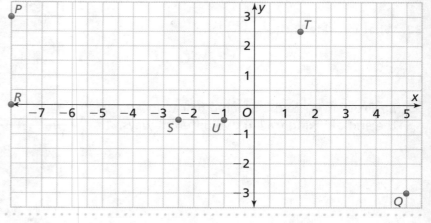

In 21–26, write the ordered pair for each point.

21. P

22. Q

23. R

24. S

25. T

26. U

In 27–30, use the map at the right.

27. Which building is located in Quadrant III?

28. Which two places have the same x-coordinate?

29. Use Structure The city council wants the location of the entrance to a new city park to be determined by the reflection of the school entrance across the y-axis. What are the coordinates of the entrance to the new city park on this map?

30. Higher Order Thinking You are at the market square $(0, 0)$ and want to get to the doctor's office. Following the grid lines, what is the shortest route?

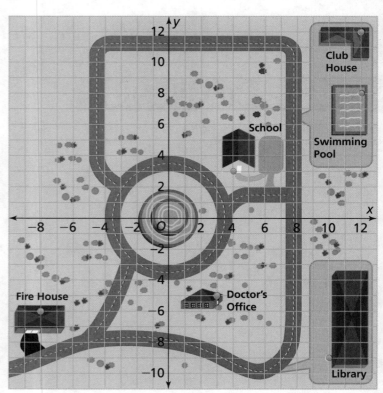

In 31–36, use the coordinate plane at the right.

31. What is located at (–0.7, –0.2)?

32. What is located at $\left(\frac{3}{10}, -\frac{1}{5}\right)$?

33. Be Precise Write the ordered pair to locate the end of hiking trail in two different ways.

34. What are the coordinates of the information center? Explain.

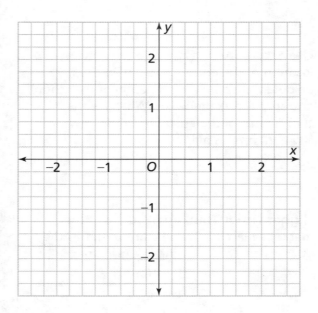

35. What are the coordinates of the point that is a reflection across the x-axis of the pond?

36. Use Structure Which picnic areas are located at points that are reflections of each other across one of the axes of the coordinate plane?

Assessment Practice

37. Graph and label each point on the coordinate plane at the right.

$A\left(\frac{3}{4}, -1\frac{1}{2}\right)$

$B(-2.75, -2.25)$

$C\left(0, 2\frac{1}{4}\right)$

$D(-1.75, 2)$

3-ACT MATH ▷ ▷ ▷

The ULTIMATE THROW

ACT 1

1. After watching the video, what is the first question that comes to mind?

2. Write the Main Question you will answer.

3. Make a prediction to answer this Main Question.

The person who threw the flying disc farther is [   ].

4. Construct Arguments Explain how you arrived at your prediction.

5. What information in this situation would be helpful to know? How would you use that information?

6. Use Appropriate Tools What tools can you use to solve the problem? Explain how you would use them strategically.

7. Model with Math Represent the situation using mathematics. Use your representation to answer the Main Question.

8. What is your answer to the Main Question? Does it differ from your prediction? Explain.

9. Write the answer you saw in the video.

10. Reasoning Does your answer match the answer in the video? If not, what are some reasons that would explain the difference?

11. Make Sense and Persevere Would you change your model now that you know the answer? Explain.

Reflect

12. Model with Math Explain how you used a mathematical model to represent the situation. How did the model help you answer the Main Question?

13. Make Sense and Persevere When did you struggle most while solving the problem? How did you overcome that obstacle?

SEQUEL

14. Reasoning Suppose each person walks to the other person's disc. They throw each other's discs toward the starting point. Where do you think each disc will land?

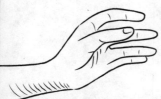

Solve & Discuss It!  ACTIVITY

Graph the points on the coordinate plane below. What picture do you make when you connect the points in order?

(3, 3), (0, 0), (−4, −4), (−9, 0), (−4, 4), (0, 0), (3, −3), (3, 3)

Name a pair of points that are the same distance from the *x*-axis. Explain your choice.

I can...
use absolute value to find distance on a coordinate plane.

Use Structure How can you use the structure of the grid to find a pair of points that are the same distance from the *x*-axis?

Focus on math practices

Use Structure How can you use the coordinate plane to find the total length of the picture you graphed?

99

? Essential Question How can you find the distance between two points on a coordinate plane?

VISUAL LEARNING

ASSESS

EXAMPLE 1 Find Vertical Distance

Scan for
Multimedia

Tammy drew a map of her neighborhood. How far is it from Li's house to school?

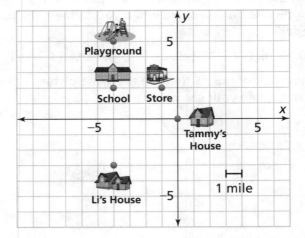

> **Reasoning** How can you use absolute values to find the distances?

Find the coordinates of Li's house and the school.

- The coordinates for Li's house are (−4, −3).

- The coordinates for the school are (−4, 2).

The absolute values of the *y*-coordinates tell you the distance between each point and the *x*-axis.

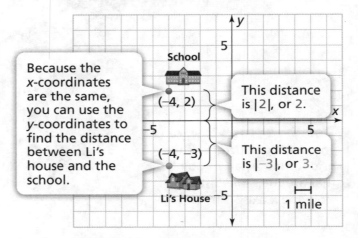

Because the x-coordinates are the same, you can use the y-coordinates to find the distance between Li's house and the school.

This distance is |2|, or 2.

This distance is |−3|, or 3.

The distance from Li's house to school is
$|2| + |-3| = 2 + 3 = 5$ miles.

✓ Try It!

What is the distance from the school to the playground? Explain how you used absolute values to find the distance.

Convince Me! To find the distance from the school to the playground, do you add or subtract the absolute values of the *y*-coordinates? Explain.

EXAMPLE 2 **Find Horizontal Distance** ACTIVITY ASSESS

The Coulter family starts at their home and stops at a rest stop to eat lunch. How much farther do they need to drive to get to the water park? Use coordinates to find the distance.

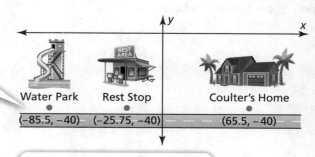

> The y-coordinates are the same. Use the absolute values of the x-coordinates to find the distance. Subtract the absolute values.

Water Park   Rest Stop   Coulter's Home
(−85.5, −40) (−25.75, −40)   (65.5, −40)

> Each unit represents 1 mile.

(−85.5, −40)   (−25.75, −40)

|−85.5| |−25.75|

85.5   −   25.75

The remaining distance to the water park is 59.75 miles.

 Try It!

What is the total distance of the Coulters' return trip after their day at the water park?

The distance of the return trip is |−85.5| ☐ |65.5| = ☐☐☐ = ☐ miles.

EXAMPLE 3 **Solve Problems Using Distance**

Point B is on the x-axis and has the same x-coordinate as point A. Point C is graphed at (−2, n). The distance from point A to point C is equal to the distance from point A to point B. What is the value of n?

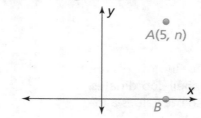

A(5, n)

B

STEP 1 Find the distance from point A to point C.

The y-coordinates are the same.

|−2| + |5| = 2 + 5 = 7 units

Add the absolute values of the x-coordinates to find the distance.

STEP 2 Find the value of n.

> The ordered pair (5, 0) describes the location of point B.

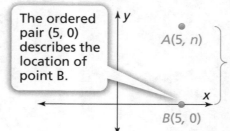

A(5, n)

B(5, 0)

} The distance from point A to point B is 7 units.

n − 0 = 7

n = 7

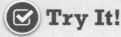 **Try It!**

Point D is in Quadrant IV and is the same distance from point B as point A. What are the coordinates of point D?

You can use absolute values to find distances between points on a coordinate plane.

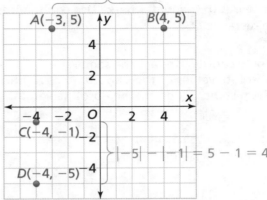

$|-3| + |4| = 3 + 4 = 7$

$A(-3, 5)$ $B(4, 5)$

$C(-4, -1)$

$D(-4, -5)$

$|-5| - |-1| = 5 - 1 = 4$

Do You Understand?

1. **Essential Question** How can you find the distance between two points on a coordinate plane?

2. **Look for Relationships** To find the distance between two points using their coordinates, when do you add their absolute values and when do you subtract them?

3. **Reasoning** Can you use absolute value to find the distance between Li's house and Tammy's house in Example 1? Explain.

Do You Know How?

In 4–9, find the distance between each pair of points.

4. (−5, 2) and (−5, 6)

5. (4.5, −3.3) and (4.5, 5.5)

6. $\left(5\frac{1}{2}, -7\frac{1}{2}\right)$ and $\left(5\frac{1}{2}, -1\frac{1}{2}\right)$

7. $\left(-2\frac{1}{4}, -8\right)$ and $\left(7\frac{3}{4}, -8\right)$

8. $\left(5\frac{1}{4}, -3\frac{1}{4}\right)$ and $\left(5\frac{1}{4}, -6\frac{1}{4}\right)$

9. $\left(-1\frac{1}{2}, -6\frac{1}{2}\right)$ and $\left(-2\frac{1}{2}, -6\frac{1}{2}\right)$

Practice & Problem Solving

Scan for
Multimedia

Leveled Practice In **10–15**, find the distance between each pair of points.

10. (−2, 8) and (7, 8)

$$\left| \,\boxed{}\, \right| + \left| \,\boxed{}\, \right|$$

$$= \boxed{} + \boxed{}$$

$$= \boxed{} \text{ units}$$

11. (−6.1, −8.4) and (−6.1, −4.2)

$$\left| \,\boxed{}\, \right| - \left| \,\boxed{}\, \right|$$

$$= \boxed{} - \boxed{}$$

$$= \boxed{} \text{ units}$$

12. $\left(12\frac{1}{2}, 3\frac{3}{4}\right)$ and $\left(-4\frac{1}{2}, 3\frac{3}{4}\right)$

$$\left| \,\boxed{}\, \right| + \left| \,\boxed{}\, \right|$$

$$= \boxed{} + \boxed{}$$

$$= \boxed{} \text{ units}$$

13. (−5, −3) and (−5, −6)

14. (−5.4, 4.7) and (0.6, 4.7)

15. $\left(7\frac{1}{2}, -5\frac{3}{4}\right)$ and $\left(7\frac{1}{2}, -1\frac{1}{4}\right)$

In **16–19**, use the map at the right.

16. Find the distance from roller coaster 1 to the swings.

17. Find the distance from the Ferris wheel to roller coaster 3.

18. Find the total distance from roller coaster 2 to roller coaster 3 and then to the water slide.

19. Higher Order Thinking Is the distance from the merry-go-round to the water slide the same as the distance from the water slide to the merry-go-round? Explain.

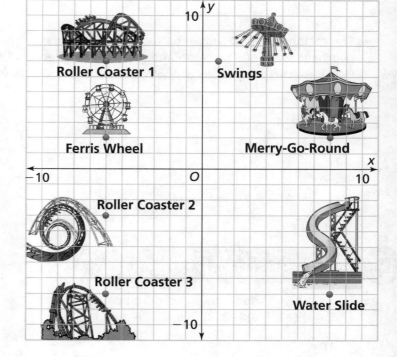

In 20 and 21, use the coordinate plane at the right.

The graph shows the locations of point *G* and point *H*.
Point *J* is graphed at $(n, -3)$. The distance from point *H*
to point *J* is equal to the distance from point *H* to point *G*.

20. What is the distance from point *H* to point *J*?

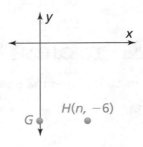

21. What is the value of *n*?

22. Use Structure Suppose *a*, *b*, and *c* are all
negative numbers. How do you find the
distance between points (a, b) and (a, c)?

23. A scientist graphed the locations of the epicenter
of an earthquake and all of the places where
people reported feeling the earthquake. She
positioned the epicenter at $(-1, 8)$ and the
farthest location reported to have felt the
quake was positioned at $(85, 8)$. If each unit on
the graph represents 1 mile, how far from its
epicenter was the earthquake felt?

24. The rectangle *ABCD* shown on the coordinate plane represents an
overhead view of a piece of land. Each unit represents 1,000 feet.
What are the dimensions of the rectangular piece of land, in feet?

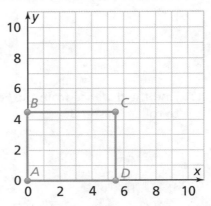

✓ **Assessment Practice**

25. You are given the following ordered pairs.
$(3.5, -1)$ $(-1.5, 3)$ $(-3, 3)$ $(3.5, 2.5)$ $(-1.5, -1.5)$

PART A
Graph the ordered pairs on the coordinate plane.

PART B
Find the two ordered pairs on the coordinate plane
that are 4.5 units apart.

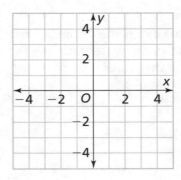

Solve & Discuss It!  ACTIVITY

Draw a polygon with vertices at $A(-1, 6)$, $B(-7, 6)$, $C(-7, -3)$, and $D(-1, -3)$. Then find the perimeter of the polygon.

Use Structure How can you use the coordinate plane to draw the polygon and find its perimeter?

I can...
find side lengths of polygons on a coordinate plane.

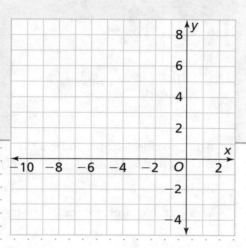

Focus on math practices

Construct Arguments What type of polygon did you draw? Use a definition to justify your answer.

? Essential Question How is distance used to solve problems about polygons in a coordinate plane?

VISUAL LEARNING
ASSESS

EXAMPLE ◉ **Find the Perimeter of a Rectangle**

Scan for Multimedia

An archaeologist used a coordinate plane to map a dig site. She marked the corners of a building with flags, as shown. How much rope does she need to go around the building?

> **Generalize** How can you use what you know about finding distances to find the perimeter of the building?

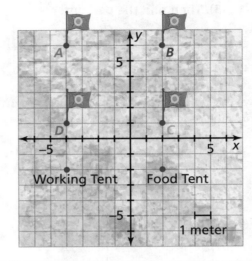

Find the length of each side of rectangle *ABCD*. Use the coordinates of the vertices of the rectangle; $A(-4, 6)$, $B(2, 6)$, $C(2, 1)$, and $D(-4, 1)$.

- *A* to $B = |-4| + |2| = 4 + 2 = 6$ m
- *B* to $C = |6| - |1| = 6 - 1 = 5$ m
- *C* to $D = |2| + |-4| = 2 + 4 = 6$ m
- *D* to $A = |6| - |1| = 6 - 1 = 5$ m

Add the side lengths to find the perimeter of rectangle *ABCD*.

Perimeter = 6 m + 5 m + 6 m + 5 m = 22 meters

The archaeologist needs 22 meters of rope.

☑ Try It!

The archaeologist later decides to extend the roped-off area so that the new perimeter goes from *A* to *B* to the food tent to the working tent and then back to *A*. How much rope does she need now?

A to *B* = ☐ m

B to food tent = ☐ m

Food tent to working tent = $|2| + \left| \boxed{} \right| = 2 + \boxed{} = \boxed{}$ m

Working tent to $A = \left| \boxed{} \right| + |6| = \boxed{} + 6 = \boxed{}$ m

The archaeologist needs ☐ meters of rope.

Convince Me! How could you use the formula for the perimeter of a rectangle to find the perimeter of the larger rectangle using two of the distances?

EXAMPLE 2 ▶ 👆 Find the Perimeter of an Irregular Polygon

A rancher maps the coordinates for a holding pen for his cows. How much fencing does the rancher need to enclose the cows' holding pen?

STEP 1 Find the side lengths.

$LM = |-16.25| - |-4.5| = 16.25 - 4.5 = 11.75$

$MN = |4| + |-6| = 4 + 6 = 10$

$NO = |-4.5| + |8.25| = 4.5 + 8.25 = 12.75$

$OP = |-12| - |-6| = 12 - 6 = 6$

$PQ = |8.25| + |-16.25| = 8.25 + 16.25 = 24.50$

$QL = |-12| + |4| = 12 + 4 = 16$

STEP 2 Add the side lengths.

$11.75 + 10 + 12.75 + 6 + 24.50 + 16 = 81$

The rancher needs 81 yards of fencing.

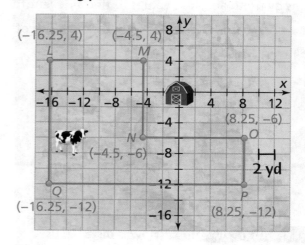

☑ **Try It!**

The rancher needs to replace the fence for the holding pen for the horses. How much fencing does he need?

The rancher needs ☐ yards of fencing.

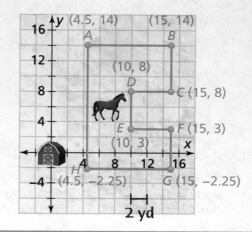

EXAMPLE 3 ▶ 👆 **Apply Distance to Geometry**

Are triangle *ABC* and triangle *BCD* isosceles? Explain.

Find the length of the green sides of each triangle.

The length of side $AC = |-5| + |1| = 5 + 1 = 6$ units.

The length of side $DC = |7| - |1| = 7 - 1 = 6$ units.

The length of side $BC = |8| - |2| = 8 - 2 = 6$ units.

The sides are the same length so the triangles are isosceles.

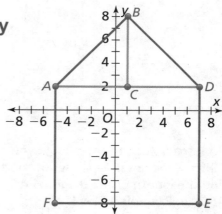

☑ **Try It!**

Joaquin says that quadrilateral *ADEF* is a square. Is he correct? Explain.

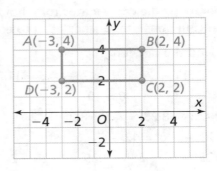

You can represent polygons on a coordinate plane and solve problems by using absolute values to find side lengths.

Add or subtract absolute values to find the length of each side.

AB: $|-3| + |2| = 3 + 2 = 5$ units

BC: $|4| - |2| = 4 - 2 = 2$ units

CD: $|-3| + |2| = 3 + 2 = 5$ units

DA: $|4| - |2| = 4 - 2 = 2$ units

Do You Understand?

1. **?Essential Question** How is distance used to solve problems about polygons in a coordinate plane?

2. **Reasoning** In Example 1, why do you add absolute values to find the distance from A to B but subtract absolute values to find the distance from B to C?

3. **Construct Arguments** Could you add or subtract the absolute values of coordinates to find the length of the diagonal AC of rectangle $ABCD$ in Example 1? Explain.

Do You Know How?

4. Find the perimeter of rectangle $MNOP$ with vertices $M(-2, 5)$, $N(-2, -4)$, $O(3, -4)$, and $P(3, 5)$.

5. Jen draws a polygon with vertices $E(-2, 3.5)$, $F(3, 3.5)$, $G(3, -1.5)$, and $H(-2, -1.5)$. Is $EFGH$ a square? Justify your answer.

6. Square $ABCD$ has vertices $A(-4.5, 4)$, $B(3.5, 4)$, $C(3.5, -4)$, and $D(-4.5, -4)$. What is the area of square $ABCD$?

Practice & Problem Solving

Scan for
Multimedia

Leveled Practice In 7 and 8, find the perimeter of each rectangle.

7. Rectangle *JKLM*: *J*(−3, 8), *K*(−3, −1), *L*(4, −1), *M*(4, 8)

$JK = |8| + |-1| = \boxed{}$

$KL = |-3| + |4| = \boxed{}$

Perimeter = $\boxed{}$ units

8. Rectangle *WXYZ*: *W*(−3, −2), *X*(4, −2), *Y*(4, −5), *Z*(−3, −5)

$WX = |-3| + |4| = \boxed{}$

$XY = |-5| - |-2| = \boxed{}$

Perimeter = $\boxed{}$ units

9. Triangle *JKL* has vertices *J*(0, 0), *K*(5, 0), and *L*(0, −3). Is triangle *JKL* equilateral? Justify your answer.

10. Polygon *WXYZ* has vertices *W*(−1.5, 1.5), *X*(6, 1.5), *Y*(6, −4.5), and *Z*(−1.5, −4.5). Is *WXYZ* a rectangle? Justify your answer.

11. What are the perimeter and area of rectangle *ABCD*?

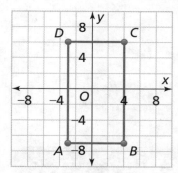

12. Mike used a coordinate plane to design the patio shown at the right. Each unit on the grid represents 1 yard. To buy materials to build the patio, Mike needs to know its perimeter. What is the perimeter of the patio?

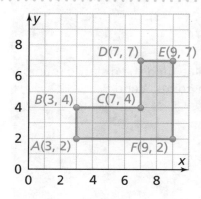

13. Jordan started at her home at point *H*. She ran to the bank (*B*), the library (*L*), the post office (*P*), the café (*C*), her school (*S*), and then back to her home, as shown. The coordinates represent the position, in miles, of each of these locations with respect to the center of town, which is located at the origin. What is the total distance that Jordan ran?

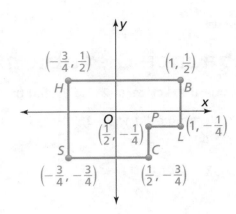

14. Use Structure Ana drew a plan for a rectangular piece of material that she will use for a quilt. The vertices are $(-1.2, -3.5)$, $(-1.2, 4.4)$, and $(5.5, 4.4)$. What are the coordinates of the fourth vertex?

15. Mr. Janas is building a pool in his backyard. He sketches the rectangular pool on a coordinate plane. The vertices of the pool are $A(-5, 7)$, $B(1, 7)$, $C(1, -1)$, and $D(-5, -1)$. If each unit represents 1 yard, how much area of the backyard is needed for the pool?

16. Vocabulary Why is absolute value used to find distances on a coordinate plane?

17. Higher Order Thinking A square on a coordinate plane has one vertex at $(-0.5, -2)$ and a perimeter of 10 units. If all of the vertices are located in Quadrant III, what are the coordinates of the other three vertices?

18. You are given the following points on a coordinate plane: $A\left(-1\frac{1}{2}, -\frac{1}{2}\right)$, $B\left(-1\frac{1}{2}, -3\right)$, and $C(4, -3)$.

PART A

Using absolute value, find the distance (number of units) between points *A* and *B*.

PART B

Select all the coordinates that are 8 units from point *C*.

- ☐ $(12, -3)$
- ☐ $(12, -11)$
- ☐ $(4, -3)$
- ☐ $(-4, -3)$
- ☐ $(4, -11)$

? Topic Essential Question

What are integers and rational numbers? How are points graphed on a coordinate plane?

Vocabulary Review

Complete each definition and then provide an example of each vocabulary word.

Vocabulary	absolute value	opposite	ordered pair	rational number

Definition	Example
1. A point on a coordinate plane is represented by a(n) _____ .	
2. The _____ of a positive integer is a negative integer.	
3. A(n) _____ is any number that can be written as the quotient of two integers.	

Use Vocabulary in Writing

Explain how the points $A\left(9, -\frac{2}{5}\right)$ and $B\left(9, \frac{2}{5}\right)$ are related. Use vocabulary words in your explanation.

Concepts and Skills Review

LESSON 2-1 **Understand Integers**

Quick Review

Integers are all of the counting numbers, their opposites, and 0. **Opposites** are integers located on opposite sides of 0 and the same distance from 0 on a number line.

Example

For each point on the number line, write the integer and its opposite.

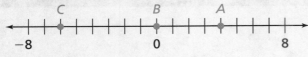

A: 4, −4 B: 0, 0 C: −6, 6

The opposite of the opposite of a number is the number itself.

Practice

For each point on the number line, write the integer and its opposite.

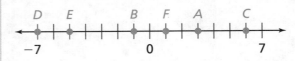

1. A **2.** B

3. C **4.** D

5. E **6.** F

LESSON 2-2 **Represent Rational Numbers on the Number Line**

Quick Review

Rational numbers are numbers that can be written as a quotient $\frac{a}{b}$, where a and b are integers and b does not equal 0. You can use number lines to represent, compare, and order rational numbers.

Example

Compare and order −0.1, 0.75, and $-\frac{1}{4}$ from least to greatest.

Plot the numbers on a number line.

So $-\frac{1}{4} < -0.1 < 0.75$, and their order from least to greatest is $-\frac{1}{4}$, −0.1, 0.75.

Practice

In 1–3, plot each rational number on the number line.

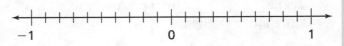

1. $\frac{3}{4}$ **2.** $-\frac{2}{5}$ **3.** 0.5

In 4–7, use <, >, or = to compare.

4. 0.25 ◯ $\frac{1}{4}$

5. $1\frac{5}{8}$ ◯ 1.6

6. 3.65 ◯ $3\frac{3}{4}$

7. $-\frac{2}{3}$ ◯ $\frac{3}{4}$

LESSON 2-3 › Absolute Values of Rational Numbers

Quick Review

The **absolute value** of a number is its distance from 0 on the number line. Distance is always positive. Absolute values are never negative.

Example

Find the absolute values and order |3|, |4|, |−2|, |−5| from *least* to *greatest*.

$$|3| = 3$$
$$|4| = 4$$
$$|−2| = 2$$
$$|−5| = 5$$

Ordered from least to greatest: |−2|, |3|, |4|, |−5|

Practice

In 1–4, find each value.

1. |−9|
2. |−2|
3. |4|
4. −|−10|

In 5–8, order the values from least to greatest.

5. |−3|, |−2|, |10|
6. |−7|, |0|, |−5|
7. |−18.5|, |18|, |−12.5|
8. |26|, |−20|, |−24.5|

LESSON 2-4 › Represent Rational Numbers on the Coordinate Plane

Quick Review

An **ordered pair** (*x*, *y*) of numbers gives the coordinates that locate a point on a **coordinate plane**. Coordinates can be whole numbers, fractions, mixed numbers, or decimals.

Example

Explain how to plot any point with coordinates (*x*, *y*).

- Start at the origin, (0, 0).
- Use the *x*-coordinate to move right (if positive) or left (if negative) along the *x*-axis.
- Then use the *y*-coordinate of the point to move up (if positive) or down (if negative) following the *y*-axis.
- Draw and label the point on the coordinate plane.

Explain how to name the location of a point on a coordinate plane.

Follow the grid line from the point to the *x*-axis to name the *x*-coordinate, and follow the grid line from the point to the *y*-axis to name the *y*-coordinate.

Practice

In 1–6, give the ordered pair for each point.

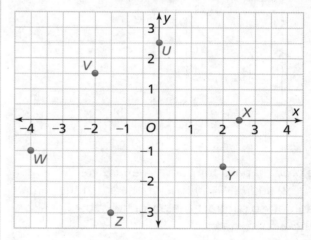

1. U
2. V
3. W
4. X
5. Y
6. Z

Quick Review

You can use absolute value to find the distance between two points that share the same *x*- or *y*-coordinate. When the *y*-coordinates are the same, use the *x*-coordinates to find the distance. When the *x*-coordinates are the same, use the *y*-coordinates. If the points are in different quadrants, add their absolute values. If the points are in the same quadrant, subtract their absolute values.

You can use what you know about finding the distance between two points to find the lengths of the sides of a polygon on a coordinate plane.

Example

Find the length of side *AB*.

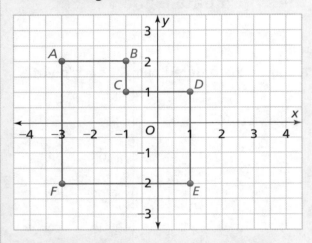

The ordered pairs for points *A* and *B* are *A*(−3, 2) and *B*(−1, 2). The points are in the same quadrant, so subtract the absolute values of the *x*-coordinates.

$$|-3| - |-1| = 3 - 1 = 2 \text{ units}$$

The length of side *AB* is 2 units.

Practice

In 1–6, find the remaining side lengths of polygon *ABCDEF*. Then find the polygon's perimeter.

1. Length of *BC*

2. Length of *CD*

3. Length of *DE*

4. Length of *EF*

5. Length of *FA*

6. Perimeter of *ABCDEF*

In 7 and 8, polygon *QRST* has vertices *Q*(−4, −1), *R*(−4, 5), *S*(2, 5), and *T*(2, −1).

7. Draw and label polygon *QRST* on the coordinate plane.

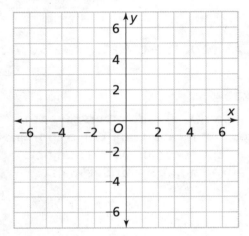

8. Construct an argument to justify whether or not polygon *QRST* is a square.

Hidden Clue

For each ordered pair, simplify the two coordinates. Then locate and label the corresponding point on the graph. Draw line segments to connect the points in alphabetical order. Use the completed picture to help answer the riddle below.

I can...
add and subtract multi-digit decimals.

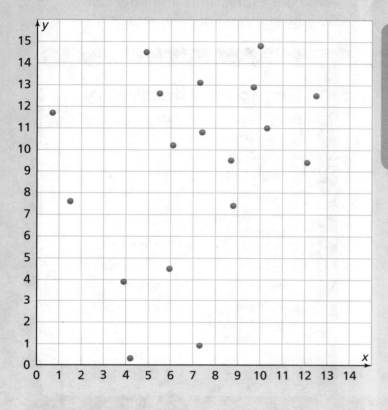

What kind of tree can you carry in your hand?

A (6.4 + 0.92, 15.74 − 2.64) ____ , ____

B (9.65 + 0.4, 16.058 − 1.2) ____ , ____

C (13.4 − 0.896, 8.6 + 4.095) ____ , ____

D (22.10 − 9.99, 0.251 + 9.16) ____ , ____

E (15.6 − 5.87, 8 + 4.95) ____ , ____

F (5.16 + 5.16, 15.6 − 4.6) ____ , ____

G (16.9 − 8.04, 5.08 + 2.27) ____ , ____

H (8.64 + 0.1, 19 − 9.45) ____ , ____

I (9.6 − 2.18, 4.8 + 6.024) ____ , ____

J (12.4 − 6.45, 0.808 + 3.61) ____ , ____

K (5.94 + 1.36, 2.76 − 1.87) ____ , ____

L (4.09 + 0.144, 4.012 − 3.7) ____ , ____

M (6.982 − 3.03, 1.5 + 2.4) ____ , ____

N (7.3 − 1.17, 0.54 + 9.63) ____ , ____

P (0.83 + 0.57, 12.65 − 4.95) ____ , ____

Q (9 − 3.6, 5.74 + 7.06) ____ , ____

R (0.18 + 0.67, 20.02 − 8.17) ____ , ____

S (15.6 − 10.7, 5.43 + 9.07) ____ , ____

TOPIC 3

NUMERIC AND ALGEBRAIC EXPRESSIONS

? Topic Essential Question

What are expressions and how can they be written and evaluated?

Topic Overview

3-1 Understand and Represent Exponents

3-2 Find Greatest Common Factor and Least Common Multiple

3-3 Write and Evaluate Numerical Expressions

3-4 Write Algebraic Expressions

3-5 Evaluate Algebraic Expressions

3-Act Mathematical Modeling: The Field Trip

3-6 Generate Equivalent Expressions

3-7 Simplify Algebraic Expressions

Topic Vocabulary

- algebraic expression
- base
- coefficient
- composite number
- equivalent expressions
- evaluate
- exponent
- factor tree
- greatest common factor (GCF)
- least common multiple (LCM)
- like terms
- numerical expression
- power
- prime factorization
- prime number
- simplify
- substitution
- term
- variable

Go online

Lesson Digital Resources

 INTERACTIVE STUDENT EDITION
Access online or offline.

 VISUAL LEARNING ANIMATION
Interact with visual learning animations.

 ACTIVITY Use with *Solve & Discuss It, Explore It,* and *Explain It* activities, and to explore Examples.

 VIDEOS Watch clips to support *3-Act Mathematical Modeling Lessons* and *STEM Projects*.

The Field Trip

The Field Trip

When was the last time your class went on a field trip? There's one thing all field trips have in common—they cost money. Schools need to find creative ways to pay for field trips. Fundraising is a great way to generate this money while also giving students the satisfaction of helping make the trip happen.

No matter where the money comes from, it's important for the school to consider every possible cost. Think about this during the 3-Act Mathematical Modeling lesson.

PRACTICE Practice what you've learned.

TUTORIALS Get help from *Virtual Nerd*, right when you need it.

MATH TOOLS Explore math with digital tools.

GAMES Play Math Games to help you learn.

KEY CONCEPT Review important lesson content.

GLOSSARY Read and listen to English/Spanish definitions.

ASSESSMENT Show what you've learned.

Did You Know?

There are **more than 600,000 bridges** in the United States.

It took workers 14 years to build the Brooklyn Bridge.

The Mackinac Bridge in Michigan contains **1,016,600 steel bolts.**

The Golden Gate Bridge, completed in 1937, has been **closed due to high winds three times.**

The Mike O'Callaghan-Pat Tillman Memorial Bridge at the Hoover Dam is made up of **30,000 cubic yards of concrete and 16 million pounds of steel.**

Your Task: Design a Bridge

Suppose the proposed maximum weight limit for a new bridge in your community is 100,000 pounds. How many and what types of vehicles can be allowed to cross the bridge? How can the weight on the bridge be controlled? You and your classmates will begin the engineering design process to understand the problem, do necessary research, and brainstorm solutions.

Review What You Know!

Vocabulary

Choose the best term from the box to complete each definition.

composite number
formula
numerical expression
prime number

1. A _____ is a rule that uses symbols to relate two or more quantities.

2. The number 12 is a _____ because it has more than two factors.

3. A _____ is a mathematical phrase that includes numbers and at least one operation.

Perimeter and Area

Use the formulas $P = 2\ell + 2w$ and $A = \ell w$, where ℓ is the length and w is the width, to find the perimeter, P, and the area, A, of each figure.

4.

13 cm

13 cm

$P =$ _____

$A =$ _____

5.

5 in.

21 in.

$P =$ _____

$A =$ _____

6.

9 m

15 m

$P =$ _____

$A =$ _____

Multiples

Write the first five multiples of each number.

7. 8

8. 9

9. 10

10. 6

11. 4

12. 3

Factors

13. How can you find the factors of 12 and 15? Explain.

Operations

14. How are the terms *difference*, *sum*, *quotient*, and *product* alike?

Language Development

Write terms and phrases related to *Numeric Expressions* and *Algebraic Expressions* in the Venn diagram.

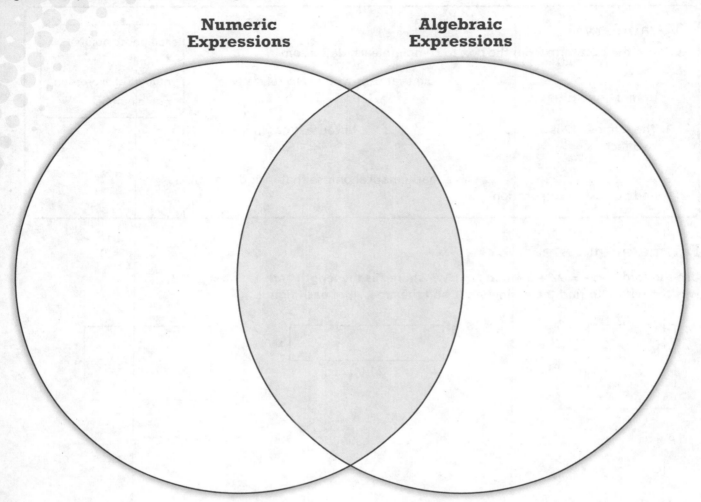

Numeric Expressions

Algebraic Expressions

In the box below, draw pictures to represent the terms and phrases in the overlap section of your diagram.

PROJECT 3A

What is the most inspiring poem you have read?

PROJECT: WRITE AN ALGEBRAIC POEM

PROJECT 3B

What equipment do you need to play your favorite sport?

PROJECT: PLAN A TEAM PURCHASE

PROJECT 3C

Where is the most interesting place you have gone swimming?

PROJECT: DESIGN A POOL PATIO

PROJECT 3D

In what ways have you seen exponents used in the real world?

PROJECT: CALCULATE WITH EXPONENTS

Solve & Discuss It!   ACTIVITY

Fold a sheet of paper in half. Record the number of sections you see when it is unfolded. Continue folding the paper in half 4 more times. Record the number of sections each time. Describe any patterns you see.

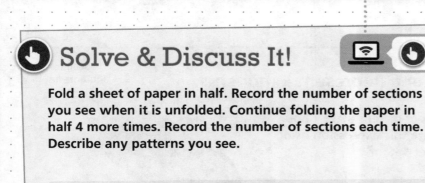

Look for Relationships How are the number of sections related to the number of folds?

I can...
write and evaluate numbers with exponents.

Focus on math practices
Use Structure How many sections will there be after 6 folds? 7 folds?

? Essential Question ❭ How can you write and evaluate numbers with exponents?

  VISUAL LEARNING   ✓ ASSESS

 EXAMPLE 1 ❭ 👁 **Understand and Represent Exponents**

Scan for Multimedia

The expression 2 × 2 × 2 represents the number of cells after 1 hour if there is 1 cell at the start. How can you write this expression using exponents? How many cells will there be after 1 hour?

Reasoning Repeated multiplication can be represented in more than one way.

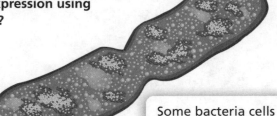

Some bacteria cells divide every 20 minutes to make 2 cells.

You can use an exponent to write repeated multiplication of a number.

The number that is repeatedly multiplied is the **base**.

$$2 \times 2 \times 2 = 2^3$$

3 factors of 2 power

The **exponent** tells how many times the base is used as a factor.

A number that can be written using exponents is called a **power**.

You can use repeated multiplication to **evaluate**, or find the value of a power.

Multiply the first two factors, 2 × 2 = 4.

$$2^3 = \overbrace{2 \times 2} \times 2 = 8$$

Then multiply that product by the last factor, 4 × 2 = 8.

Power	2^3
Value	8

There will be 8 cells after 1 hour.

✓ Try It!

There are 2 × 2 × 2 × 2 × 2 × 2 × 2 × 2 × 2 bacteria cells after 3 hours. Write the repeated multiplication as a power and then evaluate.

Convince Me! Why can you represent the number of cells after two hours as the power 2^6?

EXAMPLE **2** **Evaluate Exponents**

 ACTIVITY ASSESS

A. How can you evaluate 2^0?

The base is 2. The exponent is 0.

Make a table and look for a pattern.

Power	2^0	2^1	2^2	2^3	2^4
Value	n	2	4	8	16

Each value equals the previous value multiplied by 2.

$1 \times 2 = 2$, so the value of 2^0 is 1.

Generalize Any nonzero number raised to an exponent of zero has a value of 1.

B. How can you evaluate 1.2^4?

The base is 1.2. The exponent is 4.

Find $1.2 \times 1.2 \times 1.2 \times 1.2$.

$1.2 \times 1.2 \times 1.2 \times 1.2$ .... Multiply the first two factors.

1.44×1.2 .... Multiply by the third factor.

1.728×1.2 .... Multiply by the fourth factor.

2.0736

Power	1.2^1	1.2^2	1.2^3	1.2^4
Value	1.2	1.44	1.728	2.0736

$1.2^4 = 2.0736$

 Try It!

Evaluate $\left(\frac{1}{3}\right)^3$.

EXAMPLE **3** **Evaluate Expressions with Exponents**

Julia calculated the foil as 1.9×10^5 units thick. Thom calculated the foil as 183,000 units thick. Which calculation represents the greater thickness for the foil?

Evaluate the expression: 1.9×10^5.

Power	10^1	10^2	10^3	10^4	10^5
Value	10	100	1,000	10,000	100,000

$10^5 = 10 \times 10 \times 10 \times 10 \times 10 = 100,000$

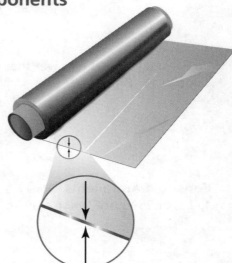

Multiply by the decimal: $1.9 \times 100,000 = 190,000$

Compare the numbers.

$190,000 > 183,000$

Julia's calculation represents the greater thickness for the foil.

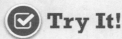 **Try It!**

Rafael calculated the foil as 1.8×10^4 units thick. Evaluate Rafael's expression.

You can represent a repeated multiplication expression using an exponent.

base

$5 \times 5 \times 5 \times 5 = \underbrace{5^4}_{\text{power}}$ exponent

You can evaluate a power using repeated multiplication.

$5^4 = 5 \times 5 \times 5 \times 5 = 625$

Do You Understand?

1. **Essential Question** How can you write and evaluate numbers with exponents?

2. Look for Relationships How many times is 4 used as a factor in the expression 4^5? Write the numerical expression as repeated multiplication.

3. Be Precise What is a power that has the same value as 1^8? Explain.

4. Construct Arguments Does 2.5×10^0 equal 0, 1, 2.5, or 25? Justify your answer.

5. Model with Math How would you write $\left(\frac{1}{2}\right)^3$ as repeated multiplication?

Do You Know How?

6. Write 81 as a repeated multiplication of 3s. Then write it as a power.

7. Write 125 as a repeated multiplication of 5s. Then write it as a power.

8. What is $0.75 \times 0.75 \times 0.75 \times 0.75 \times 0.75$ written as a power?

9. What is $\frac{3}{8} \times \frac{3}{8} \times \frac{3}{8}$ written as a power?

In **10–13**, evaluate each power.

10. $\left(\frac{1}{6}\right)^2$

11. 45^0

12. 0.1^5

13. 7^3

In **14–16**, evaluate each expression.

14. 4.5×10^4

15. 0.6×10^6

16. 3.4×10^0

Practice & Problem Solving

In 17–20, write the exponent for each expression.

17. $9 \times 9 \times 9 \times 9$

18. 1.2^9

19. $\frac{1}{6} \times \frac{1}{6} \times \frac{1}{6}$

20. 7

Leveled Practice In 21–26, evaluate each power or expression.

21. 8^3

☐ × ☐ × ☐

$8^3 =$ ☐

22. $\left(\frac{1}{5}\right)^4$

☐ × ☐ × ☐ × ☐

$\left(\frac{1}{5}\right)^4 =$ ☐

23. 0.6^2

24. $\left(\frac{1}{4}\right)^2$

25. 58^0

26. 6.2×10^3

27. A company rents two storage units. Both units are cube-shaped. What is the difference in volume of the two storage units? Note that the volume of a cube is s^3, where s is the side length. Explain.

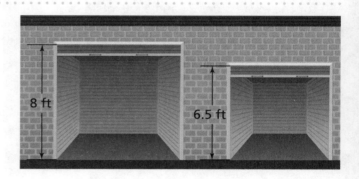

8 ft

6.5 ft

28. Jia is tiling a floor. The floor is a square with side length 12 feet. Jia wants the tiles to be squares with side length 2 feet. How many tiles does Jia need to cover the entire floor? Note that the area of a square is s^2, where s is the side length. Explain.

29. A marine biologist studies the population of seals in a research area. How many seals are in the research area?

Seal population
3.27×10^2

30. **Higher Order Thinking** Zach invested $50 and tripled his money in two years. Kayla also invested $50, and after two years the amount was equal to 50 to the third power. Who had more money after two years? Explain.

31. Malik read that the land area of Alaska is about 5.7×10^5 square miles. About how many square miles is the land area of Alaska?

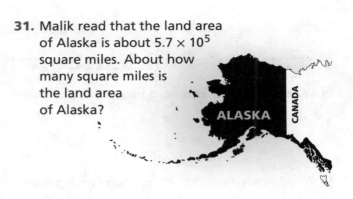

32. Explain why the expressions 10^0, 1^4, and 1×1.0^0 have the same value.

33. Solve the equation $0.3^3 = n$.

34. **Construct Arguments** The same digits are used for the expressions 2^5 and 5^2. Explain how to compare the values of the expressions.

35. **Critique Reasoning** Kristen was asked to write each of the numbers in the expression $80,000 \times 25$ using exponents. Her response was $(8 \times 10^3) \times 5^2$. Was Kristen's response correct? Explain.

36. Consider the equation $1,000,000 = 10^6$. Why is 10 used as the base to write 10^6?

37. Isabella saved 2 nickels today. If she doubles the number of nickels she saves each day, how many days, including today, will it take her to save more than 500 nickels?

✓ Assessment Practice

38. Select all expressions equivalent to $5 \times 5 \times 5 \times 5$.

☐ $5^1 \times 5^4$

☐ 5^4

☐ $5^2 \times 5^2$

☐ 4^5

☐ $4(5^1)$

39. Which expression is equivalent to $\frac{1}{36}$?

Ⓐ $\frac{1}{3} \times \frac{1}{6}$

Ⓑ $\frac{1}{4} \times \left(\frac{1}{3}\right)^3$

Ⓒ $\left(\frac{1}{2}\right)^2 \times \left(\frac{1}{3}\right)^2$

Ⓓ $\frac{1}{2} \times \frac{1}{3} \times \frac{1}{3} \times \frac{1}{3}$

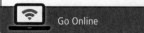
Solve & Discuss It!

ACTIVITY

Mark sets the dinner table every 2 days and dries the dishes every 3 days. If he sets the table on Day 2 and dries the dishes on Day 3, on what day would Mark first perform both chores on the same day?

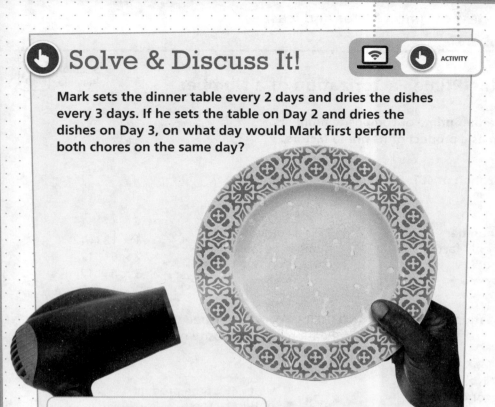

I can...
write the prime factorization and find the greatest common factor and the least common multiple of two numbers.

Look for Relationships
What is the relationship between the chores that Mark does each day?

Day	Chore

Focus on math practices

Generalize On what day will Mark do both chores on the same day again? How can you find on which days Mark does both chores without making a list?

VISUAL LEARNING

ASSESS

EXAMPLE 1 ◉ **Find the Prime Factorization of a Number**

Scan for Multimedia

Whole numbers greater than 1 are either prime or composite numbers. A composite number can be written as a product of its prime factors, called its **prime factorization**.

How can you find the prime factorization of 48?

$1 \times 5 = 5$

5 is a **prime number** because the only factors of 5 are 1 and 5.

12 is a **composite number** because it has more than two factors.

$1 \times 12 = 12$
$2 \times 6 = 12$
$3 \times 4 = 12$

ONE WAY To find the prime factorization of 48, write its factors as a product.

$48 = 2 \times 24$

Start with the least prime factor. 2 is the least prime factor of 48.

$= 2 \times 2 \times 12$

Continue using prime factors.

$= 2 \times 2 \times 2 \times 6$

$= 2 \times 2 \times 2 \times 2 \times 3$

The prime factorization of 48 is $2 \times 2 \times 2 \times 2 \times 3$ or $2^4 \times 2$.

ANOTHER WAY A **factor tree** shows the prime factorization of a composite number.

48

2 × 24

Write 48 as the product of two factors.

2 × 12

2 × 6

2 × 3

Continue the process until all of the factors are prime factors.

The prime factorization of 48 is $2 \times 2 \times 2 \times 2 \times 3$ or $2^4 \times 2$.

There is only one prime factorization for any number.

◉ **Try It!**

Find the prime factorization of 56. Start with the least prime factor.

$56 = 2 \times \boxed{}$

The prime factorization of 56 is $\boxed{} \times \boxed{} \times \boxed{} \times \boxed{}$

or $\boxed{} \times \boxed{}$.

$= 2 \times \boxed{} \times \boxed{}$

$= 2 \times \boxed{} \times \boxed{} \times \boxed{}$

Convince Me! A number is greater than 2 and it has 2 as a factor. Is the number prime or composite? Explain.

EXAMPLE 2 Find the Greatest Common Factor of Two Numbers

Keesha is putting together bags of supplies. She puts an equal number of craft sticks and an equal number of glue bottles in each bag. There are no supplies left over. What is the greatest number of bags of supplies that Keesha can make?

12 bottles of glue
42 craft sticks

Identify the **greatest common factor (GCF)** of 12 and 42. The GCF is the greatest number that is a factor of two or more numbers.

$12 = 2 \times 2 \times 3$
$42 = 2 \times 3 \times 7$

> Write the prime factorization of each number and identify common factors.

Multiply the common factors.

$2 \times 3 = 6$

The greatest common factor (GCF) of 12 and 42 is 6.
Keesha can make 6 bags of supplies.

 **Try It!**

Keesha has 24 beads to add equally to each bag. Can she still make 6 bags and have no supplies left over? Explain.

EXAMPLE 3 Use the Greatest Common Factor and the Distributive Property to Find the Sum of Two Numbers

Use the GCF and the Distributive Property to find the sum of 18 and 24.

STEP 1 Find the GCF of 18 and 24.

$18 = 2 \times 3 \times 3$
$24 = 2 \times 2 \times 2 \times 3$

> The greatest number that is a factor of both 18 and 24 is 2×3.

The GCF of 18 and 24 is 6.

STEP 2 Write each number as a product using the GCF as a factor.

$18 + 24 = 6 \times 3 + 6 \times 4$

$\quad\quad\quad = 6(3 + 4)$ ← Apply the Distributive Property.

$\quad\quad\quad = 6(7)$

$\quad\quad\quad = 42$

The sum of 18 and 24 is 42.

Try It!

Use the GCF and the Distributive Property to find the sum of 12 and 36.

EXAMPLE 4 ▶ 👆 **Find the Least Common Multiple of Two Numbers**

Grant is making picnic lunches. He wants to buy as many juice bottles as applesauce cups but no more than he needs to have an equal number of each.

8 applesauce cups per pack

How many packages of each should Grant buy?

6 juice bottles per pack

> **Look for Relationships** How are the multiples of 6 and 8 related?

The **least common multiple (LCM)** is the least multiple, not including zero, common to both numbers.

$6 = 2 \times 3$
$8 = 2 \times 2 \times 2$

> Write the prime factorization of each number.

List the greatest number of times each factor appears in either prime factorization. Multiply these factors to find the LCM.

$3 \times 2 \times 2 \times 2 = 24$

> 24 is the LCM of 6 and 8.

$6 \times 4 = 24 \qquad 8 \times 3 = 24$

Grant should buy 4 packages of juice and 3 packages of applesauce.

 Try It!

Grant also buys bottled water and juice pouches for the picnic. There are 12 bottles of water in each case and 10 juice pouches in each box. Grant wants to buy the least amount but still have as many bottles of water as juice pouches. How many of each should he buy? Explain.

KEY CONCEPT ▶

The **greatest common factor (GCF)** of two numbers is the greatest number that is a factor of both numbers.

Factors of 12: 1, 2, 3, 4, 6, 12

Factors of 40: 1, 2, 4, 5, 8, 10, 20, 40

2 and 4 are common factors of 12 and 40.

4 is the greatest common factor.

The GCF of 12 and 40 is 4.

The **least common multiple (LCM)** of two numbers is the least multiple, not including zero, common to both numbers.

Multiples of 6: 6, 12, 18, 24, 30, 36, 42, 48 . . .

Multiples of 9: 9, 18, 27, 36, 45, 54 . . .

18 and 36 are common multiples of 6 and 9.

18 is the least common multiple.

The LCM of 6 and 9 is 18.

Do You Understand?

1. **❓ Essential Question** How can you write the prime factorization and find the greatest common factor and the least common multiple of two numbers?

2. What are two different ways in which you can use prime factorization to find the prime factors of a number?

3. **Generalize** Why is the GCF of two prime numbers always 1?

4. **Construct Arguments** In Example 4, Grant finds applesauce that comes in packages of 8, but now he finds juice bottles in only packages of 3. Will the LCM change? Explain.

5. **Critique Reasoning** Sarah says that you can find the LCM of any two whole numbers by multiplying them together. Provide a counterexample to show that Sarah's statement is incorrect.

Do You Know How?

In **6–8**, write the prime factorization of each number. If the number is prime, write *prime*.

6. 33

7. 32

8. 19

In **9–11**, find the GCF for each pair of numbers.

9. 18, 36

10. 22, 55

11. 100, 48

In **12–14**, find the LCM for each pair of numbers.

12. 2, 5

13. 8, 12

14. 8, 10

Practice & Problem Solving

Leveled Practice In **15–18**, find the prime factorization of each number.
If it is prime, write *prime*.

15.
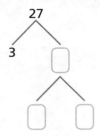
27
3

16.
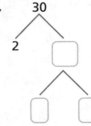
30
2

17. 26

18. 47

In **19–21**, find the GCF for each pair of numbers.

19. 21, 49

20. 8, 52

21. 32, 81

In **22–24**, use the GCF and the Distributive Property to find each sum.

22. 30 + 66

23. 34 + 51

24. 15 + 36

In **25–27**, find the LCM for each pair of numbers.

25. 12, 11

26. 4, 12

27. 5, 8

28. Critique Reasoning Gabrielle and John each
wrote the prime factorization of 64. Analyze
their work and explain any errors.

Gabrielle's Work

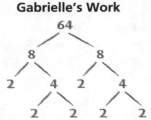

64 = 2 × 2 × 2 × 2 × 2 × 2 = 2⁶

John's Work

64 = 2 × 32
= 2 × 2 × 16
= 2 × 2 × 2 × 8
= 2 × 2 × 2 × 2 × 4
= 2 × 2 × 2 × 2 × 2 × 2

29. To celebrate its grand opening, a store is giving customers
gift certificates. Which customer is the first to get two
gift certificates?

Every 8th customer gets
a $50 gift certificate.

Every 6th customer gets
a $10 gift certificate.

30. **Model with Math** The Venn diagram at the right shows the factors of 24 and 40.

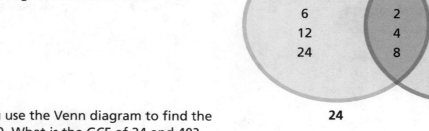

a. What is the meaning of each of the three shaded regions?

b. Explain how you use the Venn diagram to find the GCF of 24 and 40. What is the GCF of 24 and 40?

31. **Reasoning** You have 50 blueberry scones and 75 cranberry scones. You want to make as many identical bags as possible. Each bag should have an equal number of blueberry scones and an equal number of cranberry scones. What is the greatest number of bags you can fill? Explain.

32. **Make Sense and Persevere** The prime factorizations of A and B are shown. Find the value of n that needs to be listed as a prime factor of B so that the greatest common factor (GCF) of A and B is 9.

Prime factorization of A: $3 \times 3 \times 3$

Prime factorization of B: $2 \times 2 \times 3 \times n$

33. **Higher Order Thinking** Gena has 28 trading cards, Sam has 91 trading cards, and Tiffany has 49 trading cards. Use the GCF and the Distributive Property to find the total number of trading cards Gena, Sam, and Tiffany have.

34. Periodical cicada species emerge in large numbers from their larval stage at different yearly intervals. What is the GCF of the years?

Emerges every 13 years

Emerges every 17 years

35. People are waiting in line for a theater premiere. Every 5th person in line will receive a free theater ticket. Every 6th person will receive a gift card for $40. Which person is the first to receive both prizes?

36. Two volunteer groups plant trees. Group A plants the trees in clusters of 3. Group B plants the trees in clusters of 10. Both groups plant the same number of trees. What is the least number of clusters that Group B plants?

37. Find the LCM of the two numbers. Then use the LCM to find the corresponding letter in the key. Write that letter in the box. What word did you decode?

2 and 3	3 and 7	2 and 7

Decryption Key				
A = 1	B = 2	C = 3	D = 4	E = 5
F = 6	G = 7	H = 8	I = 9	J = 10
K = 11	L = 12	M = 13	N = 14	O = 15
P = 16	Q = 17	R = 18	S = 19	T = 20
U = 21	V = 22	W = 23	X = 24	Y = 25
Z = 26				

38. Rami has swimming lessons every 3 days and guitar lessons every 8 days. If he has both lessons on the first day of the month, in how many days will Rami have both lessons on the same day again?

39. A number is between 58 and 68. It has prime factors of 2, 3, and 5. What is the number?

40. A college offers shuttle service from Dickson Hall or Lot B to its campus quad. Both shuttles first depart their locations at 9:10 A.M. They run from each location to campus and back at the intervals shown. When is the next time both shuttles will depart for campus at the same time? Explain.

College Shuttle

Departs from:
Lot B
Every 10 minutes
Dickson Hall
Every 12 minutes

SHUTTLE STOP

First shuttles leave at 9:10 A.M.

✔ Assessment Practice

41. Match each pair of numbers with the pair(s) of numbers that has the same LCM.

	Same LCM as 6, 12	Same LCM as 2, 9	Same LCM as 3, 9	Same LCM as 4, 6	Same LCM as 9, 12
6, 9	☐	☐	☐	☐	☐
3, 4	☐	☐	☐	☐	☐

42. Which expression is equivalent to 48 + 60?

Ⓐ 12(4 + 5)

Ⓑ 12(8 + 5)

Ⓒ 6(6 + 10)

Ⓓ 6(8 + 12)

Solve & Discuss It!

An airline company charges additional fees for bags that do not meet the weight and size limits. For one flight, fees were charged for a total of 50 bags that were over the weight limit and 6 oversized bags. Find the total amount of fees collected for that flight.

LAX	Departures	✈
TIME **FLIGHT**	**OVERLIMIT REMARKS**	**EXTRA FEES**
10:00 JFK123	OVERWEIGHT BAGS	$49 EACH
	OVERSIZED BAGS	$75 EACH

Lesson 3-3
Write and Evaluate Numerical Expressions

 Go Online

I can...
use the order of operations to evaluate numerical expressions.

Look for Relationships You can use the order of operations to evaluate numerical expressions.

Focus on math practices

Model with Math Tamara was charged for two bags that were over the weight limit and another bag that was over the size limit. Write and evaluate a numerical expression to find the additional fees Tamara was charged for her bags.

? Essential Question How do you write and evaluate numerical expressions?

 VISUAL LEARNING   ASSESS

EXAMPLE 1 Use the Order of Operations to Evaluate Numerical Expressions

Scan for Multimedia

Some expressions look difficult because they include parentheses and brackets. You can think of brackets as "outside" parentheses.

Evaluate the following numerical expression.

$$\frac{1}{2} \times 4^2 - [2 + (3.6 \div 0.9)]$$

A **numerical expression** is a math expression that contains numbers and at least one operation. $3 + 4$, $(5)\left(\frac{3}{4}\right)$, and $8 \div 2 + 0.5$ are numerical expressions.

Order of Operations

1 Evaluate parentheses and brackets from inside out.

2 Evaluate powers.

3 Multiply and divide from left to right.

4 Add and subtract from left to right.

---

(1) Evaluate parentheses and brackets from inside out.

$\frac{1}{2} \times 4^2 - [2 + (3.6 \div 0.9)]$ ··· Evaluate inside the parentheses.

$= \frac{1}{2} \times 4^2 - [2 + 4]$ ············ Evaluate inside the brackets.

$= \frac{1}{2} \times 4^2 - 6$

(2) Evaluate powers.

$= \frac{1}{2} \times 4^2 - 6$ ··············· Evaluate the power.

$= \frac{1}{2} \times 16 - 6$

(3) Multiply and divide from left to right.

$\frac{1}{2} \times 16 - 6 = \frac{1}{2} \times \frac{16}{1} - 6$ ···················· Multiply or divide from left to right.

$= 8 - 6$

(4) Add and subtract from left to right.

$= 8 - 6$ ···························· Add or subtract from left to right.

$= 2$

✓ Try It!

Evaluate the numerical expression at the right.

Convince Me! Why is it important to follow the order of operations?

$\frac{1}{8}[6^3 + (48 \div 6)] - 20$

$= \frac{1}{8}[6^3 + \boxed{}] - 20$

$= \frac{1}{8}[\boxed{} + \boxed{}] - 20$

$= \frac{1}{8}[\boxed{}] - 20$

$= \boxed{} - 20$

$= \boxed{}$

 EXAMPLE 2 **Evaluate Numerical Expressions with Decimals and Fractions**

Evaluate the numerical expression $2.5^2 + [(6 - \frac{3}{4}) \div 2] \times 2^5$.

$2.5^2 + [(6 - \frac{3}{4}) \div 2] \times 2^5$ ·············· Evaluate inside the parentheses.

$= 2.5^2 + [5\frac{1}{4} \div 2] \times 2^5$ ·············· Evaluate inside the brackets.

$= 2.5^2 + 2\frac{5}{8} \times 2^5$ ·············· Evaluate the powers.

$= 6.25 + 2\frac{5}{8} \times 32$ ·············· Multiply from left to right.

$= 6.25 + 84$ ·············· Add from left to right.

$= 90.25$

The value of the numerical expression is 90.25.

 EXAMPLE 3 **Insert Grouping Symbols in a Numerical Expression**

Insert grouping symbols in the expression so that it has a value of 10.

$40 - 7 + 33 \times \frac{3}{4}$

Place parentheses around $40 - 7$ and evaluate.

$(40 - 7) + 33 \times \frac{3}{4}$ ◁ Evaluate inside the parentheses.

$= 33 + 33 \times \frac{3}{4}$ ◁ Multiply.

$= 33 + 24\frac{3}{4}$

$= 57\frac{3}{4}$

$57\frac{3}{4} \neq 10$, so place the grouping symbols in another location.

$40 - 7 + 33 \times \frac{3}{4}$

Place parentheses around $7 + 33$ and evaluate.

$40 - (7 + 33) \times \frac{3}{4}$ ◁ Evaluate inside the parentheses.

$= 40 - 40 \times \frac{3}{4}$ ◁ Multiply.

$= 40 - 30$

$= 10$

Inserting grouping symbols around $7 + 33$ gives the numerical expression a value of 10.

> **Be Precise** When you use math symbols correctly, you are being precise.

☑ Try It!

A. Evaluate the numerical expression: $3.2^2 - [(9 \times 4) + 9] \times \left(\frac{1}{3}\right)^2$.

B. Insert grouping symbols so that the numerical expression has a value of 80.

$6 + 12 \times \left(\frac{2}{3}\right)^2 \times 3 + 7$

3-3 Write and Evaluate Numerical Expressions **139**

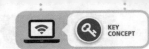
The order of operations is a set of rules used to evaluate expressions that include more than one operation.

Order of Operations

1 Evaluate inside grouping symbols, such as parentheses or brackets.

2 Evaluate powers.

3 Multiply or divide from left to right.

4 Add or subtract from left to right.

Do You Understand?

1. **? Essential Question** How do you write and evaluate numerical expressions?

2. **Make Sense and Persevere** Explain why grouping symbols can change the value of a numerical expression. Then insert grouping symbols to show four different values for the following expression.
$80 \div 8 \times 5 + 4^2$

3. In the expression $(21 - 3) \times (7 + 2) \div (12 - 4)$, what operation should you perform last? Explain.

4. **Critique Reasoning** Charles says that $2 \times 3 - 2$ is 4, and Seth says that $2 \times 3 - 2$ is 2. Who is correct? Explain.

Do You Know How?

In 5–9, evaluate each expression.

5. $5^2 + (6.7 - 3.1)$

6. $(8.2 + 5.3) \div 5$

7. $(1.5 - 0.5^2) \div [(3 + 2) \times 2]$

8. $36.8 \div [11.5 - (2.5 \times 3)]^2$

9. $6 + 4 \times 5 \div 2 - 8 \times 1.5$

In 10–12, insert grouping symbols so that the expression has the given value.

10. $12 \times 3^2 + 36$ Target value: 540

11. $32 \div 2^3 - 4$ Target value: 8

12. $2.3^2 + 9 \times 4 \div 2$ Target value: 28.58

Practice & Problem Solving

Leveled Practice In **13–18**, use the order of operations to evaluate.

13. $4^2 - (3.1 + 6.4) + 4.5$

$= 4^2 - \boxed{} + 4.5$

$= \boxed{} - \boxed{} + 4.5$

$= \boxed{} + 4.5$

$= \boxed{}$

14. $(8.7 + 3.3) \times \left(\frac{1}{2}\right)^2$

$= \boxed{} \times \left(\frac{1}{2}\right)^2$

$= \boxed{} \times \boxed{}$

$= \boxed{}$

15. $157.8 - (3^2 + 6) \times 3$

$= 157.8 - (\boxed{} + 6) \times 3$

$= 157.8 - \boxed{} \times 3$

$= 157.8 - \boxed{}$

$= \boxed{}$

16. $4.3 + (8.4 - 5.1)$

17. $1.25 \times 4 + 3 \times 2 \div \left(\frac{1}{2}\right)^3$

18. $[2^3 \times (152 \div 8)] - 52$

In **19–21**, insert grouping symbols so that the expression has the given value.

19. Target value: 32

$2 \times 9 + 7$

20. Target value: 6

$\frac{1}{3} \times 21 - 3$

21. Target value: 43

$2.5 + 5 \times 6 - 2$

22. Cory bought some baseball equipment. He used a coupon for $\frac{1}{2}$ off the price of the bat and glove. Write and evaluate a numerical expression to find the total cost of the bat, the glove, and 3 baseballs.

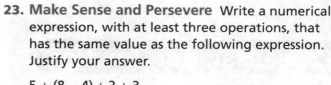

23. Make Sense and Persevere Write a numerical expression, with at least three operations, that has the same value as the following expression. Justify your answer.

$5 + (8 - 4) \div 2 + 3$

24. Use Structure How do you know which part of the numerical expression to evaluate first? Explain.

$(26 + 2.5) - [(8.3 \times 3) + (1^3 - 0.25)]$

25. Construct Arguments Evan says that the value of the numerical expression $0.2^2 + 12 \div (1.5 \times 4)$ is 32.04. Do you agree? Explain.

26. The width of the rectangular drawing is one-third the length plus 3 inches. What is the perimeter of the drawing? Write and evaluate an expression to solve the problem.

12 in.

27. Higher Order Thinking Frederick evaluates the numerical expression $[(53.7 + 37.2) - (3^3 + 3.8)] - 8.6$ and records the answer as 51.5. Lana evaluates the numerical expression $53.7 + 37.2 - 3^3 + 3.8 - 8.6$ and records the answer as 59.1. The expressions have the same numbers and operations. Explain how Frederick and Lana can both be correct.

28. Model with Math Lillian went to the gift shop on the boardwalk and bought four bags of dyed seashells at $3.99 each. She had a coupon for $1 off. Her mom paid for half of the remaining cost. Write and evaluate a numerical expression to find how much Lillian paid toward the purchase of the seashells.

29. In an ecosystem, some animals get energy by eating plants. Write and evaluate an expression to find how many pounds of plants a herd of 18 elk can eat in one week.

An elk can eat 20 pounds of plants each day.

30. Select all expressions that are equivalent to $2^4 \div [(3.2 \times 0.8) + 1.44]$.

☐ $2^4 \div [(4 \times 0.64) + 1.44]$

☐ $16 \div [(2^2 \times 0.64) + (0.72 \times 2)]$

☐ $8 \div [(3.2 \times 0.8) + (0.48 \times 3)]$

☐ $2^4 \div [2.56 + (0.48 \times 4)]$

☐ $4^2 \div [2.56 + (0.48 \times 4)]$

31. Which value is equivalent to the expression $18.9 \times [(2 \times 2.7) - 4.6] - 2^2$?

Ⓐ 1,112

Ⓑ 111.2

Ⓒ 11.12

Ⓓ 1.112

1. Vocabulary Describe the relationship between the base and the exponent in 4^3. *Lesson 3-1*

2. What is the GCF of 14 and 42? *Lesson 3-2*

3. Which pair of numbers has a GCF of 5? *Lesson 3-2*

Ⓐ 15 and 30   Ⓑ 5 and 21

Ⓒ 45 and 9   Ⓓ 20 and 55

4. What is the LCM of 12 and 9? *Lesson 3-2*

5. Evaluate the numerical expression. *Lesson 3-3*

$0.5^2 \times (20 - 2^2 \times 3) \times \left(\frac{2}{5} \times 25\right)$

6. Select all the expressions that are equal to $\left(\frac{2}{3}\right)^2$. *Lesson 3-1*

☐ $\frac{4}{9}$ ☐ $\frac{4}{3}$ ☐ $\frac{1}{3} \times \frac{1}{3}$ ☐ $\frac{1}{9} \times 4$ ☐ $\frac{2}{3} \times \frac{2}{3}$

7. Liam bought 2 vintage movie posters, 2 rock posters, and 1 rap poster. He applied a $35 gift card to the total purchase and a $\frac{1}{2}$-off coupon to the rap poster. Write and evaluate a numerical expression to show how much Liam paid for the posters. *Lesson 3-3*

Poster Prices	
Vintage Movie	$28.50
B Movie	$18.25
Rock	$29.75
Rap	$19.50

8. Eva counts up by 3s, while Jin counts up by 5s. What is the smallest number that they both say? *Lesson 3-2*

How well did you do on the mid-topic checkpoint? Fill in the stars.

☆ ☆ ☆

MID-TOPIC PERFORMANCE TASK

Monique and Raoul are helping teachers make gift bags and gather supplies for a student celebration day at Pineville Middle School.

PART A

Raoul has 72 wristbands and 96 movie passes to put in gift bags. The greatest common factor for the number of wristbands and the number of movie passes is equal to the number of gift bags Raoul needs to make. Find the number of gift bags Raoul needs to make. Then find how many wristbands and how many movie passes Raoul can put in each gift bag if he evenly distributes the items.

PART B

Monique wants to have an equal number of cups and napkins. What is the least number of packages of cups and the least number of packages of napkins Monique should buy to have an equal number of cups and napkins? Justify your answer.

Big Sale!

Cups	$3.50	12 per package
Napkins	$4.25	10 per package

PART C

Which numerical expressions show the equal number of both cups and napkins that Monique will have in Part B? Select all that apply.

☐ $2^1 \times 30$ ☐ $10^2 \times 60$ ☐ $2^2 \times 15$ ☐ 460^0 ☐ $4^0 \times 60$

PART D

The teachers have $25 to buy supplies. Write and evaluate a numerical expression to show how much more money they will need to buy the cups and napkins.

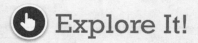 **Explore It!**

 ACTIVITY

Lesson 3-4
Write Algebraic Expressions

  Go Online

I can...
use variables to write algebraic expressions.

The table shows the number of games the Hornets won and the number of games the Lynx won.

GAMES WON

HORNETS	LYNX
3	5
6	8
9	11
n	

A. What pattern do you see in the data in the table? Explain how the pattern relates to the number of games won.

B. **Look for Relationships** Write numerical expressions to relate the number of games won by the Lynx to the number of games won by the Hornets.

Hornets	Lynx
3	3 + 2
6	
9	

C. Explain how to complete the table above for the Lynx if the Hornets won n games.

Focus on math practices

Reasoning Suppose the Lynx won g games. What mathematical expression could you write to show how many games the Hornets won? How is this expression related to the expression you wrote to find the number of games the Lynx won when the Hornets won n games? Explain.

VISUAL LEARNING   ASSESS

EXAMPLE 1   Write an Algebraic Expression Using a Pattern

Scan for Multimedia

Darius bought some comic books. How can you write an algebraic expression to represent the total cost of the comic books?

Use a variable to write an algebraic expression.

EVERY COMIC IS...

$4.00 EACH

Let n = the number of comic books. Each comic book costs $4.

Number of Comic Books	Total Cost ($)
1	4×1
2	4×2
3	4×3
4	4×4
⋮	
n	$4 \times n$

A **variable** is a letter or symbol that represents an unknown quantity.

The total cost of n comic books can be represented by the expression $4 \times n$.

An **algebraic expression** is a type of math expression that has at least one variable and at least one operation.

You can use a solid dot (•), parentheses, or no symbol at all to write the expression $4 \times n$.

$$4 \cdot n \quad \text{or} \quad 4(n) \quad \text{or} \quad 4n$$

Model with Math $4 \times n$, $4 \cdot n$, $4(n)$, and $4n$ are all ways to write the same expression.

✓ Try It!

Darius's sister Rachel bought m mystery books for $6.50 each. Show three ways to write an algebraic expression that represents the total cost of the mystery books.

Convince Me! How do you know that the expressions you wrote for the cost of the mystery books are algebraic expressions?

EXAMPLE 2   Write Algebraic Expressions

How can an algebraic expression represent a given situation?

An algebraic expression can use variables and operations to represent given situations.

A. five minutes **more than** time *t*

> addition

$t + 5$

B. ten erasers **decreased by** a number *n*

> subtraction

$10 - n$

C. *n* nectarines **shared equally** by three

> division

$n \div 3$ or $\dfrac{n}{3}$

D. 4 **times** the quantity *x* **plus** 8

> multiplication   addition

$4(x + 8)$

 Try It!

Write an algebraic expression that represents "8 minus the quantity *b* divided by 6."

EXAMPLE 3   Identify Parts of an Expression

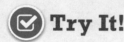

Each part of an expression that is separated by a plus sign or a minus sign is called a **term**. How many terms does the expression $12r + \dfrac{r}{2} - 19$ have? Describe the parts of the expression.

> Remember that a fraction bar also means divide.

$12r + \dfrac{r}{2} - 19$ has three terms.

terms

The terms are $12r$, $\dfrac{r}{2}$, and 19.

The first term, $12r$, is a product of two factors.

A **coefficient** is the number that is multiplied by a variable.

12 is the coefficient of *r*.

$\underset{\text{coefficient}}{\underline{12r}}$

The second term, $\dfrac{r}{2}$, is written as a fraction and represents the quotient of *r* divided by 2.

$\text{quotient} \!-\!\!\left[\begin{array}{c} r \\ \hline 2 \end{array}\right]\!\!\begin{array}{l}-\text{ dividend} \\ -\text{ divisor}\end{array}$

The third term, 19, is a constant numerical value.

 **Try It!**

How many terms does the expression $r \div 9 + 5.5$ have? Explain.

A variable, written as a letter, represents a quantity that can change. You can use a variable to write an algebraic expression that has at least one operation.

Word Phrase	Variable	Operation	Algebraic Expression
the **sum** of 8 and a number a	a	Addition	$8 + a$
five **less than** a number b	b	Subtraction	$b - 5$
the **product** of 8 and a number c	c	Multiplication	$8c$
the quotient of a number d **divided by** 2	d	Division	$\frac{d}{2}$

Do You Understand?

1. **? Essential Question** How can you write an algebraic expression?

2. **Be Precise** Identify the variable and the operation in the algebraic expression $\frac{6}{x}$.

3. **Vocabulary** Explain why $15 + \frac{1}{2}n$ is an algebraic expression.

4. **Reasoning** Could you describe the expression $2(3 + 4)$ as a product of two factors? Explain.

5. Which part of the expression $2(3 + 4)$ is the sum of two terms? Explain.

Do You Know How?

In 6 and 7, write an algebraic expression for each situation.

6. five less than y

7. six times the quantity two x plus three y

In 8–10, use the expression $\frac{w}{4} + 12.5 - 7z$.

8. How many terms does the expression have? Explain.

9. Which term has a coefficient? Explain.

10. Which term is a constant numerical value?

Practice & Problem Solving

In 11–14, write an algebraic expression for each situation.

11. 12 times a number *g*

12. *p* pennies added to 22 pennies

13. 22 divided by a number *s*

14. $12\frac{3}{4}$ less than the product of 7 and a number *x*

In 15–18, tell how many terms each expression has.

15. $5 - g$

16. $3 + \frac{1}{2}b$

17. $\frac{v}{3} + 2 \cdot 5$

18. $16.2 - (3 \cdot 4) + (14 \div 2)$

In 19 and 20, use the expression $5.3t - (20 \div 4) + 11$.

19. Which part of the expression is a quotient? Describe its parts.

20. Which part of the expression is a product of two factors? Describe its parts.

In 21 and 22, use the table at the right.

21. Model with Math Write an expression to show how much longer the round-trip to San Diego is than the round-trip to San Jose. How many terms does the expression have?

22. Make Sense and Persevere Last month, a truck driver made 5 round-trips to Los Angeles and some round-trips to San Diego. Write an expression that shows how many miles he drove in all. Identify and describe the part of the expression that shows how many miles he drove and trips he made to San Diego.

Sacramento to …	Round-Trip Distance (miles)
San Jose	236
Los Angeles	770
San Diego	1,012

23. Use the expression $y \div 3(4 - 2) + 5.5$ to complete the table. Identify the parts of the expression that correspond to the descriptions.

Description of Part	Part
Variable	
Difference	
Product	
Constant numerical value	

24. The floats in the Orlando Citrus parade may use as many citrus fruits as a small orchard produces in 6 years. If f is the number of citrus fruits a small orchard produces in 1 year, write an algebraic expression to represent the number of citrus fruits the floats in the parade may use.

25. Critique Reasoning Anthony says that the expression abc has three terms because it uses three different variables. Critique Anthony's reasoning and explain whether he is correct.

26. Yuri walked p poodles and b bulldogs on Monday. He walked the same number of poodles and bulldogs each day Tuesday through Friday as he did on Monday. Write an algebraic expression to represent how many total dogs were walked in this 5-day period.

27. Higher Order Thinking Some students equally share 2 baskets of oranges. Each basket has 12 oranges. Write an algebraic expression to represent this situation. Then explain how you chose which variable and operations to use.

28. Model with Math The figure at the right is a regular octagon with side length s. Write two algebraic expressions that use different operations to represent the perimeter of the figure.

STOP

✔ Assessment Practice

29. Which algebraic expression represents the phrase *Four more than the product 3 times the number of c cats*?

Ⓐ $4 + 3c$

Ⓑ $(4 + 3)c$

Ⓒ $3 + 4c$

Ⓓ $4 \times 3 \times c$

30. Select all of the phrases that could be represented by the algebraic expression $\frac{w}{4} - 4$.

☐ four less than the quotient of a number w and four

☐ the difference between a number w and 4

☐ four less than w divided by 4

☐ four less than a number w

☐ the quotient of four and a number w

👆 Solve & Discuss It!    ACTIVITY

A bike shop charges by the hour to rent a bike. Related items are rented for flat fees. Write an expression that represents how much it will cost to rent a bike and helmet for *h* hours. How much would it cost to rent a bike and a helmet for 3 hours?

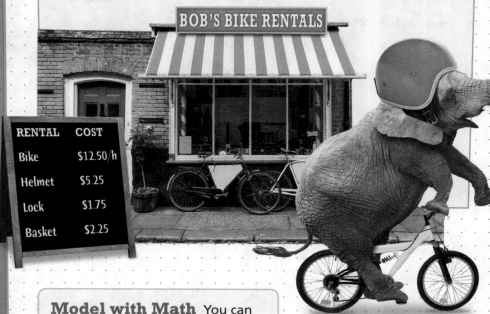

BOB'S BIKE RENTALS

RENTAL	COST
Bike	$12.50/h
Helmet	$5.25
Lock	$1.75
Basket	$2.25

I can...
evaluate an algebraic expression with whole numbers, decimals, and fractions.

Model with Math You can write an algebraic expression with decimals in the same way you do with whole numbers.

Focus on math practices
Use Structure Write an expression that represents renting a bike, a lock, and a basket for *h* hours. What is the cost of renting this equipment for 4 hours?

EXAMPLE 1 Evaluate Algebraic Expressions with Whole Numbers

Scan for Multimedia

Erik collects miniature cars. He has one large case that has 20 cars. He also has 3 same-size, smaller cases filled with cars.

Let n = the number of cars in each smaller case.

How many miniature cars does Erik have if each smaller case holds 10 cars? 12 cars? 14 cars?

> $20 + 3n$ represents the total number of cars that Erik has.

> **Use Structure** Follow the order of operations when you evaluate an expression.

To evaluate an algebraic expression, use **substitution** to replace the variable with a number.

Evaluate $20 + 3n$ when n equals 10, 12, or 14.

$20 + 3n$
$20 + 3(10)$ — Substitute 10 for n.
$= 20 + 30$
$= 50$

If each smaller case holds 10 cars, Erik has 50 cars.

$20 + 3n$
$20 + 3(12)$ — Substitute 12 for n.
$= 20 + 36$
$= 56$

If each smaller case holds 12 cars, Erik has 56 cars.

$20 + 3n$
$20 + 3(14)$ — Substitute 14 for n.
$= 20 + 42$
$= 62$

If each smaller case holds 14 cars, Erik has 62 cars.

The table summarizes the values of $20 + 3n$ for each number of cars in a smaller case.

n	$20 + 3n$
10	50
12	56
14	62

☑ Try It!

Evaluate the expression $50 - t$ when t equals 10, 20, or 25. Then complete the table to show the values.

$50 - t$ $50 - t$ $50 - t$
$50 - \boxed{}$ $50 - \boxed{}$ $50 - \boxed{}$

$= \boxed{}$ $= \boxed{}$ $= \boxed{}$

t	10	20	25
$50 - t$	☐	☐	☐

Convince Me! What does it mean to use substitution to evaluate an algebraic expression?

EXAMPLE 2 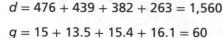 Evaluate Algebraic Equations with Decimals

Julie's family took a 4-day trip. Julie's mother wrote an equation to calculate their gas mileage, m, in miles per gallon. Let d = the number of total miles driven on the trip. Let g = the total number of gallons of gas used for the trip.

$$m = \frac{d}{g}$$

What was the gas mileage for the 4-day trip?

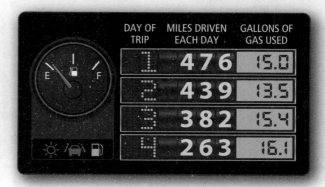

DAY OF TRIP	MILES DRIVEN EACH DAY	GALLONS OF GAS USED
1	476	15.0
2	439	13.5
3	382	15.4
4	263	16.1

STEP 1 Identify the values of the variables d and g.

$d = 476 + 439 + 382 + 263 = 1{,}560$

$g = 15 + 13.5 + 15.4 + 16.1 = 60$

STEP 2 Substitute the values of the variables into the equation and evaluate.

$$m = \frac{1{,}560}{60} = 26$$

The gas mileage was 26 miles per gallon.

Try It!

Evaluate the expression $3.4 + 12a \div 4$ for $a = 10$.

EXAMPLE 3 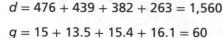 Evaluate Algebraic Expressions with Fractions

Mr. Grant wants to tile a 27-square-foot area with square tiles. Let s = the side length, in feet, of a square tile. Use the expression $27 \div s^2$ to find the number of tiles Mr. Grant needs to buy.

$s = \frac{1}{3}$ ft

Substitute $\frac{1}{3}$ for s.

$27 \div s^2$

$= 27 \div \left(\frac{1}{3} \cdot \frac{1}{3}\right)$

$= 27 \div \frac{1}{9}$

Evaluate the expression.

$27 \div \frac{1}{9}$

To divide by $\frac{1}{9}$, multiply by the reciprocal.

$= 27 \cdot \frac{9}{1}$

$= 243$

Mr. Grant needs to buy 243 tiles.

Try It!

Suppose Mr. Grant decides to buy square tiles that have side lengths of $\frac{3}{4}$ foot. How many of these tiles will he need to buy?

To evaluate an expression, use substitution to replace a variable with its numerical value.
Then use the order of operations to simplify.

$a = 9, b = 6, c = 3, d = 5$

$5a + 2b \div c + d^2$

$= 5(9) + 2(6) \div 3 + 5^2$ Replace each variable with its specific value.

$= 74$

Do You Understand?

1. **? Essential Question** How can you evaluate an algebraic expression?

2. **Construct Arguments** Why is it important to use the order of operations to evaluate algebraic expressions?

3. How is evaluating an expression with fractions like evaluating an expression with whole numbers? How is it different?

4. **Reasoning** Annalise earns $4 an hour walking pets in her neighborhood. She evaluates the expression $4h$, where h represents the number of hours, to find the amount she earns. Can any number be substituted for h? Explain.

Do You Know How?

In 5–8, evaluate each expression for $t = 8$, $w = \frac{1}{2}$, and $x = 3$.

5. $3t - 8$

6. $6w \div x + 9$

7. $t^2 - 12w \div x$

8. $5x - 2w + t$

In 9–14, evaluate each expression for the value given.

9. $z \div 4$; $z = 824$

10. $6t \div 9 - 22$; $t = 60$

11. $r \div 2.4$; $r = 16.8$

12. $9.85 \times s$; $s = 4$

13. $x \div 12$; $x = \frac{2}{3}$

14. $\frac{3}{4} + 4y \div 3$; $y = 1\frac{1}{2}$

Practice & Problem Solving

In **15–17**, evaluate each expression for $w = 5$, $x = 3$, $y = 4$, and $z = 8$.

15. $9x$

16. $3y + 6 \div 2x$

17. $w^2 + 2 + 48 \div 2z$

In **18–20**, evaluate each expression for $x = 1.8$, $x = 5$, and $x = 6.4$.

18. $x \div 4$

19. $x(3.35)$

20. $2x + 3.1$

In **21–23**, evaluate each expression for the value given.

21. $j + \frac{3}{8}$; $j = \frac{3}{4}$

22. $8 - g \div \frac{7}{8}$; $g = \frac{5}{6}$

23. $3m \div \frac{2}{5}$; $m = \frac{2}{3}$

24. Evaluate the expression for the values of b.

b	8.9	5.1	0.2
$b(3) + 20.4$			

25. Evaluate the expression for the values of j.

j	$\frac{1}{2}$	$\frac{4}{5}$	$1\frac{3}{4}$
$2j + \frac{3}{5}$			

In **26–28**, use the table at the right.

26. Model with Math Ms. White wants to rent a small car for a week. It will cost the weekly fee plus $0.30 per mile driven.

   a. Let m = the number of miles Ms. White drives during the week. Write an expression that shows the amount she will pay for the car.

   b. Evaluate the expression you wrote to find how much Ms. White will pay if she drives 100 miles.

ABC Car Rentals: Rates

Vehicle	Week	Day
Small car	$250	$100
Medium car	$290	$110
Luxury car	$325	$120
Small van	$350	$150
Large van	$390	$170

27. Mr. Black rents a luxury car for one week and a few days, d. He does not pay a per-mile fee. Evaluate the expression $325 + 120d$ to find how much Mr. Black will pay for an 11-day rental.

28. For any of the vehicles listed in the table, how many days can you rent the vehicle before it would be less expensive to rent for the week?

In 29 and 30, use the table at the right.

Necklace Length	Cost of Chain	Cost of Pendant
Long	$2.25	$4.50
Medium	$1.80	$3.72
Short	$1.15	$2.39

29. **Model with Math** Tamara is making a medium-length necklace. Write an expression that shows how much it will cost Tamara for the chain, pendant, and *b* beads that cost $0.25 each. Then find the total cost of the necklace if Tamara uses 30 beads.

30. **Higher Order Thinking** Ronnie is making short and long necklaces with only one chain and one pendant per necklace. Write an expression that shows how much it will cost Ronnie to make *s* short necklaces and *n* long necklaces. Then find the cost for 3 short necklaces and 2 long necklaces.

31. **Critique Reasoning** Katrina says that the expression $5{,}432 + 4{,}564 + 13{,}908 \div 61n$ can be evaluated by adding $5{,}432 + 4{,}564 + 13{,}908$ and then dividing by the value of $61n$. Do you agree? Explain.

32. The density, *d*, of an object can be found by using the formula $d = \frac{m}{v}$, where *m* is the mass of the object and *v* is its volume. What is the density of an object that has a mass of 73,430 kilograms and a volume of 7 m³?

33. The formula $V = s^3$ can be used to find the volume of a cube. Use the formula to find the volume, *V*, of a cube-shaped bin with side length *s* of $\frac{2}{3}$ yard.

34. Katie is evaluating the expression $15.75 \div p + 3p$ when $p = 3.15$. Explain each step that she should follow.

☑ Assessment Practice

35. An equation is shown.

    $5x + (x \div 3) = 38.4$

    Which value of *x* makes the equation true?

    Ⓐ $x = 5.1$

    Ⓑ $x = 5.2$

    Ⓒ $x = 6.1$

    Ⓓ $x = 7.2$

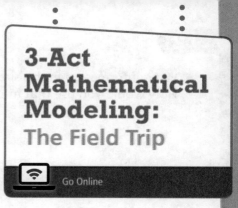

3-ACT MATH ▶ ▶ ▶

The Field Trip

3-Act Mathematical Modeling:
The Field Trip

📶 Go Online

ACT 1

1. After watching the video, what is the first question that comes to mind?

2. Write the Main Question you will answer.

3. **Construct Arguments** Make a prediction to answer this Main Question. Explain your prediction.

4. On the number line below, write a number that is too small to be the answer. Write a number that is too large.

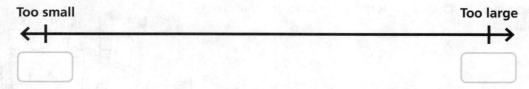

Too small   Too large

5. Plot your prediction on the same number line.

6. What information in this situation would be helpful to know? How would you use that information?

7. Use Appropriate Tools What tools can you use to solve the problem? Explain how you would use them strategically.

8. Model with Math Represent the situation using mathematics. Use your representation to answer the Main Question.

9. What is your answer to the Main Question? Is it higher or lower than your prediction? Explain why.

10. Write the answer you saw in the video.

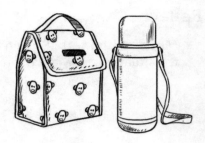

11. Reasoning Does your answer match the answer in the video? If not, what are some reasons that would explain the difference?

12. Make Sense and Persevere Would you change your model now that you know the answer? Explain.

Reflect

13. Model with Math Explain how you used a mathematical model to represent the situation. How did the model help you answer the Main Question?

14. Critique Reasoning A classmate said your model works for any number of students and adults. Do you agree? Justify your reasoning or explain your classmate's error.

15. Generalize Suppose the entire grade goes on the field trip: 283 students and 10 teachers. Each bus holds 72 people and costs $610 for transport. How much money is needed? Explain how you reused your model.

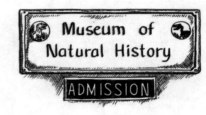

Museum of Natural History

ADMISSION

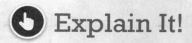

Juwon says all three expressions are equivalent.

ACTIVITY

$8n + 6$
$2(4n + 3)$
$14n$

I can...
identify and write equivalent algebraic expressions.

A. Find the value of each expression for $n = 1$.

$8n + 6$	$2(4n + 3)$	$14n$
$8(\boxed{}) + 6$	$2(4 \cdot \boxed{} + 3)$	$14(\boxed{})$
$= \boxed{} + 6$	$= 2(\boxed{} + 3)$	$= \boxed{}$
$= \boxed{}$	$= 2 \cdot \boxed{}$	
	$= \boxed{}$	

B. Find the value of each expression for $n = 2$.

$8n + 6$	$2(4n + 3)$	$14n$

C. Critique Reasoning Do you agree with Juwon that all three expressions are equivalent? Explain.

Focus on math practices

Generalize When a number is substituted for the same variable in two expressions, how many times must those two expressions have different values before you know they are not equivalent? Explain.

? Essential Question How can you identify and write equivalent expressions?

  VISUAL LEARNING ASSESS

EXAMPLE 1 **Use Properties of Operations to Write Equivalent Expressions**

Scan for Multimedia

Equivalent expressions have the same value regardless of the value that is substituted for the same variable in the expressions.

Use properties of operations to write equivalent expressions for $3(4x - 1)$ and $2x + 4$.

> **Use Structure** Think about how you can use these properties of operations for any numbers a, b, or c.

Properties of Operations

1. **Commutative Property**
   of Addition $a + b = b + a$
   of Multiplication $a \times b = b \times a$
2. **Associative Property**
   of Addition $(a + b) + c = a + (b + c)$
   of Multiplication $(a \times b) \times c = a \times (b \times c)$
3. **Distributive Property**
   across Addition $a(b + c) = a(b) + a(c)$
   across Subtraction $a(b - c) = a(b) - a(c)$

Use the Distributive and Associative Properties to write an expression that is equivalent to $3(4x - 1)$.

$3(4x - 1) = 3(4x) - 3(1)$ ·········· Distributive Property

$\quad\quad = (3 \cdot 4)x - 3$ ·········· Associative Property of Multiplication

$\quad\quad = 12x - 3$

$12x - 3$ and $3(4x - 1)$ are equivalent expressions.

> Equivalent expressions can be written in more than one way.

Use the Distributive Property in reverse order to write an expression that is equivalent to $2x + 4$.

> Look for a common factor of both terms that is greater than 1.

$2x + 4 = 2(x) + 2(2)$ ·········· Distributive Property

$\quad\quad = 2(x + 2)$ ·········· 2 is a common factor.

So, $2(x + 2)$ is equivalent to $2x + 4$.

☑ Try It!

Write an expression that is equivalent to $3y - 9$.

A common factor of 3 and 9 is ☐.

$3y - 9 = $ ☐$(y) - $ ☐$($☐$)$

$\quad\quad = $ ☐$($☐$ - $☐$)$

So, $3y - 9$ is equivalent to ☐.

Convince Me! Why can you use properties of operations to write equivalent expressions?

EXAMPLE 2 Use Properties to Identify Equivalent Expressions

Which of the expressions below are equivalent?

$8x - 4$ $4x$ $4(2x - 1)$

> **Use Structure** You can use properties of operations to determine whether expressions are equivalent.

Use the Distributive Property to simplify $4(2x - 1)$.

$4(2x - 1) = 4(2x) - 4(1)$

$\qquad = 8x - 4$

So, $4(2x - 1)$ and $8x - 4$ are equivalent expressions.

Properties of operations cannot be used to write either $8x - 4$ or $4(2x - 1)$ as $4x$.

$8x - 4 \neq 4x$

$4(2x - 1) \neq 4x$

So, neither $8x - 4$ nor $4(2x - 1)$ is equivalent to $4x$.

 Try It!

Which of the following expressions are equivalent? Explain.

$10y + 5 \quad 15y \quad 5(2y + 1)$

EXAMPLE 3 Use Substitution to Justify Equivalent Expressions

Are $6(n + 3) - 4$ and $6n + 14$ equivalent expressions?

Use properties of operations to simplify $6(n + 3) - 4$.

$6(n + 3) - 4 = 6(n) + 6(3) - 4$ Use the Distributive Property.

$\qquad = 6n + 18 - 4$

$\qquad = 6n + 14$

> **Generalize** When two expressions name the same number regardless of the value of the variable, they are equivalent.

Substitute 3 for n to justify that the expressions are equivalent.

$6(n + 3) - 4 = 6(3) + 6(3) - 4 \qquad\qquad 6n + 14 = 6(3) + 14$

$\qquad\qquad = 18 + 18 - 4 \qquad\qquad\qquad\qquad\quad = 18 + 14$

$\qquad\qquad = 32 \qquad\qquad\qquad\qquad\qquad\qquad\quad = 32$

So, $6(n + 3) - 4$ and $6n + 14$ are equivalent expressions.

 Try It!

Are $2(x - 3) + 1$ and $2x + 6$ equivalent expressions? Use substitution to justify your work.

Two algebraic expressions are equivalent if they have the same value when any number is substituted for the variable.

You can use the properties of operations to write equivalent expressions.

Properties of Operations

1 **Commutative Property**
   of Addition $a + b = b + a$
   of Multiplication $a \times b = b \times a$

2 **Associative Property**
   of Addition $(a + b) + c = a + (b + c)$
   of Multiplication $(a \times b) \times c = a \times (b \times c)$

3 **Distributive Property**
   across Addition $a(b + c) = a(b) + a(c)$
   across Subtraction $a(b - c) = a(b) - a(c)$

Do You Understand?

1. **? Essential Question** How can you identify and write equivalent expressions?

2. **Use Structure** Which property of operations could you use to write an equivalent expression for $y + \frac{1}{2}$? Write the equivalent expression.

3. **Generalize** Are z^3 and $3z$ equivalent expressions? Explain.

4. Are the expressions $3(y + 1)$ and $3y + 3$ equivalent for $y = 1$? $y = 2$? $y = 3$?

5. **Construct Arguments** Are the expressions $3(y + 1)$ and $3y + 3$ equivalent for any value of y? Explain.

Do You Know How?

In **6–8**, use properties of operations to complete the equivalent expressions.

6. $2(r + 3) = \boxed{}\,r + \boxed{}$

7. $6(4s - 1) = \boxed{}\,s - \boxed{}$

8. $8t + 2 = 2(\boxed{}\,t + \boxed{}\,)$

9. Complete the table below.

x	12x − 6	3x + 3	6(2x − 1)
1			
2			
3			

10. In Exercise 9, which expressions in the table are equivalent?

Practice & Problem Solving

Scan for
Multimedia

Leveled Practice In **11–20**, write equivalent expressions.

11. $3(m + 3) = \boxed{}m + \boxed{}$

12. $20n - 4m = 4(\boxed{}n - \boxed{}m)$

13. $3(x - 6)$

14. $2x + 10$

15. $8\left(2y + \frac{1}{4}\right)$

16. $5.7 + (3z + 0.3)$

17. $5w - 15$

18. $2x + 4y$

19. $10(y^2 + 2.45)$

20. $\frac{3}{4} \cdot (z^3 \cdot 4)$

In **21–24**, write the letters of the expressions that are equivalent to the given expression.

21. $5(2x + 3)$

  a. $10x + 15$

  b. $5x + 15 + 5x$

  c. $10x + 8$

22. $4x - 8$

  a. $2(2x - 6)$

  b. $2(2x - 4)$

  c. $x - 8 + 3x$

23. $12x - 16$

  a. $9.6x - 16 + 2.4x$

  b. $3(3x - 5)$

  c. $4(3x - 4)$

24. $2\left(6x + \frac{1}{2}\right)$

  a. $12x + 2$

  b. $12x + 1$

  c. $6x + \frac{1}{2} + 6x + \frac{1}{2}$

In **25–27**, use the signs at the right.

25. Write an algebraic expression that represents each purchase.

  a. Mr. Tonkery bought x number of soccer balls and 3 baseballs.

Soccer Balls
$15 each

Baseballs
$6 each

Sweat Socks
$5 per pair

  b. Dennis, Eddie, and Felix are on a baseball team. They each bought a baseball and x pairs of sweat socks.

26. **Make Sense and Persevere** Suppose x has the same value in both of the expressions you wrote for Exercise 25. Are the two expressions you wrote equivalent? Explain.

27. **Critique Reasoning** Wendy says that soccer balls cost $2\frac{1}{2}$ times as much as baseballs. Do you agree? Explain.

28. **Use Structure** Write an algebraic expression to represent the area of the rectangular rug. Then use properties of operations to write an equivalent expression.

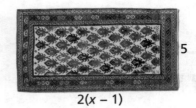

5

$2(x - 1)$

29. **Critique Reasoning** Jamie says that the expressions $6x - 2x + 4$ and $4(x + 1)$ are not equivalent because one expression has a term that is subtracted and the other does not. Do you agree? Explain.

30. Are the two expressions shown below equivalent? Explain.

$$4(n + 3) - (3 + n) \text{ and } 3n + 9$$

31. **Critique Reasoning** Chris says that the expression $4n - 2$ can be written as $2(2n - 1)$. Do you agree? Explain.

32. **Higher Order Thinking** Write an expression that has only one term and is equivalent to the expression below.

$$(f \cdot g^2) + 5 - (g^2 \cdot f)$$

33. **Construct Arguments** A Florida college golf team with 14 members is planning an awards banquet. To find the total cost of the meals, the team uses the expression $5(g + 14)$, where g is the number of guests attending the banquet. A team member says that an equivalent expression is $5g + 14$. Do you agree? Explain.

$5 per meal

☑ Assessment Practice

34. Select each expression that is equivalent to $8.5 + (2s + 0.5)$.

- ☐ $(8.5 + 2s) + 0.5$
- ☐ $(8.5 + 0.5) + 2s$
- ☐ $9 + 2$
- ☐ $2(4.5 + s)$
- ☐ $8.5(2s + 0.5)$

35. Select each expression that is equivalent to $5(n + 4)$.

- ☐ $5n + 4$
- ☐ $5n + 20$
- ☐ $15 + 5n + 5$
- ☐ $5(n + 3) + 5$
- ☐ $5n + 54$

Solve & Discuss It! ACTIVITY

Write an expression equivalent to $x + 5 + 2x + 2$.

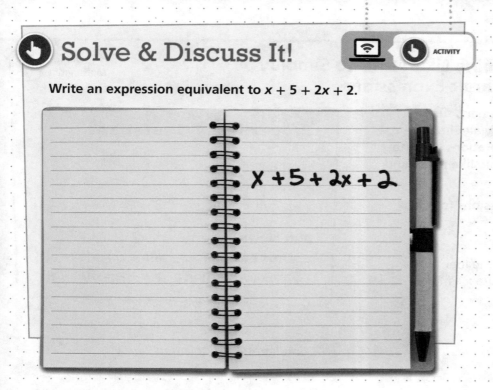

$x + 5 + 2x + 2$

Make Sense and Persevere Use what you know about algebraic expressions and properties of operations to make sense of the problem.

I can...
combine like terms in algebraic expressions.

Focus on math practices

Be Precise How do you know that the expression you wrote is equivalent to $x + 5 + 2x + 2$?

VISUAL LEARNING ASSESS

EXAMPLE 1 **Combine Like Terms to Simplify Algebraic Expressions**

Scan for Multimedia

Terms that have the same variable part, such as y and $2y$, are like terms. To simplify algebraic expressions, use properties of operations to write equivalent expressions that have no like terms and no parentheses.

Write simplified equivalent expressions for $x + x + x$ and $2y - y$.

> **Use Structure** You can use the Identity Property of Multiplication to write x as $1x$.

Properties of Operations

Identity Property
  of Addition $a + 0 = a = 0 + a$
  of Multiplication $a \times 1 = a = 1 \times a$

Distributive Property
  across Addition $a(b + c) = a(b) + a(c)$
  across Subtraction $a(b - c) = a(b) - a(c)$

Combine the like terms in $x + x + x$.

$x + x + x$ .... All three terms are like terms.

$= 1x + 1x + 1x$ .... Identity Property of Multiplication

$= (1 + 1 + 1)x$ .... Distributive Property

$= 3x$

> Add the coefficients, and write the common variable.

So, $3x$ is equivalent to $x + x + x$.

Combine the like terms in $2y - y$.

$2y - y$ .... $2y$ and y are like terms.

$= 2y - 1y$ .... Identity Property of Multiplication

$= (2 - 1)y$ .... Distributive Property

$= 1y$ or y

> Subtract the coefficients, and write the common variable.

So, y is equivalent to $2y - y$.

☑ **Try It!**

Simplify the expression $4z - z + z - 2z$.

$4z - z + z - 2z$

$= 4z - 1z + \boxed{} - \boxed{}$ .... Use the Identity Property of Multiplication.

$= (4 - 1 + \boxed{} - \boxed{})\boxed{}$ .... Use the Distributive Property.

$= \boxed{}$

The simplified expression is $\boxed{}$.

Convince Me! How do you know that the expression $2x + 4y$ is not equivalent to $6xy$?

EXAMPLE 2 **Simplify Algebraic Expressions with Fractions**

A new hiking trail includes three sections of an old trail. There is a flat section, a hilly section, and a winding section. The park ranger marked the sections of the trail in relation to the length of the flat stretch of the trail, which is *n* kilometers. What is the simplified expression that describes the length of the new trail?

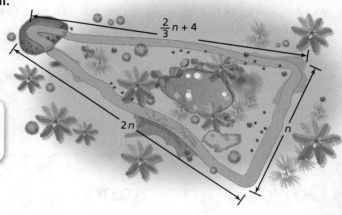

$n + 2n + \frac{2}{3}n + 4$

> Write an expression that represents the total length of the trail and simplify.

$= 1n + 2n + \frac{2}{3}n + 4$

$= \left(1 + 2 + \frac{2}{3}\right)n + 4$

$= 3\frac{2}{3}n + 4$

$3\frac{2}{3}n + 4$ is equivalent to $n + 2n + \frac{2}{3}n + 4$.

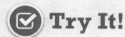 **Try It!**

Park rangers add another section to the trail, represented by the expression $\frac{1}{2}n + n + \frac{1}{2}$. Write an expression for the new total length of the trail. Then write a simplified equivalent expression.

EXAMPLE 3 **Simplify Algebraic Expressions with Parentheses and Decimals**

This summer Vanna wants to charge 2.5 times as much for mowing and raking, but her expenses ($10 per weekend) will also increase 2.5 times. The expression below can be used to find how much Vanna will make this summer mowing and raking *x* lawns in a weekend.

$2.5(20.50x + 5.50x - 10)$

How can you use properties of operations to write a simplified equivalent expression without parentheses?

Use the Distributive Property.

$2.5(20.50x + 5.50x - 10) = 2.5(26x - 10)$

$= 2.5(26x) - 2.5(10)$

$= 65x - 25$

$65x - 25$ is equivalent to $2.5(20.50x + 5.50x - 10)$.

> Simplifying expressions can make the expressions easier to evaluate.

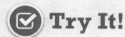 **Try It!**

Suppose Vanna increases her rate by 3.5 times and her expenses also increase by 3.5 times this summer. Write two equivalent expressions to represent how much she can earn mowing and raking grass.

You can combine like terms to write equivalent expressions. Like terms have the same variable part.

$2x + 6 + 5x + 4$ ·········· Identify like terms.

$= 2x + 5x + 6 + 4$ ·········· Commutative Property of Addition

$= 7x + 10$

$2x + 6 + 5x + 4 = 7x + 10$

Do You Understand?

1. **Essential Question** How can you simplify algebraic expressions?

2. Explain how you know which terms to combine when combining like terms.

3. **Construct Arguments** Explain why the expression $2y - y$ can be written as y.

4. Explain why the expressions $\frac{1}{2}x + \frac{1}{2}x$ and x are equivalent.

5. **Critique Reasoning** Henry wrote $4z^2 - z^2$ as 4. Are $4z^2 - z^2$ and 4 equivalent expressions? Explain.

Do You Know How?

In 6–15, simplify each expression.

6. $x + x + x + x$

7. $4y - y$

8. $7y - 4.5 - 6y$

9. $4x + 2 - \frac{1}{2}x$

10. $3 + 3y - 1 + y$

11. $x + 6x$

12. $0.5w + 1.7w - 0.5$

13. $12\frac{1}{3}b + 6\frac{2}{3} - 10\frac{2}{3}b$

14. $\frac{3}{4}x + 2 + 3x - \frac{1}{2}$

15. $3.2x + 6.5 - 2.4x - 4.4$

Practice & Problem Solving 📝 ⏻

Leveled Practice In **16–26**, combine like terms to simplify each expression.

16. $2.1x^2 + 3 - 0.5x^2 - 1$

$= (\boxed{} x^2 - \boxed{} x^2) + (3 - 1)$

$= \boxed{} x^2 + \boxed{}$

17. $\frac{2}{3}n + 6 + 3n - \frac{2}{3}$

$= (\boxed{} n + \boxed{} n) + (\boxed{} - \boxed{})$

$= \boxed{} n + \boxed{}$

18. $5 + 3w + 3 - w$

19. $5w - 5w$

20. $2x + 5 + 3x + 6$

21. $\frac{3}{4}z^3 + 4 - \frac{1}{4}z^3$

22. $3.4m + 2.4m$

23. $4.2n + 5 - 3.2n$

24. $q^5 + q^5 + q^5$

25. $3x + \frac{1}{4} + 2y + \frac{1}{4} + 7x - y$

26. $1.5z^2 + 4.5 + 6z - 0.3 - 3z + z^2$

27. Use Structure Use the table at the right. Yolanda is planning a party that will take place in three rooms.

a. Write an expression that can be used to represent the total amount Yolanda will need to rent all three rooms and the sound system for t hours.

Room	Rental Fee (per hour)	Sound System Fee
1	$25	$15
2	$20	$10
3	$50	no charge

b. How can you use a property to write a simplified equivalent expression?

In 28–30, use the diagram at the right.

28. Write an algebraic expression for the perimeter of the swimming pool.

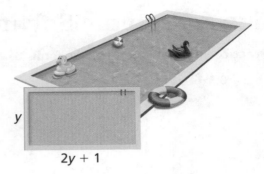

y

$2y + 1$

29. Use Structure Write a new expression equivalent to the expression you wrote for Exercise 28.

30. Justify that the two expressions are equivalent.

31. Rodney rewrote the expression $\frac{1}{2}(2x + 7)$ as $x + 3\frac{1}{2}$. Which property of operations did Rodney use?

32. Construct Arguments Annie said that she simplified the expression $6.5(x + 0.5x + 1)$ by writing the equivalent expression $6.5x + 3.25x + 6.5$. Do you agree? Explain.

33. Critique Reasoning Thea said that the expressions $4x - 3x + 2$ and $x + 2$ are equivalent. Is Thea correct? Explain.

34. Higher Order Thinking Write an equivalent expression for the expression shown below.

$$\frac{a}{3} + \frac{a}{3} + \frac{a}{3}$$

Assessment Practice

35. Select all expressions that are equivalent to $8x + 3 + 5x - 2x$.

☐ $13x + 3 - 2x$

☐ $11x + 3x$

☐ $11 + 3x$

☐ $14x$

☐ $11x + 3$

36. Select which expression is equivalent to or NOT equivalent to the given expression.

	Equivalent to $2x + 7 + 6x - x$	NOT Equivalent to $2x + 7 + 6x - x$
$2x + 13$	☐	☐
$7 + 7x$	☐	☐
$14x$	☐	☐
$7x + 7$	☐	☐

? Topic Essential Question

What are expressions and how can they be written and evaluated?

Vocabulary Review

Complete each definition with a vocabulary word.

> **Vocabulary** algebraic expression   coefficient   exponent
> factor tree   like terms   variable

1. A(n) _____ tells the number of times the base is used as a factor.

2. A letter or symbol that represents an unknown quantity is a(n) _____.

3. A diagram that shows the prime factors of a composite number is a(n) _____.

Draw a line from each pair of numbers in Column A to the *least common multiple* (*LCM*) of the numbers in Column B.

Column A	Column B
4. 9, 6	36
5. 9, 12	56
6. 8, 7	18

7. Look at the variables in each expression below. Write **Y** if the terms of each expression are *like terms*. Write **N** if they are NOT *like terms*.

   a. $3a + 3z$ **b.** $\frac{x}{3} + \frac{x}{4}$ **c.** $4j - j + 3.8j$

Use Vocabulary in Writing

Explain one way to simplify the expression $4(3q - q)$. Use vocabulary words in your explanation.

Concepts and Skills Review

Understand and Represent Exponents

Quick Review

An exponent is a way to show repeated multiplication.

Example

Use an exponent to write the expression $6 \times 6 \times 6$. Then evaluate the expression.

6 is used as a factor 3 times.

6 is the base and 3 is the exponent.

$6 \times 6 \times 6 = 6^3 = 216$

Find 6^0.

A number with an exponent of 0 is always equal to 1.

$6^0 = 1$

Practice

Write each expression using an exponent.

1. $8 \times 8 \times 8 \times 8 \times 8 \times 8 \times 8$

2. 4

3. $10 \times 10 \times 10 \times 10$

Evaluate each expression.

4. 9^2 **5.** 99^1

6. $3,105^0$ **7.** 22^2

8. 2^7 **9.** 3^4

Find Greatest Common Factor and Least Common Multiple

Quick Review

You can use prime factorization to find the greatest common factor and the least common multiple of two numbers.

Example

Find the greatest common factor (GCF) and the least common multiple (LCM) of **12 and 6.**

List the prime factors of both numbers.

12: ②$\times$ 2 $\times$③   *Identify the common factors, then multiply.*

6: ②$\times$③

GCF: $2 \times 3 = 6$

12: ②$\times$②$\times$ 3   *Identify the greatest number of times each factor appears, then multiply.*

6: 2 $\times$③

LCM: $2 \times 2 \times 3 = 12$

Practice

Find the GCF for each pair of numbers. Use the GCF and the Distributive Property to find the sum of each pair of numbers.

1. 30, 100   **2.** 8, 52

3. 28, 42   **4.** 37, 67

5. 12, 24   **6.** 8; 12

Find the LCM for each pair of numbers.

7. 4, 9   **8.** 3, 6

9. 8, 10   **10.** 3, 5

11. 12, 5   **12.** 4, 11

LESSON 3-3 ▸ Write and Evaluate Numerical Expressions

Quick Review

Use the order of operations to evaluate numerical expressions.

Example

Evaluate the expression $3^2 + 2[(21 - 9) \div 4]$.

$3^2 + 2[(21 - 9) \div 4]$ ·········· Evaluate inside the parentheses.

$= 3^2 + 2[12 \div 4]$ ·············· Evaluate inside the brackets.

$= 3^2 + 2 \times 3$ ··················· Evaluate the power.

$= 9 + 2 \times 3$ ····················· Multiply.

$= 9 + 6$ ···························· Add.

$= 15$

The value of $3^2 + 2[(21 - 9) \div 4]$ is 15.

Practice

Evaluate each expression.

1. $80 - 4^2 \div 8$

2. $92.3 - (3.2 \div 0.4) \times 2^3$

3. $\left[(2^3 \times 2.5) \div \frac{1}{2}\right] + 120$

4. $[20 + (2.5 \times 3)] - 3^3$

5. $\left[(2 \times 10^0) \div \frac{1}{3}\right] + 8$

LESSONS 3-4 AND 3-5 ▸ Write and Evaluate Algebraic Expressions

Quick Review

An algebraic expression can be written to represent a situation with an unknown quantity. Use a variable to represent the unknown quantity. An algebraic expression can be evaluated by substituting a value for the variable and performing the operations.

Example

Write an algebraic expression for 9 times the difference of 12 and a divided by 2. Then evaluate the expression for $a = 4$.

"9 times the difference of 12 and a divided by 2" is represented by $9 \times (12 - a) \div 2$.

Evaluate $9 \times (12 - a) \div 2$ when $a = 4$.

$9 \times (12 - a) \div 2$

$9 \times (12 - 4) \div 2$ — Use substitution to replace the variable with its value.

$= 9 \times 8 \div 2$

$= 72 \div 2$

$= 36$

Practice

Write an algebraic expression to represent each situation.

1. 22 less than 5 times a number f

2. 48 times a number of game markers, g

3. A number of eggs, e, divided by 12

4. 3 times the sum of m and 7

Evaluate each expression for $n = 7$, $x = 4$, $y = 8$, and $z = 1$.

5. $12x - 7$ **6.** $x^2 \div y$

7. $5z + 3n - z^3$ **8.** $y^2 \div 2x + 3n - z$

Generate Equivalent Expressions

Quick Review

Equivalent expressions are expressions that have the same value. The properties of operations and substitution can be used to write and identify equivalent expressions.

Example

Are the expressions $5x + 20$, $5(x + 4)$, and $x + 4$ equivalent?

For algebraic expressions to be equivalent, each expression must name the same value no matter what value is substituted for the variable.

x	5x + 20	5(x + 4)	x + 4
1	25	25	5
2	30	30	6
3	35	35	7

Use the Distributive Property to write $5x + 20$ as $5(x + 4)$.

$$5x + 20 = 5 \cdot x + 5 \cdot 4$$
$$= 5(x + 4)$$

Properties of operations cannot be used to write $5x + 20$ or $5(x + 4)$ as $x + 4$.

$5x + 20$ and $5(x + 4)$ are equivalent expressions.

Practice

Complete the table. Then circle the expressions that are equivalent.

1.

y	5(2.2y + 1) − 3	11y + 5 − y	11y + 2
1			
2			
3			

In 2–4, write Yes or No to indicate whether the expressions are equivalent.

2. $10x - 3 + 2x - 5$ and $4(3x - 2)$

3. $3y + 3$ and $9\left(y + \frac{1}{3}\right)$

4. $6(3x + 1)$ and $9x + 6 + 9x$

In 5–7, use properties of operations to complete the equivalent expressions.

5. $2(x + 4)$ and ____ $x +$ ____

6. $5x - 45$ and $5($ ____ $-$ ____ $)$

7. $3(x + 7)$ and ____ $x +$ ____

Simplify Algebraic Expressions

Quick Review

Combine like terms to simplify algebraic expressions.

Example

Simplify the expression $3x + 7 + 6x$.

$3x + 7 + 6x$ .... Identify the like terms, $3x$ and $6x$.

$= 3x + 6x + 7$ .... Use the Commutative Property of Addition.

$= 9x + 7$ .... Simplify.

The expression $9x + 7$ is equivalent to $3x + 7 + 6x$.

Practice

Simplify each expression.

1. $9y + 4 - 6y$

2. $3x + 5 + 7x$

3. $8x + 13 - 3x + 9$

4. $y^2 + 3y^2$

5. $4x + 15 - 3x + 10$

6. $10x + 2x - 12x$

Crisscrossed

Find each product or quotient. Write your answers in the cross-number puzzle below. Each digit and decimal point of your answer goes in its own box.

I can...
multiply and divide multi-digit decimals.

ACROSS

B 18.25 × 20.2

F 945.12 ÷ 6.6

H 7.11 ÷ 0.1

J 2.2 × 1.2

K 9.75 ÷ 1.2

L 64.2 ÷ 3

M 27.1 × 0.2

P 28.713 ÷ 0.3

S 95.3 × 0.02

U 0.009 ÷ 0.9

V 3.3456 ÷ 0.4

X 50.048 ÷ 0.08

Y 8.284 × 5.5

Z 19.698 ÷ 0.06

DOWN

A 240.5 ÷ 5

B 10.1 × 0.31

C 2.15 × 2.9

D 18.45 × 4

E 2.58 × 1.3

F 5.735 ÷ 0.5

G 5.45 × 0.4

N 62.54 ÷ 0.025

Q 0.742 ÷ 0.4

R 12.3 × 0.04

S 16.1 × 6.7

T 2.04 ÷ 3.4

U 3.3 × 0.07

W 8.85 ÷ 2.5

TOPIC 4

REPRESENT AND SOLVE EQUATIONS AND INEQUALITIES

? Topic Essential Question

What procedures can be used to write and solve equations and inequalities?

Topic Overview

Topic Vocabulary

- Addition Property of Equality
- dependent variable
- Division Property of Equality
- equation
- independent variable
- inequality
- inverse relationship
- Multiplication Property of Equality
- solution of an equation
- Subtraction Property of Equality

Lesson Digital Resources

INTERACTIVE STUDENT EDITION
Access online or offline.

VISUAL LEARNING ANIMATION
Interact with visual learning animations.

ACTIVITY Use with *Solve & Discuss It, Explore It,* and *Explain It* activities, and to explore Examples.

VIDEOS Watch clips to support *3-Act Mathematical Modeling Lessons* and *STEM Projects*.

 Go online

Checking a Bag

▶ Checking a Bag

A large plane flying across the ocean can weigh almost 1 million pounds! The heavier an airplane is, the more fuel it needs for a flight. The cost of fuel has led many airlines to add a weight restriction on luggage.

If you were to fly somewhere, what would you bring? What would you leave at home to minimize the weight of your luggage? Packing light is important, not only to avoid a fee but also to do your part to conserve fuel. Think about this during the 3-Act Mathematical Modeling lesson.

 **PRACTICE** Practice what you've learned.

TUTORIALS Get help from *Virtual Nerd*, right when you need it.

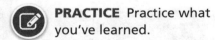 **MATH TOOLS** Explore math with digital tools.

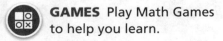 **GAMES** Play Math Games to help you learn.

KEY CONCEPT Review important lesson content.

 GLOSSARY Read and listen to English/Spanish definitions.

 ASSESSMENT Show what you've learned.

Did You Know?

The design of a bridge depends on factors such as the distance the bridge will cover, the expected number of vehicles that will cross the bridge daily, and the geographic conditions.

Beam

Beam bridges contain a horizontal beam supported at each end by piers.

Arch

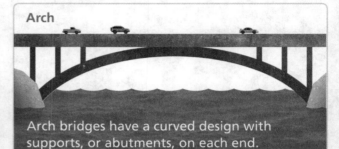

Arch bridges have a curved design with supports, or abutments, on each end.

Cantilever

Cantilever bridges contain cantilevers–horizontal beams that are fixed at only one end.

Truss

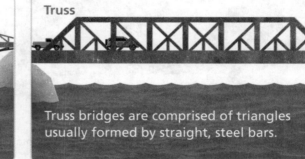

Truss bridges are comprised of triangles usually formed by straight, steel bars.

Suspension

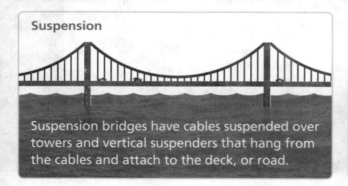

Suspension bridges have cables suspended over towers and vertical suspenders that hang from the cables and attach to the deck, or road.

Cable-stayed

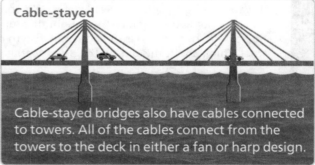

Cable-stayed bridges also have cables connected to towers. All of the cables connect from the towers to the deck in either a fan or harp design.

Your Task: Design a Bridge ▶

Now that you have defined the problem, identified the criteria and constraints, and performed some data collection, it is time to focus on the solution. You and your classmates will continue to be engineers as you brainstorm solutions and develop prototypes for your bridge.

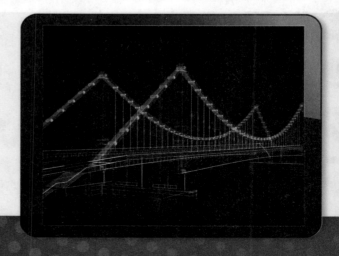

Review What You Know!

Vocabulary

Choose the best term from the box to complete each definition.

| algebraic expression |
| coefficient |
| equation |
| evaluate |
| variable |

1. In 6x, x is a(n) _____.

2. $x + 5$ is an example of a(n) _____.

3. _____ an expression to find its value.

4. The expressions on each side of the equal sign in a(n) _____ are equal.

Equality

Tell whether the equation is true or false.

5. $6 + 2 = 2 + 6$

6. $2.5 - 1 = 1 - 2.5$

7. $\frac{1}{2} \times 3 = 3 \times \frac{1}{2}$

8. $\frac{3}{4} \div 5 = \frac{3}{4} \times \frac{1}{5}$

9. $5 \div \frac{1}{3} = \frac{5}{3}$

10. $\frac{2}{3} \times 5 = \frac{10}{15}$

Expressions

Evaluate each expression.

11. $x - 2$ for $x = 8$

12. $2b$ for $b = 9$

13. $3\frac{3}{4} + y$ for $y = \frac{5}{6}$

14. $\frac{15}{x}$ for $x = 3$

15. $5.6t$ for $t = 0.7$

16. $4x$ for $x = \frac{1}{2}$

Order of Operations

17. Explain the order in which you should compute the operations in the expression below. Then evaluate the expression.

$[(33 \div 3) + 1] - 2^2$

Graphing in the Coordinate Plane

18. Describe how to plot point $A(-6, 2)$ on a coordinate plane.

Language Development

Use the graphic organizer to help you understand new vocabulary terms.

Addition Property of Equality

Definition

Example

Subtraction Property of Equality

Definition

Example

Properties of Equality

Multiplication Property of Equality

Definition

Example

Division Property of Equality

Definition

Example

**PROJECT
4A**

If you were going to try a new exercise, what would it be? Why?

PROJECT: ANALYZE AN EXERCISE ROUTINE

**PROJECT
4B**

What is the most interesting book you have read?

PROJECT: WRITE AND ILLUSTRATE A CHILDREN'S BOOK

PROJECT 4C

If you were a carpenter, what sorts of things would you build?

PROJECT: MAKE A MODEL OF A STAIRCASE

PROJECT 4D

What skills would you need if you wanted to move as slowly as a snail?

PROJECT: PLAN A RACE

I can...
determine if a value for a variable makes an equation true.

Solve & Discuss It!  ACTIVITY

Unit cubes are placed on a pan balance. There are 3 cubes on one pan and 9 cubes on the other pan. What can you do to make the pans balance?

Model with Math A pan balance can be used to represent the relationship between two quantities. You can write an equation with a variable to show this relationship.

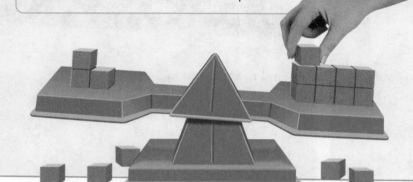

Focus on math practices

Use Structure Suppose that you added 10 cubes to the pan with 3 cubes and then added 4 cubes to the pan with 9 cubes. Would the pans balance? Write an equation to show this relationship.

EXAMPLE 1 Determine Whether a Value is a Solution of an Equation

Scan for Multimedia

Jordan received a $15.00 gift card for phone apps. He has used $4.50 of the value and wants to buy one more app to use up the balance. Which app should Jordan buy?

PHONE APPS

RECIPES $9.50

W02 SPORTS $10.50

REMOTE DESKTOP $12.00

Model with Math How can you use a bar diagram to help write an equation?

Draw a bar diagram and write an equation to show how the quantities are related.

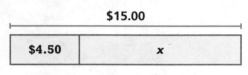

$15.00

| $4.50 | x |

$4.50 + x = $15.00

An **equation** is a mathematical sentence that uses an equal sign to show that two expressions are equal.

A **solution of an equation** is a value for the variable that makes the equation true.

Find the solution of $4.50 + x = $15.00.

Substitute the cost of each app for x and evaluate.

Try x = $9.50:

$4.50 + $9.50 = $14.00   Not a solution

Try x = $10.50:

$4.50 + $10.50 = $15.00   Solution

Try x = $12.00:

$4.50 + $12.00 = $16.50   Not a solution

The solution is $10.50, so Jordan should buy the W02 Sports app.

☑ Try It!

Tracy received a $21.00 gift card for phone apps. She has used $9.00 of the value and wants to buy one more app from the list above to use up the balance. Complete the bar diagram and use the equation $21.00 = x + $9.00 to determine which app she should buy.

| x | |

The solution is [   ] , so Tracy should buy the [   ] app.

Convince Me! What do you notice about the expression on the left side of an equation compared to the expression on the right side when a value is substituted for the variable? How do you know which value is a solution?

Maya has a total of 1,190 marbles and 5 boxes. She puts an equal number of marbles in each box.

A. Which of Maya's three friends, if any, correctly guessed the number of marbles, x, Maya has in each box?

234? 242? 240?

1,190 marbles

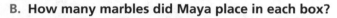

| x | x | x | x | x |

$$5x = 1{,}190$$

Substitute each guess for x and evaluate.

Try $x = 234$: $5 \times 234 \neq 1{,}190$ Not a solution

Try $x = 242$: $5 \times 242 \neq 1{,}190$ Not a solution

Try $x = 240$: $5 \times 240 \neq 1{,}190$ Not a solution

Of Maya's three friends, none correctly guessed the number of marbles in each box. No solution is given in the set of values.

B. How many marbles did Maya place in each box?

There are 1,190 marbles equally divided into 5 boxes. $1{,}190 \div 5 = 238$, so $5 \times 238 = 1{,}190$.

Maya put 238 marbles in each box.

> An equation may have a solution that is not given in the set of possible values.

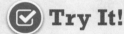 Try It!

Anthony has a total of y marbles and 4 boxes. He puts 13 marbles in each box and has none left over. Which of his friends, if any, correctly guessed how many marbles Anthony has in all? Use the equation $y \div 4 = 13$.

Substitute each guess for y and evaluate.

y marbles

| 13 | 13 | 13 | 13 |

Friend	Guess
Julianne	48 marbles
Nikos	60 marbles
Quincy	120 marbles

Try $y = 48$: ☐ $\div 4 =$ ☐

Try $y = 60$: ☐ $\div 4 =$ ☐

Try $y = 120$: ☐ $\div 4 =$ ☐

Of Anthony's three friends, ☐ correctly guessed the number of marbles he has in all.

No solution is given in the set of values.

Anthony has ☐ marbles in all.

KEY CONCEPT

A **solution of an equation** is a value for the variable that makes the equation true. Substitute values from a given set for the variable and evaluate.

$x - 4 = 12$ $x = 9, 16$

$$x - 4 = 12$$

| 9 is not a solution of this equation because $9 - 4 \neq 12$. | 16 is a solution of this equation because $16 - 4 = 12$. |

Do You Understand?

1. **? Essential Question** How can you determine whether a given number makes an equation true?

2. When is an equation true?

3. **Reasoning** Ben says that $n = 5$ is the solution of the equation $7n = 45$. How can you check whether Ben is correct?

4. A pan balance has 3 cubes on one pan and 11 cubes on the other pan. Lucy thinks she should add 7, 8, 9, or 10 cubes to make the pans balance. How can you use the equation $3 + c = 11$ to find the number of cubes Lucy should add?

Do You Know How?

In **5–8**, substitute each given value of the variable to find which, if any, is a solution of the equation.

5. $d + 9 = 35$ $d = 16, 22, 26, 36$

6. $14n = 35$ $n = 2, 3, 3.5, 4$

7. $13.4 - g = 8.1$ $g = 4.3, 5.3, 5.5, 6.5$

8. $4 = 36 \div m$ $m = 4, 6, 8, 9$

In **9–12**, tell whether each equation is true or false for $n = 8$.

9. $n = 54 - 36$ 10. $5n = 40$

11. $152 \div n = 21$ 12. $n + 46 = 54$

Name: _____

Practice & Problem Solving

In 13–16, tell which given value, if any, is a solution of the equation.

13. $t - 2.1 = 0$ $t = 2.1, 2.4, 2.6, 2.8$

14. $49 = 7r$ $r = 3, 6, 7, 9$

15. $\$4.10 = \$6.25 - y$ $y = \$2.15, \$2.95, \$3.05, \$3.15$

16. $24 \div h = 6$ $h = 1, 3, 6, 8$

17. In the past, Marcie's father rode his bike 108 miles in 7.5 hours. Her mother rode the same distance in 8 hours. Marcie plans to ride her bike 108 miles at a steady rate of 18 mph for y hours. Will she match her father's or mother's time? Use the equation $108 \div y = 18$ to justify your answer.

18. Write if $b = 6$ is a *solution* or is *not a solution* of each equation.

  a. $8b = 48$

  b. $11 - b = 6$

  c. $b + 3 = 9$

  d. $54 \div b = 9$

19. A group of 4 friends is planning a fun day trip. The equations in the table represent the number of people n who can participate in each activity for $29.

Activity	Cost ($)
Raft Trip	$6n + 5 = 29$
Amusement Park	$14n = 29$
Balloon Ride	$30n - 40 = 29$

Which activity should the friends choose if they want to spend exactly $29?

20. There are 27 pennies on one pan of a pan balance and 18 pennies on the other. To make the pans balance, Hillary thinks 5 pennies should be added to the higher pan. Sean thinks 8 pennies should be added, and Rachel thinks 9 pennies should be added. Use the equation $27 = 18 + p$ to determine who is correct.

21. Construct Arguments Gerard spent $5.12 for a drink and a sandwich. His drink cost $1.30. Did he have a ham sandwich for $3.54, a tuna sandwich for $3.82, or a turkey sandwich for $3.92? Use the equation $s + 1.30 = 5.12$ to justify your answer.

22. Higher Order Thinking Write an equation that has a solution of 12. Show how you know that 12 is the solution.

23. Gina's family is driving 255 miles to visit Tallahassee. After driving for a while, they pass a sign that reads "Tallahassee: 124 miles." Substitute the values $m = 111, 121, 131$, and 141 in the equation $255 - m = 124$ to find the number of miles the family has already driven.

24. Lisa is making a quilt that uses a pattern of triangles like the one shown. Write an equation that represents the missing side length if the perimeter is 19 centimeters.

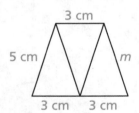

3 cm

5 cm m

3 cm   3 cm

25. Alisa's family planted 7 palm trees in their yard. The park down the street has 147 palm trees. Alisa guessed that the park has either 11 or 31 times as many palm trees as her yard has. Is either of Alisa's guesses correct? Use the equation $7n = 147$ to justify your answer.

☑ Assessment Practice

26. Trish has $26.00 to spend at a craft store. She buys fabric that costs $18.62. She also wants to buy knitting needles for $7.32, silk flowers for $7.38, or oil paints for $8.48.

Use the equation $\$18.62 + c = \$26.00$, where c is the item cost, to find the most expensive item Trish can buy. Explain how you found your answer.

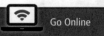
I can...
use the properties of equality to write equivalent equations.

Solve & Discuss It! ACTIVITY

Start with the equation $4 + 8 = 12$ and complete each computation listed below. Do each computation individually. Which of the computations keeps the equation true? Explain.

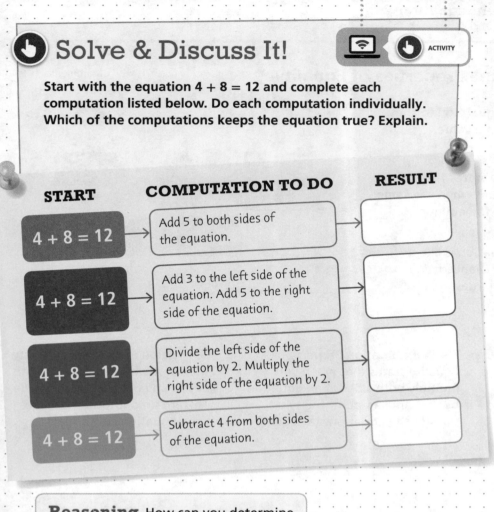

START	COMPUTATION TO DO	RESULT
$4 + 8 = 12$	Add 5 to both sides of the equation.	
$4 + 8 = 12$	Add 3 to the left side of the equation. Add 5 to the right side of the equation.	
$4 + 8 = 12$	Divide the left side of the equation by 2. Multiply the right side of the equation by 2.	
$4 + 8 = 12$	Subtract 4 from both sides of the equation.	

Reasoning How can you determine whether an equation is true?

Focus on math practices

Use Structure Complete the equation $7 + \boxed{} = 10 - \boxed{}$ by filling in the missing numbers. Describe at least two other operations with numbers that you can do to each side of the completed equation to keep it true.

VISUAL LEARNING ASSESS

EXAMPLE 1 Define Properties of Equality

Scan for Multimedia

Recall that an equation uses an equal sign to show that two expressions have the same value.

$$5 + 3 = 8$$

The **Addition Property of Equality** states that the two sides of an equation stay equal when the same amount is added to both sides of the equation.

> **Model with Math** An equation is like a balance. To keep the equation balanced, you must do the same thing to both sides.

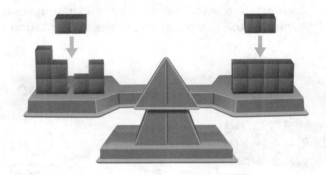

$$(5 + 3) + 2 = 8 + 2$$

The **Subtraction Property of Equality** states that when you subtract the same amount from both sides of an equation, the two sides of the equation stay equal.	The **Multiplication Property of Equality** states that when you multiply both sides of an equation by the same amount, the two sides of the equation stay equal.	The **Division Property of Equality** states that when you divide both sides of an equation by the same non-zero amount, the two sides of the equation stay equal.
$5 + 3 = 8$	$5 + 3 = 8$	$5 + 3 = 8$
$(5 + 3) - 2 = 8 - 2$	$(5 + 3) \times 2 = 8 \times 2$	$(5 + 3) \div 2 = 8 \div 2$

☑ Try It!

If $5y = 25$, which property of equality was used to keep the equation $5y - 7 = 25 - 7$ equal?

Convince Me! What other properties of equality could you apply to keep the equation $5y = 25$ equal? Give an example of each.

EXAMPLE 2 · Apply Multiplication and Division Properties of Equality

The scale balances with 1 blue *x*-block on one side and 4 green blocks on the other side. Franklin put some more green blocks on the right side and now the scale is not balanced. What can you do to make the scale balance? Which Property of Equality justifies this?

Multiply the left side of the balance by 3 to balance the scale.

$$x = 4$$
$$3 \cdot x = 4 \cdot 3$$

> The quantity 4 is multiplied by 3 on the right side of the balance.

> The Multiplication Property of Equality says that you can multiply each side of an equation by the same amount and the two sides will be equal.

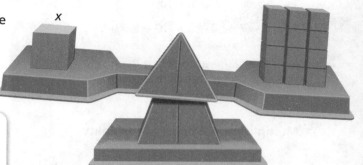

x

EXAMPLE 3 · Apply Addition and Subtraction Properties of Equality

Merijoy says, "You can add 12 to each side of the equation $y - 12 = 30$ and the equation will still be true."

George says, "You can subtract 5 from each side of the equation $y - 12 = 30$ and the equation will still be true."

Who is correct? Explain.

$$y - 12 + 12 = 30 + 12 \qquad\qquad y - 12 - 5 = 30 - 5$$

> The Addition Property of Equality says you can add the same amount to each side of an equation and the two sides will still be equal.

> The Subtraction Property of Equality says you can subtract the same amount from each side of an equation and the two sides will still be equal.

Both Merijoy and George are correct.

Try It!

A. A scale balances with four blue *x*-blocks on one side and 36 green blocks on the other side. Complete the equation to balance the scale with only one blue *x*-block.

$$4 \cdot x = 36$$
$$(4 \cdot x) \div \boxed{} = 36 \div \boxed{}$$
$$x = 9$$

B. If $25 + d = 36$, does $25 + d - 25 = 36 - 20$? Explain.

You can use the properties of equality to write equivalent equations.

Addition Property of Equality

$$7 + 3 = 10$$

$$(7 + 3) + a = 10 + a$$

> Add the same amount to each side to keep the equation balanced.

Subtraction Property of Equality

$$7 + 3 = 10$$

$$(7 + 3) - a = 10 - a$$

> Subtract the same amount from each side to keep the equation balanced.

Multiplication Property of Equality

$$7 + 3 = 10$$

$$(7 + 3) \times a = 10 \times a$$

> Multiply each side of the equation by the same amount to keep the equation balanced.

Division Property of Equality

$$7 + 3 = 10$$

$$(7 + 3) \div a = 10 \div a$$

> Divide each side of the equation by the same non-zero amount to keep the equation balanced.

Do You Understand?

1. **? Essential Question** How can you use the properties of equality to write equivalent equations?

2. A pan balance shows $7 + 5 = 12$. If 4 units are removed from one side, what needs to be done to the other side to keep the pans balanced?

3. If one side of the equation $23 + 43 = 66$ is multiplied by 3, what needs to be done to the other side of the equation to keep the sides equal?

4. **Reasoning** If one side of the equation $x + 5 = 8$ has 9 added to it and the other side has $(4 + 5)$ added to it, will the equation stay equal?

Do You Know How?

In 5 and 6, answer yes or no and explain why or why not.

5. If $23 + 37 = 60$, does $23 + 37 + 9 = 60 + 9$?

6. If $16 + 1 = 17$, does $(16 + 1) - 1 = 17 - 2$?

7. Apply the Multiplication Property of Equality to write an equation equivalent to $7n = 28$.

8. **Critique Reasoning** Tomas says that if one side of the equation $6m = 9$ is divided by 2 and the other side is divided by 3, the equation will stay equal because the result will be $3m = 3$. Is Tomas correct? Explain.

Practice & Problem Solving

In 9–12, tell which property of equality was used.

9. $5m + 4 = 19$

   $5m + 4 - 3 = 19 - 3$

10. $3t = 20$

    $3t \div 2 = 20 \div 2$

11. $\frac{n}{6} = 9$

    $\left(\frac{n}{6}\right) \times 5 = 9 \times 5$

12. $5b - 6 = 14$

    $(5b - 6) + 2 = 14 + 2$

13. If $r + 9 = 42$, does $r + 9 - 9 = 42 + 9$? Why or why not?

14. If $6s = 24$, does $6s \div 6 = 24 \div 6$? Why or why not?

15. This scale was balanced. Find the number to add that makes the scale become balanced again. Then complete the equation to make it true.

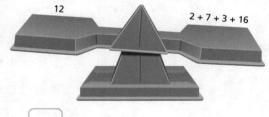

$12 + \boxed{} = 2 + 7 + 3 + 16$

16. This scale balanced with 3 green blocks on one side and 1 blue x-block on the other side. Find the number to multiply by that makes the scale balance. Then complete the equation to make it true.

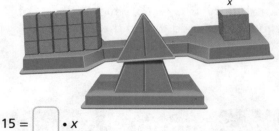

$15 = \boxed{} \cdot x$

17. You start with the equation $8x = 24$. Your friend changes the equation as follows.

    $$8x = 24 \div 4$$

    How can you make your friend's equation equivalent to the original equation?

18. A scale balanced with 1 blue x-block and 20 green blocks on the left side and 40 green blocks on the right side. A student bumped into the scale and knocked some blocks off so that only 1 blue x-block and 3 green blocks remained on the left side. How many blocks do you need to remove from the right side to make the scale balance?

19. Bobbie wrote $y + 6 = 15$. Then she wrote $(y + 6) \div 3 = 15$. Explain why the second equation is not equivalent to the first. What can Bobbie do to make the two equations equivalent?

20. Construct Arguments John wrote that $5 + 5 = 10$. Then he wrote that $5 + 5 + n = 10 + n$. Are the equations John wrote equivalent? Explain.

21. Reasoning Scientists often use a pan balance to measure mass when doing experiments. The equation $4 + 3 - 1 = 7 - 1$ represents a scientist taking away one unit of mass from each side of a pan balance. Construct an argument to explain how the scientist knows that the pans are still in balance.

22. Bryce wrote the equation $n - 3 = 4$. Lexi used a property of equality to write an equivalent equation. Write an equation Lexi could have written. Explain how you know the equations are equivalent.

23. Higher Order Thinking Emil has $1 and a quarter. Jade has 5 quarters. If Emil gives Jade $1 and Jade gives Emil 4 quarters, will they each still have the same amount of money? Explain.

Emil's money

Jade's money

24. Vocabulary If $7w = 49$, which property of equality was used to find the equivalent equation $7w \div 7 = 49 \div 7$?

25. You start with the equation $12b = 24$. What step should you take to find the quantity that equals $4b$?

26. Which equation is equivalent to $n + 4 = 11$?

- Ⓐ $(n + 4) \times 2 = 11$
- Ⓑ $(n + 4) \times 2 = 11 \div 2$
- Ⓒ $(n + 4) \times 2 = 11 \times 4$
- Ⓓ $(n + 4) \times 2 = 11 \times 2$

27. Which of the equations is **NOT** equivalent to $8p = 12$? Select all that apply.

- ☐ $8p \div 8 = 12 \div 8$
- ☐ $8p \div 8 = 12 \div 12$
- ☐ $8p + 4 = 12 + 4$
- ☐ $8p - 2 = 12 - 2$
- ☐ $8p \times 8 = 12 \times 12$

👆 Solve & Discuss It! ACTIVITY

A group of students were on a school bus. How many students were on the bus before the last stop?

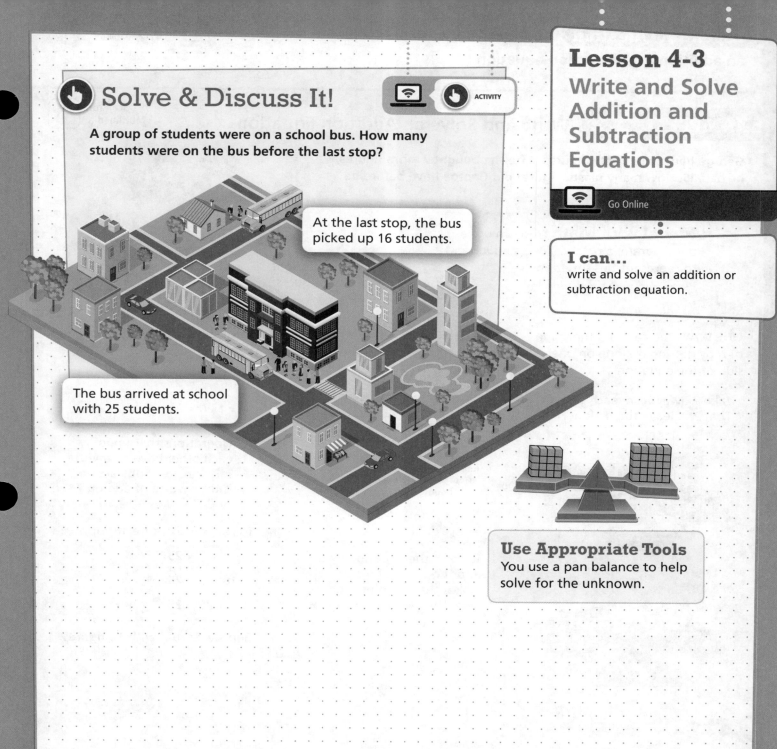

At the last stop, the bus picked up 16 students.

The bus arrived at school with 25 students.

I can...
write and solve an addition or subtraction equation.

Use Appropriate Tools
You use a pan balance to help solve for the unknown.

Focus on math practices

Reasoning How does using cubes on the pan balance demonstrate the Addition and Subtraction Properties of Equality?

? **Essential Question** How can you write and solve an addition or subtraction equation?

  VISUAL LEARNING   ASSESS

EXAMPLE 1   **Write and Solve an Addition Equation**

Scan for Multimedia

George had some plastic figures. After he bought 7 more figures, he had 25. How many plastic figures did George have before he bought more?

Model with Math You can use a bar diagram, a balance, or an equation to represent this situation.

George bought 7 more figures.

ONE WAY You can find the value of n by getting it alone on one side of the equation.

Take 7 away from each side. That will leave the n alone.

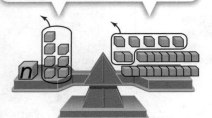

n is 18.

ANOTHER WAY Draw a bar diagram to represent the situation.

Total number of figures
25

n	7

Let n represent the number of plastic figures George had before he bought more.

He bought 7 more figures.

$n + 7 = 25$

To solve the equation, you find the value of n that makes the equation true.

Solve the addition equation.

$n + 7 = 25$

$n + 7 - 7 = 25 - 7$

$n = 18$

Operations that undo each other have an **inverse relationship**. Subtracting 7 is the inverse of adding 7.

To check, substitute 18 for n.

$n + 7 = 25$

$18 + 7 = 25$

$25 = 25$ It checks.

George started with 18 figures.

☑ Try It!

Cabrini had some markers. After she bought 12 more markers, she had 16. How many markers did Cabrini have at the start?

Let n represent the number of markers Cabrini had at the start.

Convince Me! Which property of equality is used to solve the equation $n + 12 = 16$? Could one of the other properties of equality have also been used? Explain.

Solve the addition equation.

$n + 12 = 16$

$n + 12 \boxed{} = 16 \boxed{}$

$n = \boxed{}$

Cabrini had $\boxed{}$ markers at the start.

EXAMPLE **2** Write and Solve a Subtraction Equation

 ACTIVITY ASSESS

Clive is 19 years younger than Josh. Clive is 34. Write and solve a subtraction equation to find Josh's age, y.

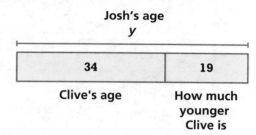

Josh's age
y

| 34 | 19 |

Clive's age   How much younger Clive is

$y - 19 = 34$

$y - 19 + 19 = 34 + 19$

$y = 53$

Josh is 53 years old.

Substitute 53 for y to check your work.

$y - 19 = 34$

$53 - 19 = 34$

$34 = 34$

EXAMPLE **3** **Solve Problems Using Equations**

Andy had some basketball cards. After he bought 12 more, he had 48 cards. How many cards did Andy have at the start?

Draw a bar diagram to represent the situation.

Total cards Andy has
48

| n | 12 |

Cards Andy   Cards Andy
originally had   bought

ONE WAY Write and solve an addition equation.

$n + 12 = 48$ Original number + Cards bought = Total cards

$n + 12 - 12 = 48 - 12$

$n = 36$

Andy had 36 cards at the start.

ANOTHER WAY Write and solve a subtraction equation.

$n = 48 - 12$ Original number = Total cards – Cards bought

$n = 36$

Andy had 36 cards at the start.

✅ **Try It!**

Vivian read 14 fewer pages than she was assigned to read. She read 60 pages. Write and solve an equation to find how many pages, p, Vivian was assigned to read.

You can use inverse relationships and the properties of equality to solve equations.

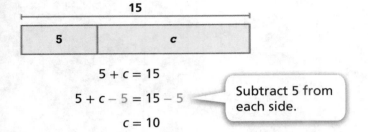

$$5 + c = 15$$
$$5 + c - 5 = 15 - 5$$
Subtract 5 from each side.
$$c = 10$$

$$m - 20 = 16$$
$$m - 20 + 20 = 16 + 20$$
Add 20 to each side.
$$m = 36$$

Do You Understand?

1. **Essential Question** How can you write and solve an addition or subtraction equation?

2. Explain how you can use the inverse relationship of addition and subtraction to solve the equation $n + 7 = 25$.

3. **Model with Math** Clare had t seashells. After she bought 8 more seashells, she had 24 seashells. Write and solve an equation to find the number of seashells Clare started with.

4. **Model with Math** The outside temperature dropped 20°F from the time Arianna ate breakfast until the time she ate dinner. When she ate dinner the temperature was 35°F. Write and solve an equation to find the outside temperature t when Arianna ate breakfast.

Do You Know How?

In 5–10, solve each equation.

5. $24 + m = 49$

6. $12 = y - 11$

7. $22 = 13 + a$

8. $t - 40 = 3$

9. $d + 11 = 15$

10. $32 = s - 19$

Practice & Problem Solving

Scan for
Multimedia

Leveled Practice In **11–16**, solve each equation.

11. $y - 12 = 89$

$y - 12 + \boxed{} = 89 + 12$

$y = \boxed{}$

12. $80 + r = 160$

$80 + r - \boxed{} = 160 - \boxed{}$

$r = \boxed{}$

13. $60 = x - 16$

$60 + \boxed{} = x - 16 + \boxed{}$

$\boxed{} = x$

14. $20 = y + 12$

15. $x + 2 = 19$

16. $z - 313 = 176$

---

17. You have some baseball trading cards. You give 21 baseball cards to a friend and have 9 left for yourself. How many baseball cards were in your original deck? Write and solve an equation to find t, the number of baseball cards in your original deck.

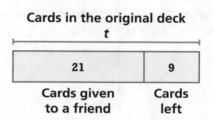

Cards in the original deck
t

21	9

Cards given to a friend   Cards left

---

18. Model with Math Joy added 26 new contacts to her phone list. She now has a total of 100 contacts. Let c represent how many contacts Joy had on her phone list before she updated it. Write an equation and solve for c.

19. Reasoning Jeremy bought a sandwich and a drink that cost him $7. His drink cost $1.75. Solve the equation $7 = s + 1.75$ to find s, the cost of Jeremy's sandwich.

20. A triathlon is about 51 kilometers. One participant completed two of the three legs of the race and traveled 42 kilometers. Solve the equation $42 + d = 51$ for the distance, d, of the third leg of the race.

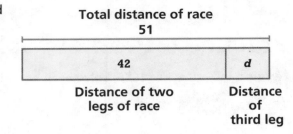

Total distance of race
51

42 | d

Distance of two legs of race | Distance of third leg

---

21. What operation should be used to solve the equation $153 = g + 45$? Solve the equation.

22. Higher Order Thinking In the equation $6 + 3y = 4y + 2$ the variable y represents the same value. Is $y = 2, 3, 4,$ or 5 the solution of this equation? Explain.

---

23. A traffic helicopter descends to hover 477 meters above the ground. Let h be the original height of the helicopter. What is a subtraction equation that represents the problem? What was the original height of the helicopter?

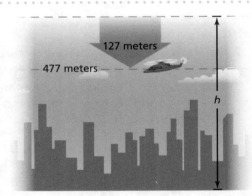

127 meters

477 meters

h

---

24. The drama club sold all the tickets for its annual production in three days. The club sold 143 tickets the first day and 295 tickets the second day. If the drama club sold 826 tickets, how many tickets were sold on the third day of sales? Solve the equation $438 + t = 826$ for the number of tickets, t, sold on the third day of ticket sales.

25. In a bag of mixed nuts, there are 35 almonds, 34 pecans, 32 walnuts, and p pistachios. The bag has a total of 134 nuts. Find the total number of almonds, pecans, and walnuts. Then write and solve an equation to find the number of pistachios in the bag.

✓ Assessment Practice

26. Which equation has $g = 6$ as the solution?

Ⓐ $g + 2 = 10$

Ⓑ $g - 1 = 10$

Ⓒ $58 + g = 60$

Ⓓ $44 - g = 38$

27. Select all the equations that have the same solution as $36 = x + 32$.

☐ $42 = 38 + x$

☐ $x + 15 = 19$

☐ $18 = x - 2$

☐ $36 = x - 32$

☐ $52 - x = 46$

Solve & Discuss It!

 ACTIVITY

A school group is planning a trip to New York City. There are 29 people going on the trip. They agreed to share the total cost of the trip equally. Let s equal each person's share of the cost. What is each person's share of the cost?

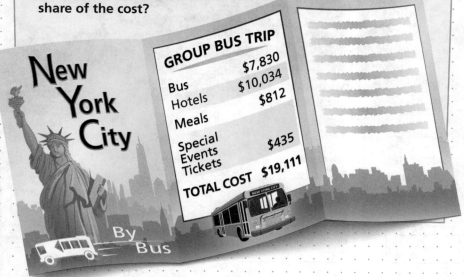

GROUP BUS TRIP

Bus $7,830
Hotels $10,034
Meals $812

Special Events Tickets $435

TOTAL COST $19,111

New York City By Bus

I can...
write and solve a multiplication or division equation.

Generalize How can you use what you know about dividing lesser numbers to write equations and solve problems involving greater numbers?

Focus on math practices

Construct Arguments Can you use the same strategy that you used above to find each person's share of the hotel bill? Explain.

VISUAL LEARNING ASSESS

EXAMPLE 1 **Write and Solve a Multiplication Equation**

Scan for Multimedia

Juan charged the same amount for each painting. How much did he charge for each painting?

Make Sense and Persevere
How do the quantities represented in the bar diagram and balance correspond to the equation?

3 paintings sold for $45.

ONE WAY You can use a balance to represent the equation.

Divide both sides into 3 equal groups.

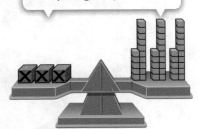

x is 15.

ANOTHER WAY Draw a bar diagram to represent the situation.

45		
x	*x*	*x*

Let *x* = the amount charged for each painting.

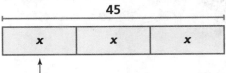

$3x = 45$

To solve the equation, find the value of *x* that makes the equation true.

Solve for *x*.

$$3x = 45$$
$$3x \div 3 = 45 \div 3$$

Use inverse operations to solve.

$$x = 15$$

To check, substitute 15 for *x*.

$$3x = 45$$
$$3(15) = 45$$
$$45 = 45$$

Juan charged $15 for each painting.

✓ Try It!

Theresia picked the same number of tomatoes each day. In 4 days she picked 52 tomatoes. How many tomatoes did Theresia pick each day?

Let *n* represent the number of tomatoes Theresia picked each day.

Convince Me! Which property of equality can you use to solve Theresia's equation? Explain.

$$4n = 52$$
$$4n \div 4 = 52 \boxed{}$$
$$n = \boxed{}$$

Theresia picked $\boxed{}$ tomatoes each day.

EXAMPLE 2 — Write and Solve for the Dividend in a Division Equation

The 15 members of the Adventure Club go on a group underwater diving trip. Student groups receive a special rate on snorkeling tickets that is half off the daily rate. Write and solve an equation to find, t, the total cost of snorkeling tickets.

STUDENT SNORKELING TRIP
Student Group Rate $\frac{1}{2}$ off $79 Ticket

Total cost of tickets
t

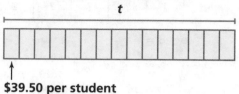

↑
$39.50 per student

$$t \div 15 = 39.50$$
$$t \div 15 \times 15 = 39.50 \times 15$$
$$t = 592.50$$

> Multiplying by 15 on both sides is the inverse of dividing by 15.

The total cost of the snorkeling tickets is $592.50.

EXAMPLE 3 — Write and Solve for the Divisor in a Division Equation

Helen puts 2,292 stickers in an album. Each page in the album holds 24 stickers. How many pages, p, did Helen fill?

Draw a bar diagram to represent the situation.

2,292 stickers

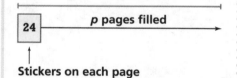

24   p pages filled

↑
Stickers on each page

$$\frac{2{,}292}{24} = p \quad \text{or} \quad 24p = 2{,}292$$

> You can use a multiplication or a division equation to represent this situation.

ONE WAY Solve the division equation $\frac{2{,}292}{24} = p$.

Divide to solve for p.

```
         95R12
   24)2292
     −216
      132
     −120
       12
```

Helen filled 95 album pages.

ANOTHER WAY Solve the multiplication equation $24p = 2{,}292$.

$$\frac{24p}{24} = \frac{2{,}292}{24}$$
$$p = 95.5$$

Check.

$$24p = 2{,}292$$
$$24(95.5) = 2{,}292$$

> Evaluate the equation for $p = 95.5$.

Helen filled 95 album pages.

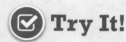 Try It!

Meghann is reading a 630-page book. She reads 18 pages each day. Write and solve a division equation to find the number of days, d, it will take Meghann to finish her book.

You can multiply or divide both sides of an equation by the same number and it will remain balanced.

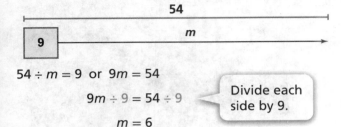

$54 \div m = 9$ or $9m = 54$

$9m \div 9 = 54 \div 9$ — Divide each side by 9.

$m = 6$

$p \div 8 = 7$

$p \div 8 \times 8 = 7 \times 8$ — Multiply each side by 8.

$p = 56$

Do You Understand?

1. **Essential Question** How can you write and solve a multiplication or division equation?

2. Which property of equality would you use to solve the equation $8n = 16$?

3. Which property of equality would you use to solve the equation $a \div 9 = 2$?

4. There are 30 students in the drama club. They are carpooling in 5 vans to perform a play. They want each van to carry an equal number of students. Let s be the number of students in each van. Write and solve a multiplication equation to find the number of students in each van.

Do You Know How?

In 5–8, explain how to solve each equation.

5. $18m = 36$

6. $t \div 3 = 10$

7. $12 = 2y$

8. $22 = a \div 5$

In 9–12, solve each equation.

9. $23d = 2{,}392$

10. $74f = 6{,}179$

11. $y \div 11 = 987$

12. $r \div 187 = 9$

Practice & Problem Solving

Scan for
Multimedia

In 13–16, explain how to get the variable alone in each equation.

13. $8y = 56$

14. $t \div 15 = 3$

15. $u \div 8 = 12$

16. $31y = 310$

In 17–20, solve each equation.

17. $d \div 2 = 108$

18. $7,200 = 800s$

19. $x \div 3 = 294$

20. $99 = 3x$

In 21 and 22, write a division equation and a multiplication equation to represent each problem.

21. Lolo typed 1,125 words in 15 minutes. Let w represent the number of words typed each minute. If Lolo typed the same number of words each minute, how many words did she type in 1 minute?

22. In 12 weeks Felipé earns $4,500 doing yard work. He earns the same amount each week. Let m stand for the amount earned each week. How much does Felipé make in 1 week?

23. Model with Math Abel has 3,330 toothpicks. He wants to use them all to make a floor mat with 18 equal rows. Use the bar diagram to write a division equation. Then solve the equation to find how many toothpicks Abel should use in each row.

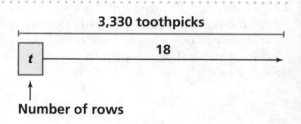

3,330 toothpicks

18

t

Number of rows

24. Model with Math Emily took an airplane trip. Her plane flew an equal number of miles each hour. Let m stand for the miles flown each hour. Write an equation to represent one way you can find how many miles Emily's plane flew each hour.

In 25 and 26, use the triangle.

25. The area of the isosceles triangle is 44 square centimeters. Use the equation $\frac{1}{2}(8h) = 44$ to find the height of the triangle.

26. If the perimeter of the triangle is 32 centimeters, what is the length of each of the two sides? Write and solve an equation.

[Triangle diagram with height h and base labeled 8 cm]

27. Kelsey and her 4 sisters spent an equal amount of time cleaning their home. Their parents added their times. They found that each of the 5 girls spent 3 hours cleaning. Let c be the total number of hours the girls spent cleaning. Write and solve a division equation to find the total number of hours the girls spent cleaning.

28. **Higher Order Thinking** Veronica traveled 562 miles to Venice, Florida. She drove 85 miles every day. On the last day of her trip she only drove 52 miles. Write and solve an equation to find the number of days Veronica traveled. Explain each step of your problem-solving strategy.

29. **Generalize** A movie theater sells 11,550 tickets for 50 sold-out showings of the same movie. Write a division equation that you can use to find the number of people who bought tickets for each showing. Use what you know about dividing with larger numbers to solve the equation.

☑ Assessment Practice

30. In October, Calvin's school used 4,920 pounds of sand to protect the building against flooding during different tropical storms. One bag contains 40 pounds of sand.

    Which of the following equations can be used to find how many bags of sand, b, Calvin's school used in October?

    Ⓐ $4{,}920b = 40$

    Ⓑ $b \div 40 = 4{,}920$

    Ⓒ $40b = 4{,}920$

    Ⓓ $b \div 4{,}920 = 40$

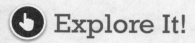 Explore It!

The cost of T-shirts for four different soccer teams are shown below.

| Team **A** | Team **B** | Team **C** | Team **D** |

I can...
write and solve equations that involve rational numbers.

A. Lorna is on Team A. Ben is on another team. They paid a total of $21.25 for both team T-shirts. Write an equation to represent the cost of Ben's shirt.

B. Dario also plays soccer and he says that, based on the price of Ben's T-shirt, Ben is on Team B. Is Dario correct? Explain.

Focus on math practices

Generalize How is solving for unknowns involving money like solving for unknowns involving whole numbers?

Essential Question How can you write and solve equations involving rational numbers?

  VISUAL LEARNING   ASSESS

EXAMPLE 1 **Solve Addition Equations with Fractions**

Scan for Multimedia

A 6-foot piece of fruit snack is cut into two pieces. What is the length of the shorter piece of fruit snack?

$3\frac{3}{4}$ feet

Use a bar diagram to show how the quantities are related and to write an equation.

| | 6 | |
Length of fruit snack

| $3\frac{3}{4}$ | x |

Length of longer piece   Length of shorter piece

$$3\frac{3}{4} + x = 6$$

Solve for x.

$$3\frac{3}{4} + x = 6$$

$$3\frac{3}{4} + x - 3\frac{3}{4} = 6 - 3\frac{3}{4}$$

Use inverse relationships and properties of equality.

$$x = 5\frac{4}{4} - 3\frac{3}{4}$$

$$x = 2\frac{1}{4}$$

The shorter piece is $2\frac{1}{4}$ feet long.

✓ Try It!

Suppose you cut the shorter piece of fruit snack from the example above into two pieces. The longer of the two pieces is $1\frac{3}{8}$ feet long. Complete the bar diagram to represent the equation. Then find the length of the shorter piece.

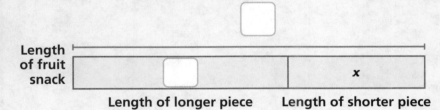

Length of fruit snack

| | x |

Length of longer piece   Length of shorter piece

$$1\frac{3}{8} + x = 2\frac{1}{4}$$

$$1\frac{3}{8} + x - \boxed{} = 2\frac{1}{4} - \boxed{}$$

$$x = 1\frac{10}{8} - \boxed{}$$

$$x = \boxed{}$$

The shorter piece is $\boxed{}$ foot long.

Convince Me! How does the equation change if you know the length of the shorter piece is $\frac{7}{8}$ foot and you want to know the length of the longer of the two pieces?

ACTIVITY ASSESS

Use inverse relationships to solve each equation.

A.

$$y - \frac{4}{9} = 5\frac{1}{3}$$

$$y - \frac{4}{9} + \frac{4}{9} = 5\frac{1}{3} + \frac{4}{9}$$

$$y = 5\frac{7}{9}$$

B.

$$\frac{3}{8}n = \frac{3}{4}$$

$$\left(\frac{8}{3}\right)\frac{3}{8}n = \left(\frac{8}{3}\right)\frac{3}{4}$$

$$n = \frac{8}{3} \times \frac{3}{4}$$

$$n = \frac{24}{12} \text{ or } 2$$

> Multiplying by $\frac{3}{8}$ is the same as dividing by $\frac{3}{8}$.

C.

$$\frac{p}{5} = 8$$

$$\frac{5}{1} \cdot \frac{1}{5}p = \frac{5}{1} \cdot 8$$

$$p = 5 \cdot 8$$

$$p = 40$$

> Multiply by the reciprocal of $\frac{1}{5}$, or $\frac{5}{1}$.

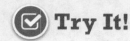 **Try It!**

Solve $\frac{5}{9}y = 25$ for y.

EXAMPLE **3** Solve Multiplication Equations with Decimals

Molly bought these oranges for $7.15. She paid the same amount for each orange. Write and solve an equation to find m, the cost of each orange.

Draw a bar diagram to represent the situation.

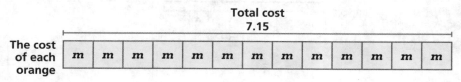

Oranges

$$13m = 7.15$$

$$13m \div 13 = 7.15 \div 13$$

$$m = 0.55$$

Molly paid $0.55 for each orange.

> **Use Structure** How can you use the operations in an equation to determine how to solve the equation?

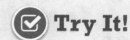 **Try It!**

Molly also buys a bag of 8 apples for $3.60. Write and solve an equation to find how much Molly paid for each apple.

EXAMPLE 4 Solve Addition, Subtraction, and Division Equations with Decimals

Use inverse relationships to solve each equation.

A.
$$m + 5.43 = 9.28$$
$$m + 5.43 - 5.43 = 9.28 - 5.43$$
$$m = 3.85$$

B.
$$y - 6.2 = 2.9$$
$$y - 6.2 + 6.2 = 2.9 + 6.2$$
$$y = 9.1$$

C.
$$x \div 2.5 = 40$$
$$x \div 2.5 \times 2.5 = 40 \times 2.5$$
$$x = 100$$

Try It!

Carmen spent $12.50 for a new notebook and a compass. The notebook cost $6.35. Write and solve an equation to find c, the cost of the compass.

KEY CONCEPT

You can solve equations using properties of equality and inverse relationships.

Addition Equation

13.6

| 5.2 | c |

$$5.2 + c = 13.6$$
$$5.2 + c - 5.2 = 13.6 - 5.2$$
$$c = 8.4$$

Subtract 5.2 from each side.

Subtraction Equation

y

| $\frac{2}{3}$ | $\frac{4}{9}$ |

$$y - \frac{2}{3} = \frac{4}{9}$$
$$y - \frac{2}{3} + \frac{2}{3} = \frac{4}{9} + \frac{2}{3}$$
$$y = 1\frac{1}{9}$$

Add $\frac{2}{3}$ to each side.

Multiplication Equation

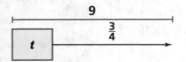

$$\frac{3}{4}t = 9$$
$$\frac{4}{3} \cdot \frac{3}{4}t = \frac{4}{3} \cdot \frac{9}{1}$$
$$t = \frac{36}{3} \text{ or } 12$$

Multiply each side by $\frac{4}{3}$.

Division Equation

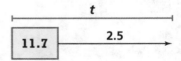

$$t \div 2.5 = 11.7$$
$$t \div 2.5 \times 2.5 = 11.7 \times 2.5$$
$$t = 29.25$$

Multiply each side by 2.5.

Do You Understand?

1. **? Essential Question** How can you write and solve equations involving rational numbers?

2. **Construct Arguments** Why are inverse relationships important for solving equations?

3. **Critique Reasoning** Johnny says that he solved the equation $x - 3.5 = 7.2$ by adding 3.5 to the left side of the equation. Explain whether Johnny is correct.

4. **Generalize** When solving an equation involving a mixed number, such as $y + \frac{3}{4} = 4\frac{1}{2}$, what do you need to do to the mixed number?

5. **Construct Arguments** How is solving an equation with fractions like solving an equation with whole numbers? How is it different?

Do You Know How?

In **6–14**, solve each equation.

6. $t - \frac{2}{3} = 25\frac{3}{4}$

7. $\frac{f}{2} = \frac{5}{8}$

8. $13.27 = t - 24.45$

9. $r \div 5.5 = 18.2$

10. $\frac{7}{10} = x - \frac{3}{5}$

11. $1.8x = 40.14$

12. $17.3 + v = 22.32$

13. $9 = \frac{3}{8}y$

14. $1\frac{3}{4} + z = 2\frac{2}{3}$

Practice & Problem Solving

Leveled Practice In **15–22**, solve each equation.

15.　　　　$w - 3.2 = 5.6$

$w - 3.2 + \boxed{} = 5.6 + \boxed{}$

$w = \boxed{}$

16.　　　　$9.6 = 1.6y$

$9.6 \div \boxed{} = 1.6y \div \boxed{}$

$\boxed{} = y$

17.　　　　$48.55 + k = 61.77$

$48.55 + k - \boxed{} = 61.77 - \boxed{}$

$k = \boxed{}$

18.　　　　$m \div 3.54 = 1.5$

$m \div 3.54 \times \boxed{} = 1.5 \times \boxed{}$

$m = \boxed{}$

19. $7\frac{1}{9} = 2\frac{4}{5} + m$

20. $a + 3\frac{1}{4} = 5\frac{2}{9}$

21. $\frac{1}{8} \cdot y = 4$

22. $k - 6\frac{3}{8} = 4\frac{6}{7}$

23. Mr. Marlon buys these tickets for his family to visit the water park. The total cost is $210. Write and solve an equation to find the cost of each ticket.

24. Higher Order Thinking Without solving, tell which equation below has a greater solution. Explain.

$$\frac{5}{8}m = 2\frac{3}{4} \qquad\qquad \frac{5}{9}m = 2\frac{3}{4}$$

25. Make Sense and Persevere A high school track team's long jump record is 21 feet $2\frac{1}{4}$ inches. This year, Tim's best long jump is 20 feet $9\frac{1}{2}$ inches. If long jumps are measured to the nearest quarter inch, how much farther must Tim jump to break the record?

26. **Make Sense and Persevere** About how many gallons of fuel does it take to move the space shuttle 3 miles from its hangar to the Vehicle Assembly Building?

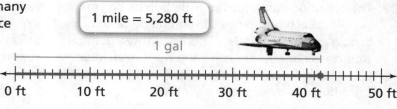

1 mile = 5,280 ft

1 gal

0 ft   10 ft   20 ft   30 ft   40 ft   50 ft

27. Is the solution of $b \times \frac{5}{6} = 25$ greater than or less than 25? How can you tell before computing?

28. What is the width of a rectangle with a length of $\frac{3}{7}$ ft and an area of 2 ft^2? Write an equation to show your work.

29. **Model with Math** Helen is filling the pool shown for her little brother. She can carry $1\frac{7}{8}$ gallons of water each trip. Write and solve an equation to find how many trips Helen needs to make.

Holds $10\frac{1}{2}$ gallons

30. After the pool was full, Helen's little brother and his friend splashed g gallons of water out of the pool. There are $7\frac{7}{8}$ gallons still left in the pool. Write and solve an equation to find how much water was splashed out of the pool.

31. Grace solved the equation $2\frac{1}{2}y = \frac{5}{8}$. Her steps for the solution are shown in the table but are all mixed up. Write her steps in the correct order on the right side of the table.

Scrambled Steps	Solution Steps in Order
$2\frac{1}{2}y = \frac{5}{8}$	
$y = \frac{10}{40}$ or $\frac{1}{4}$	
$\frac{5}{2}y = \frac{5}{8}$	
$y = \frac{5}{8} \cdot \frac{2}{5}$	

32. The scientific name for the little bumps on your tongue is *fungiform papillae*. Each bump can contain many taste buds. The number of taste buds a person has varies. There are three general classifications of taste: supertaster, medium taster, and nontaster. Suppose a supertaster has 8,640 taste buds. Solve the equation $4.5n = 8{,}640$ to find the number of taste buds, n, a nontaster may have.

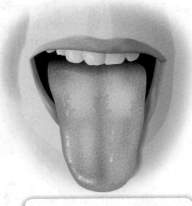

A supertaster may have 4.5 times as many taste buds as a nontaster.

33. **Model with Math** In one study, the number of women classified as supertasters was 2.25 times the number of men classified as supertasters. Suppose 72 women were classified as supertasters. Write an equation that represents the number of men, m, who were classified as supertasters. Then solve the equation. How many men were classified as supertasters?

34. **Use Structure** A fraction, f, multiplied by 5 equals $\frac{1}{8}$. Write an algebraic sentence to show the equation. Then solve the equation and explain how you solved it.

35. Yelena needs to swim a total of 8 miles this week. So far, she swam $5\frac{3}{8}$ miles. Use the equation $5\frac{3}{8} + m = 8$ to find how many more miles Yelena needs to swim.

36. Can any equation that is written using addition be written as an equivalent equation using subtraction? Explain your reasoning and give an example containing decimals that shows your reasoning.

37. **Critique Reasoning** Oscar is 12 years old and his little sister is 6. Oscar uses a to represent his age. He says that he can use the expression $a \div 2$ to always know his sister's age. Do you agree? Explain.

✅ Assessment Practice

38. Which value for y makes the equation $0.26y = 0.676$ true?

   Ⓐ $y = 0.17576$

   Ⓑ $y = 0.26$

   Ⓒ $y = 2.6$

   Ⓓ $y = 26$

39. Which value for x makes the equation $0.435 + x = 0.92$ true?

   Ⓐ $x = 1.355$

   Ⓑ $x = 0.595$

   Ⓒ $x = 0.495$

   Ⓓ $x = 0.485$

1. **Vocabulary** Describe the relationship between equations and the properties of equality. *Lessons 4-1 and 4-2*

In 2–4, write an equation for the situation. Then solve the equation.

2. A fraction f multiplied by 4 equals $\frac{1}{2}$. *Lesson 4-5*

3. When 832 is divided by n, the result is 16. *Lesson 4-4*

4. When 10 is subtracted from x, the result is 6. *Lesson 4-3*

5. Select all the equations that are equivalent to $n - 9 = 12$. *Lesson 4-2*

   ☐ $n - n - 9 = 12 - n$ ☐ $n - 9 + 12 = 12 - 9$ ☐ $n - 9 + 9 = 12 + 9$

   ☐ $n - 9 - n = 12 - n$ ☐ $n - 9 + 9 = 12 - 12$

6. Select all the values for d that make the equation $9 = 18 \div d$ true. *Lesson 4-1*

   ☐ 2   ☐ 0.5   ☐ $\frac{10}{5}$ ☐ 162   ☐ $\frac{1}{4}$

7. The area, A, of a triangle is 15.3 square centimeters. Its base, b, is 4.5 centimeters. The formula for finding the area of a triangle is $A = \frac{1}{2}bh$. Write and solve an equation to find the height, h, of the triangle. *Lessons 4-4 and 4-5*

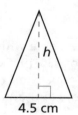

4.5 cm

How well did you do on the mid-topic checkpoint? Fill in the stars.

MID-TOPIC PERFORMANCE TASK

Ronald carved $3\frac{3}{8}$ feet of a totem pole. He says that the totem pole is $\frac{3}{4}$ complete.

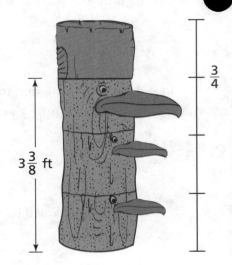

$3\frac{3}{8}$ ft

$\frac{3}{4}$

PART A

If h represents the height, in feet, of the finished totem pole, then $\frac{3}{4}h = 3\frac{3}{8}$ represents this situation. Which equations show the use of a reciprocal to write an equivalent equation that can be used to solve for h? Select all that apply.

☐ $\frac{3}{4}h + \frac{3}{4} = 3\frac{3}{8} + \frac{3}{4}$

☐ $\frac{3}{4}h \times \frac{4}{3} = 3\frac{3}{8} \times \frac{4}{3}$

☐ $\frac{3}{4}h \times \frac{3}{4} = 3\frac{3}{8} \times \frac{3}{4}$

☐ $\frac{3}{4}h - \frac{3}{4} = 3\frac{3}{8} - \frac{3}{4}$

☐ $\frac{3}{4}h \times \frac{4}{3} = 3\frac{3}{8} \times \frac{3}{4}$

PART B

Use the equation in Part A to determine the height of the finished totem pole. Then write and solve an equation to find the height, s, of the section that has not been carved.

PART C

Ronald spent $10.50 on tools and x dollars on the wood for the totem pole. His total cost for the totem pole is $19.35. The equation $10.50 + x = $19.35 represents this situation. What is the cost of the wood Ronald used?

PART D

To make the same totem pole with wood that costs y dollars, Ronald would have to spend a total of $35.19. Explain which property of equality Ronald could use to solve the equation $10.50 + y = $35.19 and why that property can be used. Then show how to use that property to solve for y.

Solve & Discuss It!

ACTIVITY

The record time for the girls' 50-meter freestyle swimming competition is 24.49 seconds. Camilla has been training and wants to break the record. What are some possible times Camilla would have to swim to break the current record?

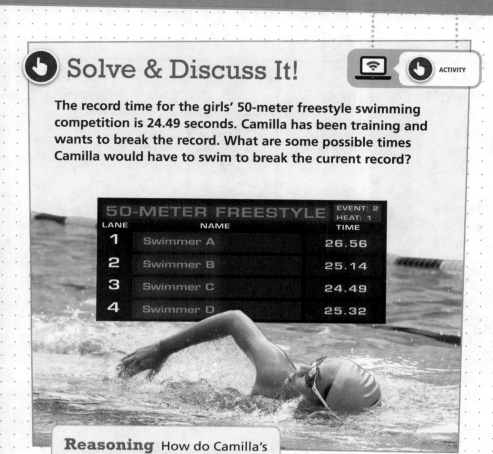

50-METER FREESTYLE EVENT: 2 HEAT: 1

LANE	NAME	TIME
1	Swimmer A	26.56
2	Swimmer B	25.14
3	Swimmer C	24.49
4	Swimmer D	25.32

Reasoning How do Camilla's possible times compare to 24.49 seconds?

I can...
understand and write an inequality that describes a real-world situation.

Focus on math practices

Be Precise Fran won a blue ribbon for growing the heaviest pumpkin. It weighed 217 pounds. What could be the weights of other pumpkins in the contest? How could you show the weights of the other pumpkins using a mathematical statement? Explain.

Essential Question How can you write an inequality to describe a situation?

VISUAL LEARNING   ASSESS

EXAMPLE 1 👁 Understand Inequalities

Scan for Multimedia

An inequality is a mathematical sentence that contains < (less than), > (greater than), ≤ (less than or equal to), ≥ (greater than or equal to), or ≠ (not equal to).

How can you write an inequality to describe the ages of the children who must be accompanied by an adult at the sledding hill?

VALLEY SLED HILL

NOTICE: CHILDREN UNDER THE AGE OF 8 MUST BE ACCOMPANIED BY AN ADULT

Model with Math How can you use an inequality to represent more than one value?

What are some ages of children who must be accompanied by an adult?

You can show some of the ages on a number line.

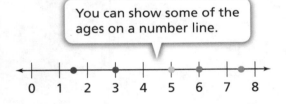

Let a represent the ages of children who must be accompanied by an adult. Use the *less than* symbol (<) to write the inequality.

$$a < 8$$

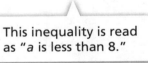

This inequality is read as "a is less than 8."

☑ Try It!

Use the number line to show some of the ages of people who do not need to be accompanied by an adult. Write an inequality to represent the ages of people, n, who do not need to be accompanied by an adult.

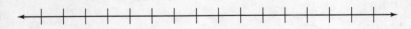

Convince Me! How do you know to which group an 8-year-old belongs, those who must be accompanied by an adult or those who do not need to be accompanied by an adult? Explain.

EXAMPLE **2** Write Inequalities

  ACTIVITY ASSESS

Write an inequality to represent each situation.

A. The length of a piece of wire, *l*, is longer than $20\frac{1}{4}$ feet.

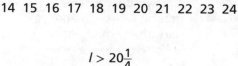

The possible lengths of wire are greater than $20\frac{1}{4}$.

14 15 16 17 18 19 20 21 22 23 24

$$l > 20\frac{1}{4}$$

B. The number of students, *s*, is at most 30.

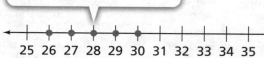

The possible numbers of students are less than or equal to 30.

25 26 27 28 29 30 31 32 33 34 35

$$s \le 30$$

C. The cost of the pizza, *c*, will be at least $8.00.

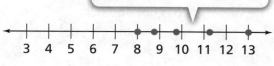

The possible costs of the pizza are greater than or equal to 8.

3 4 5 6 7 8 9 10 11 12 13

$$c \ge \$8.00$$

D. Zoe's age, *z*, is not 11 years old.

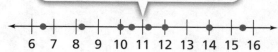

Zoe can be any age except 11.

6 7 8 9 10 11 12 13 14 15 16

$$z \ne 11$$

Be Precise The *not equal to* symbol ($\ne$) tells you that the values on the two sides of the inequality are not equal, but it does not tell you which quantity is greater.

☑ Try It!

Write an inequality to represent each situation.

a. Harry is taller than 60 inches.

b. Sherry is not 4 years old.

c. Hank has at least $7.50.

Inequality symbols can be used to describe situations that have more than one possible solution.

Inequality Symbols

Symbol	Meaning
<	less than
≤	less than or equal to
>	greater than
≥	greater than or equal to
≠	not equal to

This symbol contains a less than sign and part of an equal sign.

This symbol contains a greater than sign and part of an equal sign.

Do You Understand?

1. **Essential Question** How can you write an inequality to describe a situation?

2. **Generalize** What is the difference between an equation with a variable and an inequality with a variable?

3. Would it be more efficient to use an inequality or to list all of the quantities less than 6? Explain.

4. **Generalize** How are the symbols for *greater than* (>) and *greater than or equal to* (≥) related?

Do You Know How?

In 5–12, write an inequality for each situation.

5. A number, n, is greater than 22.

6. The value, v, does not equal $2\frac{1}{2}$.

7. Sally's age, a, is at most 15.

8. The width of the picture, w, is shorter than 8.5 inches.

9. Steve's height, h, is at least 48 inches.

10. Vera's baby brother's age, b, is not 24 months.

11. The number of quarters, q, in the jar is less than 75.

12. The length of the fish a fisherman catches, f, must be at least 10 inches for him to keep it.

Practice & Problem Solving

Scan for
Multimedia

In 13–22, write an inequality for each situation.

13. Up to 12 people, *p*, can ride in the van.

14. A number of days, *d*, of sunshine is not 28.

15. The distance of the race, *r*, is farther than 6.2 miles.

16. The value, *v*, of the bracelet is less than $85.25.

17. The number of people, *p*, that a restaurant can seat at one time is no more than 171.

18. The time, *t*, a customer has left on a parking meter is at least 25 minutes.

19. The bill, *b*, was less than $45.

20. The girls live *b* blocks apart; they do not live $7\frac{1}{2}$ blocks apart.

21. The speed of the truck, *s*, must be no less than 34 miles per hour.

22. The number of baseball games, *x*, that Karen went to last year is more than 5.

23. Mia is taller than Gage. If *m* represents Mia's height and *g* represents Gage's height, write an inequality that shows the relationship between their heights.

24. Taryn sold gift-wrapping paper for a school fund-raiser. She sold at least 15 rolls of paper. Write an inequality to represent the amount of money, *d*, she earned for the fund-raiser.

$8.00 per roll

25. A city in New England just experienced its greatest 1-day snowfall. Write an inequality to represent a snowfall that would beat this record.

19.7 inches of snow

26. The first bookcase, *a*, in a library can hold 1 less book than the second bookcase. The second bookcase holds 2,492 books. Write an inequality to represent the number of books the first bookcase can hold.

27. A certain airplane must carry no more than 134 passengers during a flight. Write an inequality to represent the number of passengers, *p*, that would **NOT** be allowed during this flight.

28. Higher Order Thinking To ride a certain roller coaster, a rider must be at least 42 inches tall. To represent this situation, Elias wrote $h \geq 42$ and Nina wrote $h > 42$. Who is correct? Explain.

42" STOP YOU MUST BE THIS TALL TO GO ON THIS RIDE

☑ Assessment Practice

29. Miguel earns extra money working two weekends with his dad. He is saving to buy a new bike that costs $140.

Heather says that Miguel needs to earn more than $6 for each hour that he works to have enough money to buy the bike. Her work is shown below. Write an inequality to explain why she is incorrect.

Heather's Solution

Weekend 1:   16 hours
Weekend 2: + 7 hours
              23 hours

$140 ÷ 23 hours > $6.00 per hour

Miguel has to earn more than $6.00 per hour.

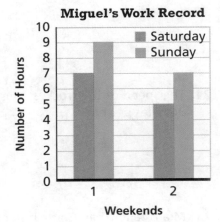

Miguel's Work Record

Number of Hours / Weekends

Saturday
Sunday

Solve & Discuss It! ACTIVITY

Henry is thinking of a number that is less than 17. What number could he be thinking of?

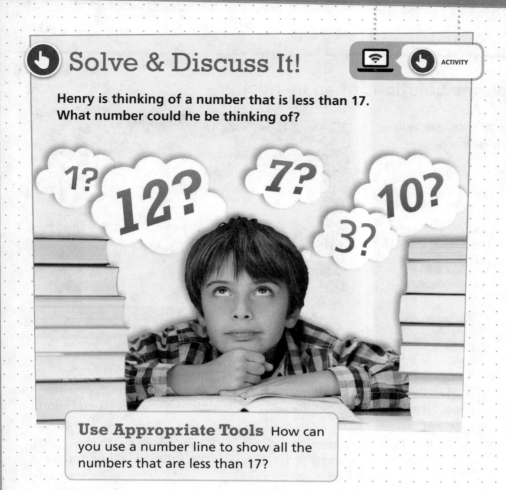

1?
12?
7?
10?
3?

Use Appropriate Tools How can you use a number line to show all the numbers that are less than 17?

I can...
write and represent solutions of inequalities.

Focus on math practices

Reasoning Could Henry be thinking of 17? Explain.

VISUAL LEARNING   ASSESS

EXAMPLE 1 **Graph the Solutions of an Inequality**

Scan for Multimedia

An inequality uses >, <, ≥, ≤, or ≠ to compare two expressions. Graph all the solutions of $x > 5$.

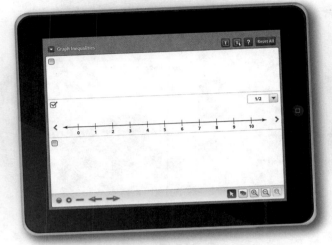

STEP 1 To graph $x > 5$, draw an open circle at 5 on a number line.

The open circle shows that 5 is **NOT** a solution.

0 1 2 3 4 5 6 7 8 9 10

STEP 2 Find some solutions and plot them on a number line.

7 and 9 are solutions because 7 > 5 and 9 > 5.

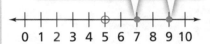

0 1 2 3 4 5 6 7 8 9 10

STEP 3 Start at the open circle and shade the solutions you found.

Draw an arrow to show that the solutions go on forever.

0 1 2 3 4 5 6 7 8 9 10

Be Precise Inequalities have *infinitely many* solutions. This means that there is an unlimited number of solutions.

☑ **Try It!**

Graph all of the solutions of $x < 8$.

To graph $x < 8$, draw a(n) [   ] circle at 8 on the number line.

0 1 2 3 4 5 6 7 8 9 10

7 and 4 are two of the many possible solutions of the inequality.

Shade the solutions to the [   ] of the [   ] circle you drew at 8.

Convince Me! How does the graph of the inequality change when the *less than* sign is changed to a *greater than* sign? How does it stay the same?

EXAMPLE 2 Graph to Solve an Inequality

The Barbeque Beef dinner entrée is the most expensive menu item. Some of the costs of the entrées are shown at the right. What are all the possible costs of the menu items?

Write and graph an inequality.

The possible costs of the menu items, m, are less than or equal to $12.25.

$m \leq 12.25$ ← There are too many possible costs to list, so it is more efficient to show the costs on a graph.

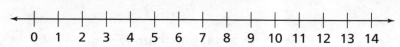
0 1 2 3 4 5 6 7 8 9 10 11 12 13 14

The closed circle shows that 12.25 is a solution of the inequality.

FLAMINGO
RESTAURANT

DINNER ENTRÉES

The Burger.................. $8.75

Barbeque Beef........... $12.25

Pasta........................ $7.50

Chicken Taco............. $10.00

Try It!

There are no menu items on the children's menu at the Flamingo Restaurant that cost more than $8.50. What are all the possible costs of the items on the children's menu?

0 1 2 3 4 5 6 7 8 9 10 11 12 13 14

EXAMPLE 3 Substitute to Solve an Inequality

A long jumper who jumps at least 18 feet qualifies for the finals. Which athletes, if any, qualify for the finals?

Write an inequality to represent the situation.
$y \geq 18$

Amir: $22\frac{1}{3} \geq 18$ Solution

Jake: $16 \not\geq 18$ Not a solution

Tyrell: $18\frac{1}{2} \geq 18$ Solution

Ryan: $20\frac{1}{2} \geq 18$ Solution

Amir, Tyrell, and Ryan qualify for the finals because $22\frac{1}{3}$, $18\frac{1}{2}$, and $20\frac{1}{2}$ are solutions.

Long Jump Results	
Amir	$22\frac{1}{3}$ ft
Jake	16 ft
Tyrell	$18\frac{1}{2}$ ft
Ryan	$20\frac{1}{2}$ ft

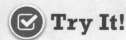 Try It!

Which athletes, if any, would qualify for the finals if the length of a jump that qualifies for the finals were at least $20\frac{1}{2}$ feet?

An inequality uses these symbols: $<$, $>$, $\leq$, or $\geq$ to compare two expressions.

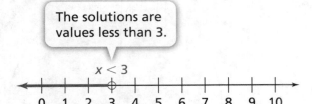

The solutions are values less than 3.

$x < 3$

The solutions are values greater than or equal to 5.

$y \geq 5$

Do You Understand?

1. **Essential Question** How can you represent the solutions of an inequality?

2. In Example 1, why is 9 a solution of $x > 5$?

3. Explain why 2 is **NOT** a solution of $x > 5$.

4. How many solutions does the inequality $x > 12$ have? Explain.

5. **Generalize** How do the graphs of the solutions of inequalities involving *greater than* ($>$) and *greater than or equal to* ($\geq$) compare?

Do You Know How?

In 6 and 7, write the inequality that each graph represents.

6.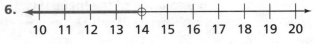

$z \bigcirc \square$

7.

$d \bigcirc \square$

In 8–11, substitute each given value of the variable to find which, if any, is a solution of the inequality.

8. $w < 8$ $w = 4.3, 5.3, 8.3, 9$

9. $t > 25$ $t = 24, 25, 25.1, 27$

10. $g \leq 4$ $g = 0, 4, 5, 6$

11. $y \geq 8$ $y = 4, 5, 6, 7$

Practice & Problem Solving

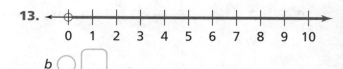 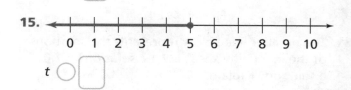

In 12–15, write the inequality that each graph represents.

12.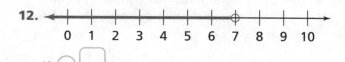

y ○ ☐

13.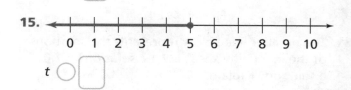

b ○ ☐

14.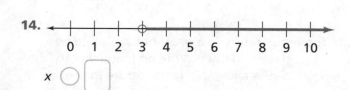

x ○ ☐

15.

t ○ ☐

In 16–19, graph each inequality on a number line.

16. $h \geq 9$

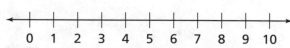

17. $p < 3$

18. $t \leq 6$

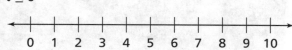

19. $s > 1$

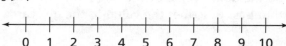

In 20–27, name three solutions of each inequality.

20. $x > 10.5$

21. $r < 19$

22. $y \geq 200$

23. $m \leq 82$

24. $x \geq 12$

25. $q \leq 3.5$

26. $v > 35$

27. $m < 2.5$

28. The inequality $w \leq 1,500$ describes the maximum weight in pounds, w, allowed by law in a freight elevator. Is a total weight of either 1,505 pounds or 1,600 pounds allowed in a freight elevator? Explain.

29. Reasoning Graph the inequalities $x > 2$ and $x < 2$ on the same number line. What value, if any, is not a solution of either inequality? Explain.

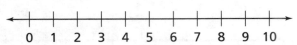

30. Model with Math Death Valley is the hottest place in the United States. The highest temperature ever recorded there was 134°F. The lowest temperature recorded there was 15°F. Write two inequalities that would describe the temperature, in degrees Fahrenheit, in Death Valley at any time since temperatures have been recorded.

31. The number line below represents the solutions of the inequality $x > 7$. Is 7.1 a solution? Is 7.01 a solution? Explain.

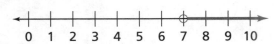

32. The temperature in a greenhouse should be 65 degrees or higher. Write an inequality to describe the allowable temperature in the greenhouse.

33. Higher Order Thinking Francine received a gift card to buy cell phone apps. She says that the card's value is enough to buy any of the apps shown at the right. Let v be the dollar value of the gift card. Write an inequality that best describes the value of the gift card.

34. The maximum load on a small plane is 400 pounds. Let w represent the weight on the plane. Write an inequality to describe the allowable weight on the plane.

35. Jillian is thinking of a whole number that is greater than 21. What numbers, if any, make the inequality $n > 21$ true for $n = 0, 1, 2, 3, 4, \ldots$?

✓ Assessment Practice

36. Select all the given values of y that make the inequality $3y < 25$ true.

☐ 6.5

☐ 7

☐ 8

☐ 8.5

☐ 9

37. Tania started a graph to show the inequality $y < 3.7$. Finish labeling the number line and draw the graph.

3.0 3.1   4.0

Checking a **Bag**

ACT 1

1. After watching the video, what is the first question that comes to mind?

2. Write the Main Question you will answer.

3. Construct Arguments Predict an answer to this Main Question. Explain your prediction.

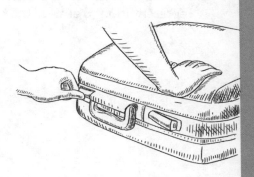

4. On the number line below, write a number that is too small to be the answer. Write a number that is too large.

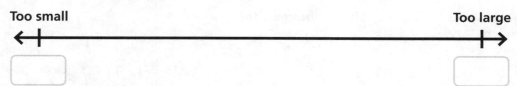

Too small

Too large

5. Plot your prediction on the same number line.

6. What information in this situation would be helpful to know? How would you use that information?

7. Use Appropriate Tools What tools can you use to solve the problem? Explain how you would use them strategically.

8. Model with Math Represent the situation using mathematics. Use your representation to answer the Main Question.

9. What is your answer to the Main Question? Is it higher or lower than your prediction? Explain why.

10. Write the answer you saw in the video.

11. Reasoning Does your answer match the answer in the video? If not, what are some reasons that would explain the difference?

12. Make Sense and Persevere Would you change your model now that you know the answer? Explain.

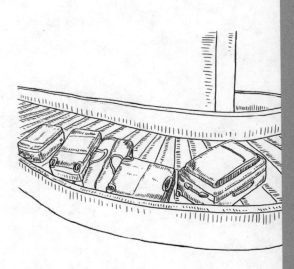

Reflect

13. Model with Math Explain how you used a mathematical model to represent the situation. How did the model help you answer the Main Question?

14. Was an *equation* or an *inequality* more useful to answer the Main Question? Explain.

15. Be Precise A different airline has a weight limit of 40 pounds for a checked bag. Explain how the answer would change for this airline.

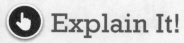 **Explain It!**

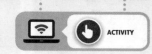 ACTIVITY

Max is shipping a present to his grandmother.

Lesson 4-8
Understand Dependent and Independent Variables

 Go Online

I can...
identify dependent and independent variables.

A. What are three factors that will affect the weight of the box? What are three factors that will not affect the weight of the box?

B. How might the size of the box and the contents of the box affect the weight of the box?

Focus on math practices

Model with Math Describe another situation in which changing one factor results in changes to another factor.

? Essential Question What does it mean for one variable to be dependent on another variable?

 EXAMPLE 1 Dependent and Independent Variables

Scan for Multimedia

An orchard sells apples by the pound. Each day, *p* pounds of apples are sold and the amount of money taken in, *m*, is recorded. Which variable, *p* or *m*, depends on the other variable?

Reasoning When you think about how total cost is dependent on the amount and price of items sold, you are reasoning quantitatively.

Fresh-Picked **APPLES**

A **dependent variable** changes in response to another variable.

The amount of money, *m*, taken in depends on the number of pounds, *p*, so *m* is the dependent variable.

An **independent variable** causes the dependent variable to change.

The number of apples sold, *p*, affects the amount of money taken in, *m*, so *p* is the independent variable.

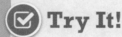 **Try It!**

A baker used a certain number of cups of batter, *b*, to make *p* pancakes. Which variable, *p*, pancakes or *b*, batter is the dependent variable? Explain.

Convince Me! If the baker doubles the number of cups of batter used, *b*, what would you expect to happen to the number of pancakes made, *p*? Explain.

EXAMPLE 2

Multiple Independent or Dependent Variables

A bike shop rents beach cruiser bikes and mountain bikes. Customers can rent these items by the day or the week. What are the independent and dependent variables involved in the cost of rental?

JOE'S BIKES
THE BEST BIKES ON THE BEACH

Bike Rental Prices

	Price Per Day	Price Per Week
Beach cruiser	$18	$50
Mountain bike	$30	$90

STEP 1

Identify the variables involved in the cost of rental.

Beach cruiser, *b*	Mountain bike, *m*	Length of rental, *l*

Price per day, *d*	Price per week, *w*	Total rental cost, *t*

STEP 2

Determine whether the variables are independent or dependent.

Beach cruiser, *b*	Mountain bike, *m*	Length of rental, *l*	Price per day, *d*	Price per week, *w*	Total rental cost, *t*
Dependent on the rate per day or week	Dependent on the rate per day or week	Independent and causes the total rental cost to change	Independent and causes the total rental cost to change	Independent and causes the total rental cost to change	Dependent on the bike and length of time rented

Try It!

Jenna wants to rent a mountain bike by the week. Identify the independent variables that affect the total rental cost.

KEY CONCEPT

A **dependent variable** changes in response to another variable, called an independent variable. An **independent variable** causes the change in a dependent variable. It is *independent* because its value is not affected by other variables.

The distance a car travels, *d*, is dependent on the speed, *s*, at which it travels. Speed is the independent variable, and distance is the dependent variable.

Do You Understand?

1. **? Essential Question** What does it mean for one variable to be dependent on another variable?

2.

Jake and Viola record the number of miles, *m*, they bike to help track the number of calories, *c*, they burn in an hour.

Critique Reasoning Viola says the number of calories, *c*, they burn is the dependent variable. Do you agree? Explain.

3. **Reasoning** In the biking problem above, identify at least one other independent variable that could affect the dependent variable.

Do You Know How?

In 4–11, identify the independent variable and the dependent variable.

4. The amount of money, *m*, earned if *t* raffle tickets are sold

5. The number of hours, *h*, worked and the amount of money, *m*, earned

6. The number of shelves, *s*, in a bookcase and the number of books, *b*, the bookcase can hold

7. The number of pages, *p*, you read in your book in *h* hours

8. The number of gallons, *g*, of water a garden hose produces after running for *m* minutes

9. The number of peaches, *y*, a farmer harvests in *x* bushels

10. The number of hours, *h*, you spend driving at a speed of *r* miles per hour

11. Name at least two independent variables that could result in a change in a monthly electric bill.

Name: _____

Practice & Problem Solving

In 12–15, identify the independent variable and the dependent variable.

12. The pages, *p*, in a book and the weight, *w*, of the book

13. The number of hamburgers, *h*, sold and the dollar amount of sales, *s*, taken in

14. The pounds, *p*, of flour you buy and the number of bread loaves, *b*, you want to make

15. The temperature, *t*, of water and the number of minutes, *m*, the water is in the freezer

16. Write your own situation. Identify the independent and dependent variables.

17. Name at least two independent variables that could result in a change in the price of a basket of grapefruits.

18. Critique Reasoning You spend *c* dollars for *p* identical pairs of pants. A friend claims that because *c* increases if you increase *p*, and *p* increases if you increase *c*, either *c* or *p* could be the independent variable. Is your friend right or wrong? Explain.

19. The number of oranges in a bag and the cost of the bag of oranges are related. What is the independent variable in this relationship? Explain.

20. The dependent variable *g* represents the growth of a plant. What variables can represent independent variables in this situation?

In 21 and 22, use the table at the right.

21. The table shows distances driven by the Williams family each day of their vacation. What is an independent variable that would affect the total distance they drove each day?

Family Vacation

Day	Distance
1	480 mi
2	260 mi
3	40 mi
4	150 mi
5	100 mi
6	320 mi

22. Name at least two dependent variables that could affect the amount of money the Williams family spends on meals during their vacation.

23. The cost of a salad at a restaurant depends on many factors. List at least two independent variables that could affect the cost of a salad.

24. Julian drove from New York to Florida. List at least two independent variables that could affect the number of days Julian took to make the trip.

25. The number of incorrect answers and the score on a math test are related. What is the dependent variable in this relationship? Explain.

26. **Higher Order Thinking** Write a situation in which time, t, is an independent variable. Then write a situation in which time, t, is a dependent variable.

☑ Assessment Practice

27. Jonas is concerned about the amount of water he uses to wash his laundry. He made a table to show the number of gallons of water used by different washing machines to complete a load of laundry.

Type of Washing Machine	Age of Washing Machine (years)	Gallons of Water
Older Top Loading	6	42
New Standard Model	4	28
Energy Efficient	2	14

PART A

Use variables to represent the independent and dependent quantities shown in the table.

PART B

Use variables to represent the dependent variable and the independent variable in this sentence.

Jonas records the total cost of the water he uses and the number of gallons of water he uses.

Solve & Discuss It!  ACTIVITY

The table below shows how many candles are in different numbers of boxes. Find a pattern that explains the relationship between the values of c and b. Use words and numbers to describe the pattern. How many candles will there be in 10 boxes?

Number of Candles, c	Number of Boxes, b
8	2
12	3
16	4

Look for Relationships How can you get from each value in the left column to its matching value in the right column?

I can...
use patterns to write and solve equations with variables.

Focus on math practices
Use Structure Write a rule that explains how you get from the values in the right column of the table above to the values in the left column.

? **Essential Question** How can you use a pattern to write and solve an equation?

EXAMPLE 1 Find a Pattern to Write an Equation

Scan for Multimedia

The table shows the cost of weekend tickets to the Slide and Splash Water Park. Find a pattern that relates the number of tickets, n, and the cost, c, of the tickets. How much would 6 tickets cost?

Use Structure How does finding the cost of 1 ticket help you find a pattern that relates the variables?

Slide and Splash Water Park

Number, n	Cost, c
3	$16.50
4	$22.00
5	$27.50
6	

Look for a pattern in the table that relates c, the dependent variable and n, the independent variables.

n		c
3	3 × 5.50	16.50
4	4 × 5.50	22.00
5	5 × 5.50	27.50

5.5 times the value of n equals the value of c.

Write an equation to describe the relationship.

5.5 times the value of n = the value of c

$$5.5n = c$$

or

$$c = 5.5n$$

Find the cost of 6 tickets.

$$c = 5.5n$$
$$c = 5.5(6)$$ ← Substitute 6 for n.
$$c = 33$$

The cost of 6 tickets is $33.00.

☑ Try It!

The table shows the number of yards, y, that a professional bicyclist rides in s seconds. Find a pattern that relates the variables. If the cyclist maintains this speed, how far would the cyclist ride in 8 seconds?

Convince Me! How do you know that the equation you wrote describes the pattern in the table?

Seconds, s	Yards, y
2	24.4
3	36.6
5	61
6	73.2

Ethan owes his mother $75. He repays his mother a set amount each week. How much will Ethan owe his mother after 12 weeks?

Make a table and look for a pattern that relates the variables.

Week, w	Pattern	Amount Owed, a
0	$75 - 5(0)$	75
1	$75 - 5(1)$	70
2	$75 - 5(2)$	65
3	$75 - 5(3)$	60
4	$75 - 5(4)$	55

To find the pattern, start with the amount owed. The amount owed decreases by $5 each week.

Write an equation to describe the relationship.

Amount still owed		Loan amount		Amount paid after w weeks
a	$=$	$\$75$	$-$	$5w$

Let a stand for the amount still owed.

Let w stand for the number of weeks.

Find how much Ethan will owe after 12 weeks.

$a = 75 - 5w$

$a = 75 - 5(12)$

$a = 75 - 60$

$a = 15$

Ethan will owe $15 after 12 weeks.

 **Try It!**

If Ethan continues to pay $5 per week, how many more weeks will he need to pay his mother after 12 weeks? Explain.

You can use patterns in a table to write an equation that relates the independent and dependent variables.

j	1	4	7	8	9
m	3	12	21	24	27

The dependent variable m is 3 times the independent variable j: $m = 3j$.

Do You Understand?

1. **Essential Question** How can you use a pattern to write and solve an equation?

2. **Make Sense and Persevere** How do you find a pattern that relates the values in a table?

3. **Reasoning** In Example 2, what happens to the value of the dependent variable, a, the amount still owed, when the value of the independent variable, w, the number of weeks Ethan pays $5, is increased by 1?

4. **Look for Relationships** Use the pattern in the table below to write an equation.

x	y
1	7
2	12
3	17
4	22

Do You Know How?

5. The table shows Brenda's age, b, when Talia's age, t, is 7, 9, and 10. Find the pattern and then write a rule and an equation that represents the pattern. Then find Brenda's age when Talia is 12.

Talia's Age, t	Brenda's Age, b
7	2
9	4
10	5
12	b

In 6 and 7, use the table below.

x	4	5	6	7	8
y	1	3	5		

6. Use the equation $y = 2x - 7$ to complete the table.

7. State the rule for the pattern in words.

Practice & Problem Solving

Scan for Multimedia

In 8 and 9, write a rule and an equation that represents the pattern in each table.

8.

x	1	2	3	4	5
y	33	34	35	36	37

9.

m	0	1	2	3	4
n	0	3	6	9	12

In 10 and 11, write a rule and an equation that represents the pattern in each table. Then complete the table.

10.

g	32	37	42	47	52
k	17	22	27		

11.

x	0	9	18	27	36
y	0	1	2		

12. To celebrate its 125th anniversary, a company produced 125 expensive teddy bears. These "125 Karat Teddy Bears" are made of gold thread and have diamonds for eyes. The table shows the approximate cost of different numbers of these bears. Write an equation that can be used to find c, the cost of n bears.

Cost of "125 Karat Teddy Bears"

Number, n	Cost, c
4	$188,000
7	$329,000
11	$517,000

13. Andrea attends the county fair. The fair charges for admission and for each ride.

a. Use the pattern in the table to the find the cost for Andrea to ride 5 rides or 8 rides. Then write an equation for the pattern.

Rides, r	Cost, c
3	$15.50
4	$18.00
5	
6	$23.00
8	

b. Find the cost, c, for 12 rides.

General Admission $8.00
Rides $2.50

In 14 and 15, write an equation that best describes the pattern in each table.

14.

w	2	4	6	8	10
z	0	2	4	6	8

15.

x	0	$\frac{1}{2}$	1	$1\frac{1}{2}$	2	$2\frac{1}{2}$
y	0	2	4	6	8	10

In 16–19, use the equation to complete each table.

16. $t = 5d + 5$

d	0	1	2	3	4
t	5	10	15	☐	☐

17. $y = \frac{1}{2}x - 1$

x	2	4	6	8	10
y	0	1	2	☐	☐

18. $y = 2x + 1$

x	0	1	2	3
y	1	3	☐	☐

19. $b = \frac{a}{2} - 2$

a	17	14	11	8	5
b	☐	☐	☐	☐	☐

20. **Higher Order Thinking** Maya wrote the equation $h = d + 22$ to represent the relationship shown in the table. Is this equation correct? Explain.

h	3	5	7	9
d	33	55	77	99

☑ Assessment Practice

21. The table below shows the total cost for the number of movie tickets purchased. Write an equation that represents the relationship between these two quantities. Use the equation to find the cost of 6 tickets.

Number of Tickets	3	5	7	9
Cost	$26.25	$43.75	$61.25	$78.75

Solve & Discuss It!   ACTIVITY

Nancy walks 4 blocks to Maria's house. Together, they continue the walk. The walk can be described as $n = m + 4$, where n is the number of blocks Nancy walks and m is the number of blocks Maria walks. Describe how the equation, data table, and graph reflect the walk.

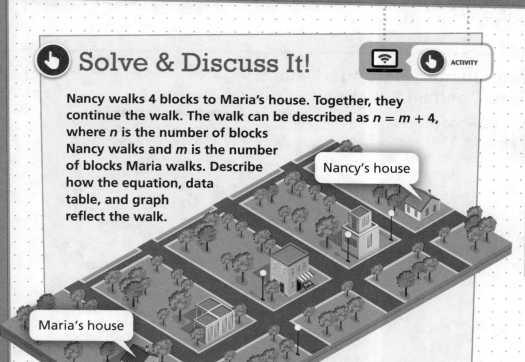

Nancy's house

Maria's house

I can...
analyze the relationship between dependent and independent variables in tables, graphs, and equations.

Look for Relationships How can you use the values in one row of the data table to describe the relationship shown in the equation, data table, and graph?

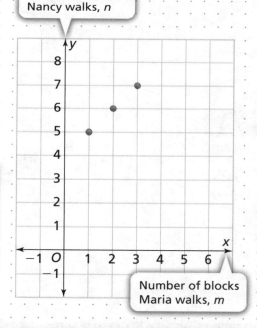

Number of blocks Nancy walks, n

Number of blocks Maria walks, m

$n = m + 4$	
m	n
1	5
2	6
3	7

Focus on math practices

Model with Math Draw a line through the points on the graph. What ordered pair on the line includes $m = 5$? Explain what that ordered pair represents.

? Essential Question How can you analyze the relationship between dependent and independent variables using tables, graphs, and equations?

EXAMPLE 1   **Relate Quantities Using a Table, a Graph, and an Equation**

Scan for Multimedia

The booster club members want to raise $50 to donate to a local charity. They buy pom poms for $0.55 each. How many pom poms do they need to sell to reach their fundraising goal?

BOOSTER CLUB
FUND RAISER
$1 EACH
POM POMS

Look for Relationships How can you use a table, a graph, and an equation to analyze the relationship between independent and dependent variables?

The booster club raises $0.45 for each pom pom they sell.

STEP 1 Make a table to relate the number of pom poms sold, n, to the amount of money raised, r.

The amount raised depends on the number of pom poms sold.

n	r
10	$4.50
50	$22.50
110	$49.50

STEP 2 Graph the ordered pairs on the coordinate plane.

Money raised, r

This point represents the number of pom poms sold to raise $50.

Number of pom poms sold, n

STEP 3 Write an equation that describes the relationship.

The amount of money raised, r, is 0.45 times the number of pom poms sold, n.

$$r = 0.45n$$

Substitute $r = 50$ and solve for n.

$$50 = 0.45n$$

$$50 \div 0.45 = 0.45n \div 0.45$$

$$111.11 \approx n$$

The booster club must sell at least 112 pom poms to raise $50.

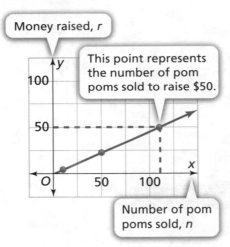

✓ **Try It!**

The booster club now raises $0.41 for each pom pom they sell. Complete the table and graph. Write and solve an equation to find how many pom poms they need to sell to raise $50.

n	r
50	$20.50
100	$41.00
150	

Money raised, r

Number of pom poms sold, n

Convince Me! How does finding three values for x and y help you represent the relationship between x and y?

The temperature was 6°C at 8 A.M. and increased 2°C each hour for 6 hours one spring day. What was the temperature after 6 hours?

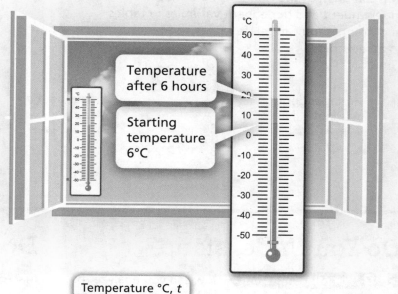

Temperature after 6 hours

Starting temperature 6°C

STEP 1 Make a table to relate the number of hours, *n*, to the temperature, *t*.

The temperature, *t*, depends on the number of hours passed, *n*.

n	t
0	6
2	10
4	14
6	18

STEP 2 Graph the ordered pairs on the coordinate plane.

STEP 3 Write an equation that describes the relationship.

$t = 6 + 2n$

$t = 6 + 2(6)$ Substitute $n = 6$ and solve for *t*.

$t = 6 + 12$

$t = 18$

The temperature was 18°C after 6 hours.

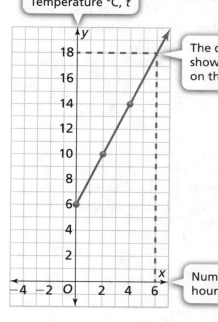

Temperature °C, *t*

The dashed blue segments show that (6, 18) is a point on the line.

Number of hours, *n*

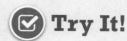 **Try It!**

A company makes decorations for pens. All the supplies cost $5, and the company plans to sell the decorations for $2 apiece. Analyze the relationship between the number of decorations sold and the profit by completing the table and the graph. Use the table and the graph to write and solve an equation to find the number of decorations that must be sold for the company to make a $15 profit.

Independent variable

Dependent variable

x	y
3	☐
☐	☐
☐	☐

Profit, *y*

Decorations sold, *x*

You can analyze the relationship between independent and dependent variables in tables and graphs. You can relate tables and graphs to an equation.

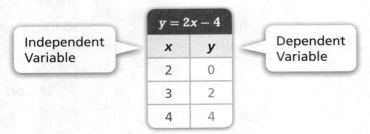

Independent Variable

Dependent Variable

$y = 2x - 4$	
x	y
2	0
3	2
4	4

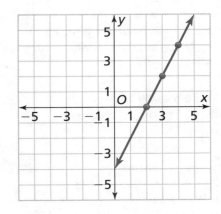

Do You Understand?

1. **? Essential Question** How can you analyze the relationship between dependent and independent variables using tables, graphs, and equations?

2. **Reasoning** Using the relationship in Example 1, how many pom poms must the booster club sell to raise $75 for charity? Explain.

3. **Construct Arguments** For every 4 bananas a grocery store sells, it sells 2 apples. Mary wrote the equation $4b \times 2 = a$, where b = the number of bananas sold and a = the number of apples sold. Does Mary's equation correctly represent the relationship of bananas sold to apples sold? Explain.

Do You Know How?

In 4–6, use the equation $d = 4t$.

4. Complete the table.
   d = distance
   t = time

$d = 4t$	
t	d
1	⬜
2	⬜
3	⬜

5. Name four ordered pairs found on the line plotted using this equation.

6. Describe the relationship between the variables.

In 7, complete the table and graph to show the relationship between the variables in the equation $d = 5 + 5t$.

7. d = distance
   t = time

$d = 5 + 5t$	
t	d
0	⬜
2	⬜
⬜	⬜

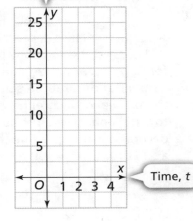

Distance, d

Time, t

Practice & Problem Solving

Scan for
Multimedia

In 8 and 9, complete the table and graph to show the relationship between the variables in each equation.

8. A rectangle is $\frac{1}{2}$ inch longer than it is wide.

Let w = width.
Let ℓ = length.
Graph $\ell = w + \frac{1}{2}$.

$\ell = w + \frac{1}{2}$	
w	**ℓ**
1	
2	

Length, ℓ

9. The sale price is $5 less than the regular price.

Let s = the sale price.
Let r = the regular price.
Graph $s = r - 5$.

$s = r - 5$	
r	**s**
10	
20	

Sale price, s

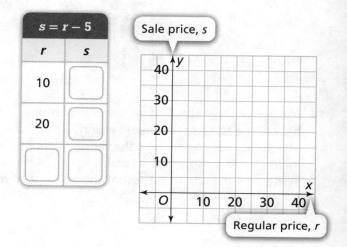

Width, w

Regular price, r

10. The points (2, 4) and (−2, −4) are plotted on the coordinate plane using the equation $y = a \cdot x$. How can you use the coordinates to find the value of a?

11. Without using a table or graph, identify three other points that a graph of the equation in Exercise 10 will pass through.

12. Reasoning The Jackson family is planning a weekend vacation. They plan to rent a car from the ABC Car Rental Company. Let m represent the number of miles the family will drive. Let c represent the cost for renting a car. Write an equation that shows what the cost for renting a car will be.

EXIT 32

ABC
CAR RENTAL
NEXT EXIT   COMPANY

Weekend Special
$40 + $0.10 per mile

In 13, write an equation. Complete the table and graph to solve the problem.

13. A puppy weighs 1 pound. What does the puppy weigh after 4 weeks?

Puppy gains $\frac{1}{2}$ pound each week.

Weight, in pounds, y

x	y
0	
2	

Number of weeks, x

14. **Model with Math** During a movie matinee, the film projector broke. The theater manager refunded the ticket price to everyone attending. Let n represent the number of people watching the movie. Let r represent the total amount of money refunded. Write an equation to represent the amount of money refunded.

MOVIE PRICES

ADULTS	$8.50
CHILDREN AND SENIORS	$7.00
MATINEES: ALL AGES	$5.00

15. **Higher Order Thinking** Write an algebraic equation that matches the values shown in the table at the right. Explain how you solved the problem.

x	y
1	8
2	11
3	14
4	17

☑ **Assessment Practice**

16. For every hour Sonia worked, she hand made 2 seashell necklaces for her gift shop.

PART A

Write an equation that describes the relationship shown in the graph on the right.

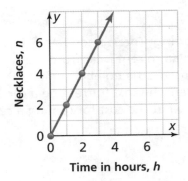

Necklaces, n

Time in hours, h

PART B

Describe the relationship between the variables in the graph and the equation.

? Topic Essential Question

What procedures can be used to write and solve equations and inequalities?

Vocabulary Review

Complete each definition with a vocabulary word.

> **Vocabulary**   dependent variable   independent variable   inequality   equation

1. In the equation $y = x + 9$, the variable x is the _____.

2. A(n) _____ has an infinite number of solutions.

3. In the equation $y = x - 9$, the variable y is the _____.

Draw a line from each equation to the property of equality it illustrates.

4. $(6 + 3) - 3 = 9 - 3$ Addition Property of Equality

5. $(6 + 3) \times 3 = 9 \times 3$ Division Property of Equality

6. $(6 + 3) + 3 = 9 + 3$ Multiplication Property of Equality

7. $(6 + 3) \div 3 = 9 \div 3$ Subtraction Property of Equality

Use Vocabulary in Writing

Describe how to solve $\frac{3}{7}n = 27$. Use vocabulary words in your explanation.

Concepts and Skills Review

LESSON **4-1** **Understand Equations and Solutions**

Quick Review

The solution of an equation makes the equation true. Substitute each of the given values into the equation for the variable to determine which value, if any, is a solution of the equation.

Example

Which value of x is a solution of the equation?

$x + 4.8 = 19$ $x = 13, 14.2, 15.8$

Try $x = 13$: $13 + 4.8 \neq 17.8$ ✗
Try $x = 14.2$: $14.2 + 4.8 = 19$ ✔
Try $x = 15.8$: $15.8 + 4.8 \neq 20.6$ ✗

Practice

Tell which value of the variable, if any, is a solution of the equation.

1. $d + 9 = 25$ $d = 6, 14, 16, 21$

2. $c - 8 = 25$ $c = 17, 28, 33, 35$

3. $2y = 30$ $y = 10, 12, 24, 36$

4. $150 \div h = 50$ $h = 2, 3, 4, 5$

5. $f - 13.2 = 28.9$ $f = 38.7, 42.2, 45.8, 51.4$

LESSON **4-2** **Apply Properties of Equality**

Quick Review

The properties of equality allow you to apply the same operation with the same amount to both sides of an equation.

Example

The properties of equality are illustrated in the table.

Properties of Equality	
Addition Property of Equality	$4 + 3 = 7$ So, $4 + 3 + 2 = 7 + 2$
Subtraction Property of Equality	$9 + 8 = 17$ So, $9 + 8 - 5 = 17 - 5$
Multiplication Property of Equality	$3 \times 5 = 15$ So, $3 \times 5 \times 2 = 15 \times 2$
Division Property of Equality	$16 + 2 = 18$ So, $(16 + 2) \div 2 = 18 \div 2$

Practice

1. If $6 + 2 = 8$, does $6 + 2 + 3 = 8 + 3$? Why or why not?

2. If $8 - 1 = 7$, does $8 - 1 - 2 = 7 - 3$? Why or why not?

3. If $4 + 6 = 10$, does $(4 + 6) \times 3 = 10 \times 3$? Why or why not?

4. If $5 + 4 = 9$, does $(5 + 4) \div 3 = 9 \div 4$? Why or why not?

Write and Solve Addition, Subtraction, Multiplication, and Division Equations

Quick Review

Use the **inverse relationship** of addition and subtraction or multiplication and division to solve equations. To check, substitute your answer back into the original equation.

Example

$23 + y = 57$

$23 + y - 23 = 57 - 23$

$y = 34$

$a - 12 = 16$

$a - 12 + 12 = 16 + 12$

$a = 28$

$9z = 63$

$9z \div 9 = 63 \div 9$

$z = 7$

$c \div 4 = 24$

$c \div 4 \times 4 = 24 \times 4$

$c = 96$

Practice

Solve for x.

1. $8x = 64$

2. $x + 2 = 11$

3. $x \div 20 = 120$

4. $x - 17 = 13$

5. $x \div 12 = 2$

6. $8 + x = 25$

7. $7x = 77$

8. $x - 236 = 450$

9. $26 = 13x$

10. $x + 21.9 = 27.1$

11. $2{,}448 \div 48 = x$

12. $x + 15 = 31$

Write and Solve Equations with Rational Numbers

Quick Review

You can use inverse relationships and properties of equality to solve each equation.

Example

Solve $w + 4\frac{1}{3} = 7$.

Subtract $4\frac{1}{3}$ from both sides.

$w + 4\frac{1}{3} - 4\frac{1}{3} = 7 - 4\frac{1}{3}$

$w = 2\frac{2}{3}$

Solve $\frac{3}{5}n = \frac{2}{3}$.

Multiply both sides by the reciprocal of $\frac{3}{5}$.

$\frac{5}{3} \times \frac{3}{5}n = \frac{5}{3} \times \frac{2}{3}$

$n = \frac{10}{9}$ or $1\frac{1}{9}$

Practice

In 1–8, solve for x.

1. $x + 3\frac{5}{8} = 7\frac{1}{4}$

2. $x - \frac{4}{8} = 4\frac{1}{4}$

3. $x \div 15 = 8\frac{1}{3}$

4. $\frac{4}{2}x = 6$

5. $\frac{x}{3} = 9$

6. $14x = 73.5$

7. $12x = 19.2$

8. $17.9 - x = 12.8$

9. Tomas buys a bag of 5 peaches for $3.55. Write and solve an equation to find how much money, m, Tomas paid for each peach.

10. Krys has $1.54 and spends $0.76. Write and solve an equation to find how much money, m, Krys has left.

Quick Review

An **inequality** is a mathematical sentence that contains < (less than), > (greater than), ≤ (less than or equal to), ≥ (greater than or equal to), or ≠ (not equal to).

Example

Situation	Inequality
The age of the house, a, is greater than 3 years.	$a > 3$
The cost of the house, c, is at least \$50,000.	$c \geq 50{,}000$
The number of windows, w, is fewer than 10.	$w < 10$
The number of people, n, living in the house is at most 5.	$n \leq 5$
The number of trucks, t, in the garage is not 2.	$t \neq 2$

Practice

Write an inequality for each situation.

1. Up to 5 people, p, visited Mary today.

2. The value, v, of the hat is less than \$9.

3. The number of guests, g, coming for dinner is not 8.

4. The distance of the race, d, is at least 6 miles.

5. The time it takes to get to Grandma's house, t, is longer than 2 hours.

Quick Review

To graph the solutions of an inequality on a number line, use an open circle for < or > and a closed circle for ≤ or ≥. If the values of the variable are less than the given number, shade to the left on the number line. If the values of the variable are greater than the given number, shade to the right on the number line.

Example

"Molly is less than 15 years old" is represented by the inequality $x < 15$. Write three ages that could represent Molly's age.

To graph the inequality on a number line, draw an open circle at 15 and shade to the left of 15 because x is less than 15. Draw an arrow to show all numbers less than 15.

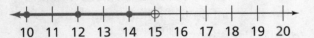

There are many solutions. Molly could be 10, 12, 14, or any age less than 15 years.

Practice

Write the inequality that each graph represents.

1.
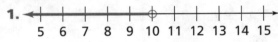

2.
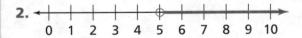

3.
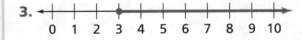

4.
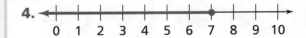

Understand Dependent and Independent Variables

Quick Review

Think about how the values of variables affect each other.

To identify the **dependent variable**, ask yourself which variable depends on the other.

To identify the **independent variable**, ask yourself which variable causes the change.

Example

The spirit squad is washing cars. The equation $m = 2c$ represents the money they make, m, for washing c cars. Identify the dependent variable and the independent variable.

The amount of money the spirit squad makes **depends** on the number of cars they wash. The dependent variable is m.

The number of cars washed changes the amount of money made. The independent variable is c.

Practice

Identify the dependent variable and the independent variable in each situation.

1. The distance traveled, d, and the speed, s

2. The calories, c, in a snack and the amount of the snack, a

3. The amount of money you have spent, s, and how much money you have left, m

4. The number of apple slices remaining, r, and the number of apple slices eaten, e

---

Use Patterns to Write and Solve Equations

Quick Review

Look for patterns between two related variables to find rules and write equations.

Example

Write a rule and an equation that represents the pattern. Then complete the table.

x	3	4	5	6	7
y	12	16	20	24	28

Find the rule and write an equation.

12 is 3 × 4
16 is 4 × 4
20 is 5 × 4

Rule: The value of y is 4 times the value of x.

Equation: $y = 4x$

Evaluate the equation for $x = 6$ and $x = 7$.

$y = 4 \times 6 = 24$

$y = 4 \times 7 = 28$

Practice

1. Find the pattern and then write a rule and an equation that represents the pattern. Then complete the table.

x	0	2	10	16	20
y	0	1	5		

2. Use the equation to complete the table.

$y = 6x + 1$

x	1	2	3	4	5
y					

Quick Review

A table, equation, or graph can be used to analyze the relationship between dependent and independent variables. Ordered pairs that make an equation true can be used to graph the equation.

Example

Complete the table and graph to show the relationship between the variables in the equation $t = s + 1$.

A restaurant has a special that when you buy one sandwich you get a second sandwich for $1.

Let s = price of one sandwich.

Let t = total price of two sandwiches.

Step 1 Make a table. Include at least three values.

$t = s + 1$	
s	t
$1.50	$2.50
$2	$3
$3	$4

Step 2 Graph each ordered pair on a coordinate plane. Then draw a line through the points.

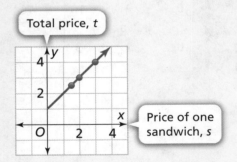

Total price, t

Price of one sandwich, s

Practice

1. The cross country team practices by jogging on the town's streets. The average jogging rate is 6 miles per hour. One member jogged for 3.5 hours one weekend. How many miles did the team member jog?

a. Complete the table to relate the number of miles to the number of hours jogged.

x	y
1	
2	
3	

b. Graph the ordered pairs on the coordinate plane.

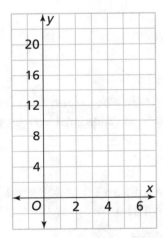

c. Write an equation that describes the relationship. Then solve the problem.

2. Alex is making puppets for a show. He bought all the string needed for $125. It costs $18 for the remaining materials to make each puppet. What is the total cost to make 50 puppets?

Riddle Rearranging

Find each quotient. Then arrange the answers in order from least to greatest. The letters will spell out the answer to the riddle below.

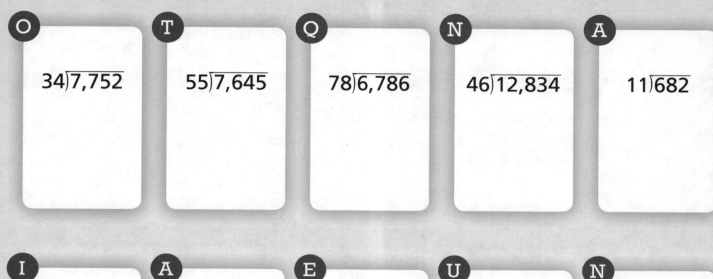

O $34\overline{)7,752}$

T $55\overline{)7,645}$

Q $78\overline{)6,786}$

N $46\overline{)12,834}$

A $11\overline{)682}$

I $81\overline{)15,309}$

A $97\overline{)11,931}$

E $72\overline{)5,256}$

U $83\overline{)8,051}$

N $68\overline{)4,624}$

What has two sides but can sometimes look like a line?

○ ○

○ ○ ○ ○ ○ ○ ○ ○

GLOSSARY

ENGLISH

SPANISH

A

absolute deviation from the mean Absolute deviation measures the distance that the data value is from the mean. You find the absolute deviation by taking the absolute value of the deviation of a data value. Absolute deviations are always nonnegative.

desviación absoluta de la media La desviación absoluta mide la distancia a la que un valor se encuentra de la media. Para hallar la desviación absoluta, tomas el valor absoluto de la desviación de un valor. Las desviaciones absolutas siempre son no negativas.

Example Data set: 0, 1, 1, 2, 2, 2, 2, 3, 3, 5, 5, 10. The absolute deviations of the values in the data set are:

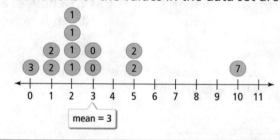

absolute value The absolute value of a number *a* is the distance between *a* and zero on a number line. The absolute value of *a* is written as $|a|$.

valor absoluto El valor absoluto de un número a es la distancia entre a y cero en la recta numérica. El valor absoluto de a se escribe como $|a|$.

Example -7 is 7 units from 0, so $|-7| = 7$.

Addition Property of Equality The two sides of an equation stay equal when the same amount is added to both sides of the equation.

propiedad de suma de la igualdad Se puede sumar el mismo número a ambos lados de una ecuación y los lados siguen siendo iguales.

Example
$$4 + 2 = 6$$
$$(4 + 2) + 3 = 6 + 3$$
$$(4 + 2) + a = 6 + a$$

additive inverses Two numbers that have a sum of 0.

inversos de suma Dos números cuya suma es 0.

Example 7 and -7 are additive inverses.

algebraic expression An algebraic expression is a mathematical phrase that consists of variables, numbers, and operation symbols.

expresión algebraica Una expresión algebraica es una frase matemática que consiste en variables, números y símbolos de operaciones.

Example $x - 7$, $n + 2$, and $5d$ are algebraic expressions.

ENGLISH	SPANISH

Associative Property of Addition For any numbers a, b, and c:
$(a + b) + c = a + (b + c)$

propiedad asociativa de la suma Para los números cualesquiera a, b y c:
$(a + b) + c = a + (b + c)$

Example $(3 + 25) + 4 = 3 + (25 + 4)$
$(m + 25) + 4 = m + (25 + 4)$

Associative Property of Multiplication For any numbers a, b, and c:
$(a \cdot b) \cdot c = a \cdot (b \cdot c)$

propiedad asociativa de la multiplicación Para los números cualesquiera a, b y c:
$(a \cdot b) \cdot c = a \cdot (b \cdot c)$

Example $(16 \cdot 26) \cdot 55 = 16 \cdot (26 \cdot 55)$
$(m \cdot 56) \cdot 4 = m \cdot (56 \cdot 4)$

base The base is the repeated factor of a number written in exponential form.

base La base es el factor repetido de un número escrito en forma exponencial.

Example $3^4 = 3 \times 3 \times 3 \times 3$
In the expression 3^4, 3 is the base and 4 is the exponent.

base of a parallelogram A base of a parallelogram is any side of the parallelogram.

base de un paralelogramo La base de un paralelogramo es cualquiera de los lados del paralelogramo.

Example

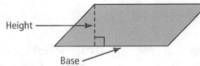

base of a prism A base of a prism is one of a pair of parallel polygonal faces that are the same size and shape. A prism is named for the shape of its bases.

base de un prisma La base de un prisma es una de las dos caras poligonales paralelas que tienen el mismo tamaño y la misma forma. El nombre de un prisma depende de la forma de sus bases.

Example

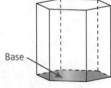

ENGLISH

SPANISH

base of a pyramid A base of a pyramid is a polygonal face that does not connect to the vertex.

base de una pirámide La base de una pirámide es una cara poligonal que no se conecta con el vértice.

Example

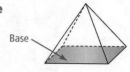

Base

base of a triangle The base of a triangle is any side of the triangle.

base de un triángulo La base de un triángulo es cualquiera de los lados del triángulo.

Example

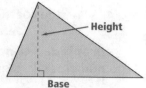

Height

Base

box plot A box plot is a statistical graph that shows the distribution of a data set by marking five boundary points where data occur along a number line. Unlike a dot plot or a histogram, a box plot does not show frequency.

diagrama de cajas Un diagrama de cajas es un diagrama de estadísticas que muestra la distribución de un conjunto de datos al marcar cinco puntos de frontera donde se hallan los datos sobre una recta numérica. A diferencia del diagrama de puntos o el histograma, el diagrama de cajas no muestra la frecuencia.

Example

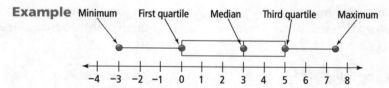

Minimum   First quartile   Median   Third quartile   Maximum

−4 −3 −2 −1 0 1 2 3 4 5 6 7 8

C

categorical data Categorical data consist of data that fall into categories.

datos por categorías Los datos por categorías son datos que se pueden clasificar en categorías.

Example Data collected about gender is an example of categorical data because the data have values that fall into the categories "male" and "female."

circle graph A circle graph is a graph that represents a whole divided into parts.

gráfica circular Una gráfica circular es una gráfica que representa un todo dividido en partes.

Example **Favorite Types of Music**

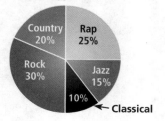

Country 20%   Rap 25%   Rock 30%   Jazz 15%   10% Classical

ENGLISH	SPANISH
circumference of a circle The circumference of a circle is the distance around the circle.	**circunferencia de un círculo** La circunferencia de un círculo es la distancia alrededor del círculo.

Example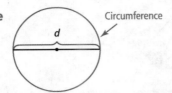

coefficient A coefficient is the number part of a term that contains a variable.	**coeficiente** Un coeficiente es la parte numérica de un término que contiene una variable.

Example In the expression $3x + 4y + 12$, the coefficients are 3 and 4.

Commutative Property of Addition For any numbers a and b: $a + b = b + a$	**propiedad conmutativa de la suma** Para los números cualesquiera a y b: $a + b = b + a$

Example $25 + 56 = 56 + 25$
$x + 72 = 72 + x$

Commutative Property of Multiplication For any numbers a and b: $a \cdot b = b \cdot a$	**propiedad conmutativa de la multiplicación** Para los números cualesquiera a y b: $a \cdot b = b \cdot a$

Example $17 \cdot 6 = 6 \cdot 17$
$47x = x \cdot 47$

composite number A composite number is a whole number greater than 1 with more than two factors.	**número compuesto** Un número compuesto es un número entero mayor que 1 con más de dos factores.

Example The factors of 15 are 1, 3, 5, and 15. Because 15 has more than two factors, it is a composite number.

constant A constant is a term that only contains a number.	**constante** Una constante es un término que solamente contiene un número.

Example In the expression $3x + 4y + 12$, 12 is a constant.

constant speed The speed stays the same over time.	**velocidad constante** Tasa de velocidad que se mantiene igual a través del tiempo.

conversion factor A conversion factor is a rate that equals 1.	**factor de conversión** Un factor de conversión es una tasa que es igual a 1.

Example $\dfrac{60 \text{ minutes}}{1 \text{ hour}}$

ENGLISH

SPANISH

coordinate plane A coordinate plane is formed by a horizontal number line called the *x*-axis and a vertical number line called the *y*-axis.

plano de coordenadas Un plano de coordenadas está formado por una recta numérica horizontal llamada eje de las *x* y una recta numérica vertical llamada eje de las *y*.

Example

D

data distribution To describe a data distribution, or how the data values are arranged, you evaluate its measures of center and variability, and its overall shape. See distribution of a data set.

distribución de datos Cómo se distribuyen los valores.

dependent variable A dependent variable is a variable whose value changes in response to another (independent) variable.

variable dependiente Una variable dependiente es una variable cuyo valor cambia en respuesta a otra variable (independiente).

deviation from the mean Deviation indicates how far away and in which direction a data value is from the mean. Data values that are less than the mean have a negative deviation. Data values that are greater than the mean have a positive deviation.

desviación de la media La desviación indica a qué distancia y en qué dirección un valor se aleja de la media. Los valores menores que la media tienen una desviación negativa. Los valores mayores que la media tienen una desviación positiva.

Example Data set: 0, 1, 1, 2, 2, 2, 2, 3, 3, 5, 5, 10. The deviations of the values in the data set are:

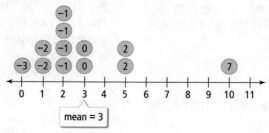

diameter A diameter is a segment that passes through the center of a circle and has both endpoints on the circle. The term diameter can also mean the length of this segment.

diámetro Un diámetro es un segmento que atraviesa el centro de un círculo y tiene sus dos extremos en el círculo. El término diámetro también puede referirse a la longitud de este segmento.

Example

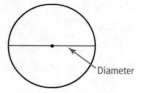

ENGLISH	SPANISH

dimensional analysis A method to convert measures by including measurement units when multiplying by a conversion factor.

análisis dimensional Método que usa factores de conversión para convertir una unidad de medida a otra unidad de medida.

Ejemplo: $64 \; \cancel{onzas} \times \dfrac{1 \; taza}{8 \; \cancel{onzas}} = \dfrac{64}{8} \; tazas$

$= 8 \; tazas$

Example $3.5 \; \cancel{ft} \times \dfrac{12 \; in.}{1 \; \cancel{ft}}$

$= 3.5 \times 12 \; in.$

$= 42 \; in.$

---

distribution (of a data set) The distribution of a data set describes the way that its data values are spread out over all possible values. This includes describing the frequencies of each data value. The shape of a data display shows the distribution of a data set. *See data distribution*.

distribución (de un conjunto de datos) La distribución de un conjunto de datos describe la manera en que sus valores se esparcen sobre todos los valores posibles. Eso incluye la descripción de las frecuencias de cada valor. La forma de una exhibición de datos muestra la distribución de un conjunto de datos.

Example The distribution of this data set shows that the data are clustered around 2 and 7, and there is one stray data value at 12.

Ages of Cats at a Local Shelter

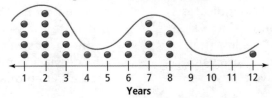

Years

Distributive Property Multiplying a number by a sum or difference gives the same result as multiplying that number by each term in the sum or difference and then adding or subtracting the corresponding products.

$a \cdot (b + c) = a \cdot b + a \cdot c$ and

$a \cdot (b - c) = a \cdot b - a \cdot c$

propiedad distributiva Multiplicar un número por una suma o una diferencia da el mismo resultado que multiplicar ese mismo número por cada uno de los términos de la suma o la diferencia y después sumar o restar los productos obtenidos.

$a \cdot (b + c) = a \cdot b + a \cdot c$ and

$a \cdot (b - c) = a \cdot b - a \cdot c$

Example $36(14 + 85) = (36)(14) + (36)(85)$

Division Property of Equality The two sides of an equation stay equal when both sides of the equation are divided by the same non-zero amount.

propiedad de división de la igualdad Ambos lados de una ecuación se pueden dividir por el mismo número distinto de cero y los lados siguen siendo iguales.

Example $4 + 2 = 6$

$(4 + 2) \div 3 = 6 \div 3$

$(4 + 2) \div a = 6 \div a$

edge of a three-dimensional figure An edge of a three-dimensional figure is a segment formed by the intersection of two faces.

arista de una figura tridimensional Una arista de una figura tridimensional es un segmento formado por la intersección de dos caras.

Example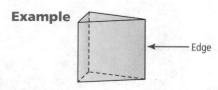

equivalent expressions Equivalent expressions are expressions that always have the same value.

expresiones equivalentes Las expresiones equivalentes son expresiones que siempre tienen el mismo valor.

Example 2(12) and 20 + 4 are equivalent expressions.

equivalent ratios Equivalent ratios are ratios that express the same relationship.

razones equivalentes Las razones equivalentes son razones que expresan la misma relación.

Example 2 : 3 and 4 : 6 are equivalent ratios.

evaluate an algebraic expression To evaluate an algebraic expression, replace each variable with a number, and then follow the order of operations.

evaluar una expresión algebraica Para evaluar una expresión algebraica, reemplaza cada variable con un número y luego sigue el orden de las operaciones.

Example To evaluate the expression $x + 2$ for $x = 4$, substitute 4 for x.
$x + 2 = 4 + 2 = 6$

expand an algebraic expression To expand an algebraic expression, use the Distributive Property to rewrite a product as a sum or difference of terms.

desarrollar una expresión algebraica Para desarrollar una expresión algebraica, usa la propiedad distributiva para reescribir el producto como una suma o diferencia de términos.

Example The expression $(5 - x)(y)$ is a product that can be expanded using the Distributive Property.
$(5 - x)(y) = 5(y) - x(y)$
$= 5y - (xy)$
$= 5y - xy$

exponent An exponent is a number that shows how many times a base is used as a factor.

exponente Un exponente es un número que muestra cuántas veces se usa una base como factor.

Example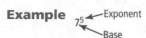

ENGLISH

SPANISH

expression An expression is a mathematical phrase that can involve variables, numbers, and operations. See algebraic expression or numerical expression.

expresión Una expresión es una frase matemática que puede tener variables, números y operaciones. Ver expresión algebraica o expresión numérica.

Example $4 + 9$
$2x$

face of a three-dimensional figure A face of a three-dimensional figure is a flat surface shaped like a polygon.

cara de una figura tridimensional La cara de una figura tridimensional es una superficie plana con forma de polígono.

Example

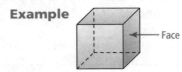

Face

factor tree A factor tree shows the prime factorization of a composite number.

árbol de factores Diagrama que muestra la descomposición en factores primos de un número.

Example

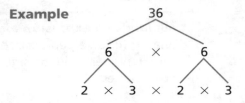

frequency table A frequency table shows the number of times a data value or values occur in the data set.

tabla de frecuencias Tabla que muestra la cantidad de veces que un valor o un rango de valores aparece en un conjunto de datos.

Example

Running Times	Tally	Frequency
14:00–15:59	IIII	4
16:00–17:59	IIIII I	6
18:00–19:59	II	2

gap A gap is an area of a graph that contains no data points.

Espacio vacío o brecha Un espacio vacío o brecha es un área de una gráfica que no contiene ningún valor.

Example

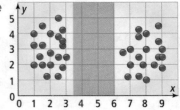

ENGLISH

SPANISH

greatest common factor The greatest common factor (GCF) of two or more whole numbers is the greatest number that is a factor of all of the numbers.

máximo común divisor El máximo común divisor (M.C.D.) de dos o más números enteros no negativos es el número mayor que es un factor de todos los números.

Example The greatest common factor of 12 and 10 is 2.
The greatest common factor of 24 and 6 is 6.

H

height of a parallelogram The height of a parallelogram is the perpendicular distance between opposite bases.

altura de un paralelogramo La altura de un paralelogramo es la distancia perpendicular que existe entre las bases opuestas.

Example Height

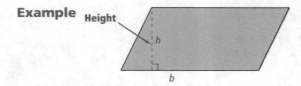

height of a prism The height of a prism is the length of a perpendicular segment that joins the bases.

altura de un prisma La altura de un prisma es la longitud de un segmento perpendicular que une a las bases.

Example

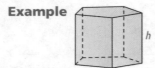

height of a pyramid The height of a pyramid is the length of a segment perpendicular to the base that joins the vertex and the base.

altura de una pirámide La altura de una pirámide es la longitud de un segmento perpendicular a la base que une al vértice con la base.

Example

height of a triangle The height of a triangle is the length of the perpendicular segment from a vertex to the base opposite that vertex.

altura de un triángulo La altura de un triángulo es la longitud del segmento perpendicular desde un vértice hasta la base opuesta a ese vértice.

Example

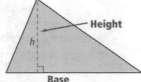
Base

ENGLISH

histogram A histogram is a statistical graph that shows the shape of a data set with vertical bars above intervals of values on a number line. The intervals are equal in size and do not overlap. The height of each bar shows the frequency of data within that interval.

Example

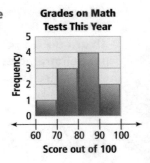

Grades on Math Tests This Year

I

Identity Property of Addition The sum of 0 and any number is that number. For any number n, $n + 0 = n$ and $0 + n = n$.

    Example $0 + 41 = 41$
                $x + 0 = x$

Identity Property of Multiplication The product of 1 and any number is that number. For any number n, $n \cdot 1 = n$ and $1 \cdot n = n$.

    Example $1 \cdot 67 = 67$
                $x \cdot 1 = x$

independent variable An independent variable is a variable whose value determines the value of another (dependent) variable.

inequality An inequality is a mathematical sentence that uses $<$, $\leq$, $>$, $\geq$, or $\neq$ to compare two quantities.

    Example $13 > 7$
                $17 + c \leq 25$

integers Integers are the set of positive whole numbers, their opposites, and 0.

    Example ..., -3, -2, -1, 0, 1, 2, 3, ...

SPANISH

histograma Un histograma es una gráfica de estadísticas que muestra la forma de un conjunto de datos con barras verticales encima de intervalos de valores en una recta numérica. Los intervalos tienen el mismo tamaño y no se superponen. La altura de cada barra muestra la frecuencia de los datos dentro de ese intervalo.

propiedad de identidad de la suma La suma de 0 y cualquier número es ese número. Para cualquier número n, $n + 0 = n$ and $0 + n = n$.

propiedad de identidad de la multiplicación El producto de 1 y cualquier número es ese número. Para cualquier número n, $n \cdot 1 = n$ and $1 \cdot n = n$.

variable independiente Una variable independiente es una variable cuyo valor determina el valor de otra variable (dependiente).

desigualdad Una desigualdad es una oración matemática que usa $<$, $\leq$, $>$, $\geq$, o $\neq$ para comparar dos cantidades.

enteros Los enteros son el conjunto de los números enteros positivos, sus opuestos y 0.

interquartile range The interquartile range (IQR) is the distance between the first and third quartiles of the data set. It represents the spread of the middle 50% of the data values.

rango intercuartil El rango intercuartil es la distancia entre el primer y el tercer cuartil del conjunto de datos. Representa la ubicación del 50% del medio de los valores.

Example Data set: 1, 3, (6), 10, 11, |14, 15, (20), 23, 40

First quartile   Third quartile

The interquartile range of the data set is 20 − 6, or 14.

inverse operations Inverse operations are operations that undo each other.

operaciones inversas Las operaciones inversas son operaciones que se cancelan entre sí.

Example Addition and subtraction are inverse operations because they undo each other.
$4 + 3 = 7$ and $7 - 4 = 3$

Multiplication and division are inverse operations because they undo each other.
$4 \times 3 = 12$ and $12 \div 4 = 3$

Inverse Property of Addition Every number has an additive inverse. The sum of a number and its additive inverse is zero.

propiedad inversa de la suma Todos los números tienen un inverso de suma. La suma de un número y su inverso de suma es cero.

Example 5 and −5 are additive inverses.
$5 + (-5) = 0$ and $(-5) + 5 = 0$

inverse relationship Operations that undo each other have an inverse relationship.

relaciones inversas Relaciones entre operaciones que se "cancelan" entre sí, como la suma y la resta o la multiplicación y la división (excepto la multiplicación o división por 0).

Example Adding 5 is the inverse of subtracting 5.

isolate a variable When solving equations, to isolate a variable means to get a variable with a coefficient of 1 alone on one side of an equation. Use the properties of equality and inverse operations to isolate a variable.

aislar una variable Cuando resuelves ecuaciones, aislar una variable significa poner una variable con un coeficiente de 1 sola a un lado de la ecuación. Usa las propiedades de igualdad y las operaciones inversas para aislar una variable.

Example To isolate x in $2x = 8$, divide both sides of the equation by 2.

ENGLISH

SPANISH

K

kite A quadrilateral with two pairs of adjacent sides that are equal in length.

cometa Cuadrilátero con dos pares de lados adyacentes de igual longitud.

Example

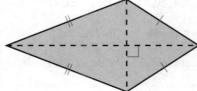

L

least common multiple The least common multiple (LCM) of two or more numbers is the least multiple, not including zero, shared by all of the numbers.

mínimo común múltiplo El mínimo común múltiplo (m.c.m.) de dos o más números es el múltiplo menor, sin incluir el cero, compartido por todos los números.

Example The LCM of 4 and 6 is 12.
The LCM of 3 and 15 is 15.

like terms Terms that have identical variable parts are like terms.

términos semejantes Los términos que tienen partes variables idénticas son términos semejantes.

Example Like terms
$y + 2.5 - 3y$

M

mean The mean represents the center of a numerical data set. To find the mean, sum the data values and then divide by the number of values in the data set.

media La media representa el centro de un conjunto de datos numéricos. Para hallar la media, suma los valores y luego divide por el número de valores del conjunto de datos.

Example Data set: 2, 4, 5, 15, 23, 12, 9

$$\text{mean} = \frac{2 + 4 + 5 + 15 + 23 + 12 + 9}{7} = \frac{70}{7} = 10$$

ENGLISH

mean absolute deviation The mean absolute deviation is a measure of variability that describes how much the data values are spread out from the mean of a data set. The mean absolute deviation is the average distance that the data values are spread around the mean.

$$MAD = \frac{\text{sum of the absolute deviations of the data values}}{\text{total number of data values}}$$

SPANISH

desviación absoluta media La desviación absoluta media es una medida de variabilidad que describe cuánto se alejan los valores de la media de un conjunto de datos. La desviación absoluta media es la distancia promedio que los valores se alejan de la media.

$$\text{desviación absoluta media} = \frac{\text{suma de las desviaciones absolutas de los valores}}{\text{número total de valores}}$$

Example Data set: 0, 1, 1, 2, 2, 2, 2, 3, 3, 5, 5, 10.
The mean absolute deviation of the data set is 1.8.

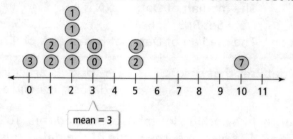

mean = 3

$$\text{mean absolute deviation} = \frac{3+2+2+1+1+1+1+0+0+2+2+7}{12}$$

$$= \frac{22}{12}$$

$$\approx 1.8$$

---

measure of variability A measure of variability describes the spread of values in a data set. There may be more than one measure of variability for a data set.

medida de variabilidad Una medida de variabilidad describe la distribución de los valores de un conjunto de datos. Puede haber más de una medida de variabilidad para un conjunto de datos.

Example Data set: 4, 5, 5, 6, 6, 7, 8, 11

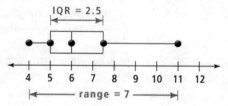

---

measures of center A measure of center is a value that represents the middle of a data set. There may be more than one measure of center for a data set.

medida de tendencia central Una medida de tendencia central es un valor que representa el centro de un conjunto de datos. Puede haber más de una medida de tendencia central para un conjunto de datos.

Example Data set: 4, 5, 5, 6, 6, 7, 8, 11

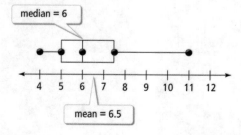

ENGLISH

SPANISH

median The median represents the center of a numerical data set. For an odd number of data values, the median is the middle value when the data values are arranged in numerical order. For an even number of data values, the median is the average of the two middle values when the data values are arranged in numerical order.

mediana La mediana representa el centro de un conjunto de datos numéricos. Para un número impar de valores, la mediana es el valor del medio cuando los valores están organizados en orden numérico. Para un número par de valores, la mediana es el promedio de los dos valores del medio cuando los valores están organizados en orden numérico.

Example Data Set A: 3, 5, 6, 10, 11, 13, 18, 21, 25
The median of Data Set A is 11.
Data Set B: 3, 5, 6, 10, 11, 13, 18, 21, 25, 30
The median of Data Set B is $\frac{11 + 13}{2}$, or 12.

mode The item, or items, in a data set that occurs most frequently.

modo El artículo, o los artículos, en un conjunto de datos que ocurre normalmente.

Example In a parking lot there are 18 red cars, 10 blue cars, and 12 silver cars. The mode of the data set is *red*.

Multiplication Property of Equality The two sides of an equation stay equal when both sides of the equation are multiplied by the same amount.

propiedad multiplicativa de la igualdad Ambos lados de una ecuación se pueden multiplicar por el mismo número distinto de cero y los lados siguen siendo iguales.

Example
$$4 + 2 = 6$$
$$(4 + 2) \times 3 = 6 \times 3$$
$$(4 + 2) \times a = 6 \times a$$

N

negative numbers Negative numbers are numbers less than zero.

números negativos Los números negativos son números menores que cero.

Example The number −5 can represent a temperature of 5 degrees below zero.

net A net is a two-dimensional pattern that you can fold to form a three-dimensional figure. A net of a figure shows all of the surfaces of that figure in one view.

modelo plano Un modelo plano es un diseño bidimensional que puedes doblar para formar una figura tridimensional. Un modelo plano de una figura muestra todas las superficies de la figura en una vista.

Example This is the net of a triangular prism.

ENGLISH

SPANISH

numerical expression A numerical expression is a mathematical phrase that consists of numbers and operation symbols.

expresión numérica Una expresión numérica es una frase matemática que contiene números y símbolos de operaciones.

Example 9 – 17
8 + (28 • 53)

opposites Opposites are two numbers that are the same distance from 0 on a number line, but in opposite directions.

opuestos Los opuestos son dos números que están a la misma distancia de 0 en la recta numérica, pero en direcciones opuestas.

Example 17 and −17 are opposites.

ordered pair An ordered pair identifies the location of a point in the coordinate plane. The x-coordinate shows a point's position left or right of the y-axis. The y-coordinate shows a point's position up or down from the x-axis.

par ordenado Un par ordenado identifica la ubicación de un punto en el plano de coordenadas. La coordenada x muestra la posición de un punto a la izquierda o a la derecha del eje de las y. La coordenada y muestra la posición de un punto arriba o abajo del eje de las x.

Example

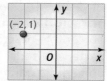

The x-coordinate of the point (−2, 1) is the −2, and the y-coordinate is the 1.

origin The origin is the point of intersection of the x- and y-axes on a coordinate plane.

origen El origen es el punto de intersección del eje de las x y el eje de las y en un plano de coordenadas.

Example The ordered pair that describes the origin is (0, 0).

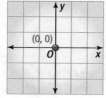

ENGLISH

SPANISH

outlier An outlier is a piece of data that does not seem to fit with the rest of a data set.

valor extremo Un valor extremo es un valor que parece no ajustarse al resto de los datos de un conjunto.

Example This data set has two outliers.

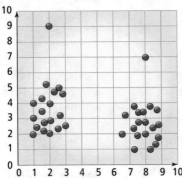

P

percent A percent is a ratio that compares a number to 100.

porcentaje Un porcentaje es una razón que compara un número con 100.

Example $\frac{25}{100} = 25\%$

percent equation The percent equation describes the relationship between a part and a whole. You can use the percent equation (part = percent × whole) to solve percent problems.

ecuación de porcentaje La ecuación de porcentaje describe la relación entre una parte y un todo. Puedes usar la ecuación de porcentaje para resolver problemas de porcentaje. parte = por ciento • todo

Pi Pi (π) is the ratio of a circle's circumference, C, to its diameter, d.

Pi Pi (π) es la razón de la circunferencia de un círculo, C, a su diámetro, d.

Example

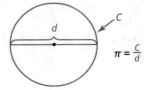

$\pi = \frac{C}{d}$

polyhedron A polyhedron is a three-dimensional figure made of flat polygon-shaped surfaces called faces.

poliedro Figura tridimensional compuesta de superficies planas que son polígonos.

Example A rectangular prism is a polyhedron.

positive numbers Positive numbers are numbers greater than zero.

números positivos Los números positivos son números mayores que cero.

Example The number +3 can represent a temperature of 3 degrees above zero. +3 is usually written 3.

ENGLISH	SPANISH

power A power is a number expressed using an exponent.

potencia Una potencia es un número expresado con un exponente.

Example 3^4 and 3^5 are powers of 3.

prime factorization The prime factorization of a composite number is the expression of the number as a product of its prime factors.

descomposición en factores primos La descomposición en factores primos de un número compuesto es la expresión del número como un producto de sus factores primos.

Example The prime factorization of 30 is 2 • 3 • 5.

prime number A prime number is a whole number greater than 1 with exactly two factors, 1 and the number itself.

número primo Un número primo es un número entero mayor que 1 con exactamente dos factores, 1 y el número mismo.

Example The factors of 5 are 1 and 5. So 5 is a prime number.

quadrant The x- and y-axes divide the coordinate plane into four regions called quadrants.

cuadrante Los ejes de las x y de las y dividen el plano de coordenadas en cuatro regiones llamadas cuadrantes.

Example

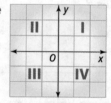

The quadrants are labeled I, II, III, and IV.

quartile The quartiles of a data set divide the data set into four parts with the same number of data values in each part.

cuartil Los cuartiles de un conjunto de datos dividen el conjunto de datos en cuatro partes que tienen el mismo número de valores cada una.

Example Data set: −5, −1, 4, 7, 8, 8, 11
First quartile: −1
Second quartile (median): 7
Third quartile: 8

range The range is a measure of variability of a numerical data set. The range of a data set is the difference between the greatest and least values in a data set.

rango El rango es una medida de la variabilidad de un conjunto de datos numéricos. El rango de un conjunto de datos es la diferencia que existe entre el mayor y el menor valor del conjunto.

rate A rate is a ratio involving two quantities measured in different units.

tasa Una tasa es una razón que relaciona dos cantidades medidas con unidades diferentes.

ENGLISH

SPANISH

ratio A ratio is a relationship in which for **every** x units of one quantity there are y units of another quantity.

razón Una razón es una relación en la cual por cada x unidades de una cantidad hay y unidades de otra cantidad.

Example The ratio of the number of squares to the number of circles shown below is 4 to 3, or 4 : 3.

rational numbers A rational number is a number that can be written in the form $\frac{a}{b}$ or $-\frac{a}{b}$, where a is a whole number and b is a positive whole number. The rational numbers include the integers.

números racionales Un número racional es un número que se puede escribir como $\frac{a}{b}$ or $-\frac{a}{b}$, donde a es un número entero no negativo y b es un número entero positivo. Los números racionales incluyen los enteros.

Example $\frac{1}{3}$, -5, 6.4, $0.\overline{6}$ are all rational numbers.

reciprocals Two numbers are reciprocals if their product is 1. If a nonzero number is named as a fraction, $\frac{a}{b}$, then its reciprocal is $\frac{b}{a}$.

recíprocos Dos números son recíprocos si su producto es 1. Si un número distinto de cero se expresa como una fracción, $\frac{a}{b}$, entonces su recíproco es $\frac{b}{a}$.

Example The reciprocal of $\frac{2}{3}$ is $\frac{3}{2}$.

simplify an algebraic expression To simplify an algebraic expression, combine the like terms of the expression.

simplificar una expresión algebraica Para simplificar una expresión algebraica, combina los términos semejantes de la expresión.

Example $4x + 7y + 6x + 9y = (4x + 6x) + (7y + 9y)$
$$= 10x + 16y$$

solution of an equation A solution of an equation is a value of the variable that makes the equation true.

solución de una ecuación Una solución de una ecuación es un valor de la variable que hace que la ecuación sea verdadera.

Example The solution of $m - 15 = 12$ is $m = 27$, because $27 - 15 = 12$.

solution of an inequality The solutions of an inequality are the values of the variable that make the inequality true.

solución de una desigualdad Las soluciones de una desigualdad son los valores de la variable que hacen que la desigualdad sea verdadera.

Example The solutions of $17 + c > 25$ are $c > 8$.

ENGLISH	SPANISH

statistical question A statistical question is a question that investigates an aspect of the real world and can have variety in the responses.

pregunta estadística Una pregunta estadística es una pregunta que investiga un aspecto de la vida diaria y puede tener varias respuestas.

> **Example** "How old are students in my class?" is a statistical question. "How old am I?" is not a statistical question.

substitution To evaluate an algebraic expression, use substitution to replace the variable with a number.

sustitución Reemplazo de la variable de una expresión por un número.

> **Example** Substitute 4 for *n*.
> $12 + n$
> $12 + 4 = 16$

Subtraction Property of Equality The two sides of an equation stay equal when the same amount is subtracted from both sides of the equation.

propiedad de resta de la igualdad Se puede restar el mismo número de ambos lados de una ecuación y los lados siguen siendo iguales.

> **Example** $4 + 2 = 6$
> $(4 + 2) - 3 = 6 - 3$
> $(4 + 2) - a = 6 - a$

surface area of a three-dimensional figure The surface area of a three-dimensional figure is the sum of the areas of its faces. You can find the surface area by finding the area of the net of the three-dimensional figure.

área total de una figura tridimensional El área total de una figura tridimensional es la suma de las áreas de sus caras. Puedes hallar el área total si hallas el área del modelo plano de la figura tridimensional.

> **Example**

> Surface area = $6s^2$
> $= 6(2)^2$
> $= 6(4)$
> $= 24$

T

term A term is a number, a variable, or the product of a number and one or more variables.

término Un término es un número, una variable o el producto de un número y una o más variables.

> **Example** In the expression $3x + 4y + 12$, the terms are $3x$, $4y$, and 12.

terms of a ratio The terms of a ratio are the quantities *x* and *y* in the ratio.

términos de una razón Los términos de una razón son la cantidad *x* y la cantidad *y* de la razón.

> **Example** The terms of the ratio 4 : 3 are 4 and 3.

ENGLISH

SPANISH

unit price A unit price is a unit rate that gives the price of one item.

precio por unidad El precio por unidad es una tasa por unidad que muestra el precio de un artículo.

Example $\frac{\$2.95}{5}$ fluid ounces $= \frac{\$.59}{1}$ fluid ounce, or $.59 per fluid ounce

unit rate The rate for one unit of a given quantity is called the unit rate.

tasa por unidad Se llama tasa por unidad a la tasa que corresponde a 1 unidad de una cantidad dada.

Example $\frac{130 \text{ miles}}{2 \text{ hours}} = \frac{65 \text{ miles}}{1 \text{ hour}}$, or 65 miles per hour

variability Variability describes how much the items in a data set differ (or vary) from each other. On a data display, variability is shown by how much the data on the horizontal scale are spread out.

variabilidad La variabilidad describe qué diferencia (o variación) existe entre los elementos de un conjunto de datos. Al exhibir datos, la variabilidad queda representada por la distancia que separa los datos en la escala horizontal.

variable A variable is a letter that represents an unknown value.

variable Una variable es una letra que representa un valor desconocido.

Example In the expression $3x + 4y + 12$, x and y are variables.

vertex of a three-dimensional figure A vertex of a three-dimensional figure is a point where three or more edges meet.

vértice de una figura tridimensional El vértice de una figura tridimensional es un punto donde se unen tres o más aristas.

Example

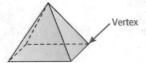

Vertex

x-axis The x-axis is the horizontal number line that, together with the y-axis, forms the coordinate plane.

eje de las x El eje de las x es la recta numérica horizontal que, junto con el eje de las y, forma el plano de coordenadas.

Example

ENGLISH

SPANISH

x-coordinate The x-coordinate is the first number in an ordered pair. It tells the number of horizontal units a point is from 0.

coordenada x La coordenada x (abscisa) es el primer número de un par ordenado. Indica cuántas unidades horizontales hay entre un punto y 0.

Example The x-coordinate is −2 for the ordered pair (−2, 1). The x-coordinate is 2 units to the left of the y-axis.

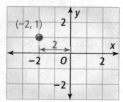

Y

y-axis The y-axis is the vertical number line that, together with the x-axis, forms the coordinate plane.

eje de las y El eje de las y es la recta numérica vertical que, junto con el eje de las x, forma el plano de coordenadas.

Example

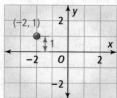

---

y-coordinate The y-coordinate is the second number in an ordered pair. It tells the number of vertical units a point is from 0.

coordenada y La coordenada y (ordenada) es el segundo número de un par ordenado. Indica cuántas unidades verticales hay entre un punto y 0.

Example The y-coordinate is 1 for the ordered pair (−2, 1). The y-coordinate is 1 unit up from the x-axis.

Z

Zero Property of Multiplication The product of 0 and any number is 0. For any number n, $n \cdot 0 = 0$ and $0 \cdot n = 0$.

propiedad del cero en la multiplicación El producto de 0 y cualquier número es 0. Para cualquier número n, $n \cdot 0 = 0$ and $0 \cdot n = 0$.

Example $36 \cdot 0 = 0$
$x(0) = 0$

ACKNOWLEDGEMENTS

Photographs

CVR: Rattanasak Khuentana/Shutterstock, HTWE/Shutterstock, Vaclav Volrab/Shutterstock, Deckorator/Shutterstock; **4**: Nerthuz/Fotolia; **7** (T) Ballda/Shutterstock, (B) Dmitry Kalinovsky/Shutterstock; **8** (T) Jamie Hooper/Shutterstock, (B) PhotocechCZ/Shutterstock; **9** (C) Timothy Masters/Fotolia, (CL) Coprid/Fotolia; **14** (BR) Pearson Education, (T) Maxim Pavlov/Fotolia; **15**: Pixelrobot/Fotolia; **16**: Zelfit/Fotolia; **19**: Steve Lovegrove/Fotolia; **20**: Snvv/Fotolia; **21**: Wckiw/Fotolia; **22** (TCL) Mara Zemgaliete/Fotolia, (TL) olllinka2/Fotolia; **26** (CR) Sergey Nivens/Shutterstock, (TL) Jason Edwards/National Geographic Creative/Corbis; **33**: Alexander Zelnitskiy/Fotolia; **34** (C): Jaddingt/Fotolia, (TC) Bombybamby/Fotolia; **35**: Maksim Shebeko/Fotolia; **38** (TR) hotshotsworldwide/Fotolia, (TC) Jupiter Images, (TL) Jupiter Images; **39**: Amphaiwan/Fotolia; **45**: Gabe9000c/Fotolia; **46**: Vectorace/Fotolia, TeddyandMia/Shutterstock, DaryaSuperman/Shutterstock; **47** (TCR) D3d/Fotolia, (TR) Kazyavka/Fotolia, Jane Kelly/Shutterstock; **51** (TC) Vipman4/Fotolia, (TL) Iagodina/Fotolia; **54** (BC): Kosmos111/Fotolia, (BCL) Tashatuvango/Fotolia, (BL) Piai/Fotolia; **55**: Deniskolt/Fotolia; **64** (BCL) Macrovector/Fotolia, (BCR) KEG/Shutterstock, (Bkgrd) Natbasil/Fotolia, (BR) Igor Stevanovic/Shutterstock, (C) Kudryashka/Fotolia, (CL) Zimmytws/Fotolia, (CR) Kenishirotie/Fotolia, (T) Poltorak/Fotolia, (TC) David Franklin/Fotolia, (TCR) Mizar_21984/Fotolia, (TL) Straghertni/Fotolia; **67** (T) Maridav/Shutterstock, (B) Tomertu/Shutterstock; **68** (T) Bunyarit Klinsukhon/Shutterstock, (B) S.Narongrit/Shutterstock; **69** (CL): Africa Studio/Shutterstock, (TL) Sagir/Shutterstock; **75**: Alexander Potapov/Fotolia, (BC) Catmando/Fotolia, (C) Andrey Kuzmin/Fotolia, (CL) Dengol/Fotolia, (CR) Andrea Izzotti/Fotolia; **77** (CL) Fenkieandreas/Fotolia, (CR) Fenkieandreas/Fotolia; **81** (TC) Underverse/Fotolia, (TL) Viper/Fotolia; **83**: Curiosity/Shutterstock; **99**: Catmando/Fotolia; **115**: Ryan Burke/DigitalVision Vectors/Getty Images; **117**: Mary Rice/Shutterstock; **118** (B) Logra/Shutterstock, (TCL) Garytog/Fotolia, (TL) Javen/Fotolia, (TR) Kenneth Keifer/Fotolia; **121** (T) 88studio/Shutterstock, (B) Taka1022/Shutterstock; **122** (T) Kateryna Mostova/Shutterstock, (B) Maren Winter/Shutterstock; **123**: Picsfive/Fotolia; **127** (BCR) latitude59/Fotolia, (BR) Johan Larson/Fotolia; **129** (C) Css101/Fotolia, (CL) Gvictoria/Fotolia, (CR) Photka/Fotolia; **135** (BCR) Thawats/Fotolia, (BR) Valeriy Kirsanov/Fotolia; **142** (BR) Josefpittner/Fotolia, (CL) Volodymyr Vechirnii/Fotolia; **145** (TC) Anna Bogatirewa/Shutterstock, (TL) Bazzier/Fotolia; **151** (CR): Kletr/Fotolia; **153**: Irina Kildiushova/Shutterstock; **161** (Bkgrd) Picsfive/Fotolia, (C) WavebreakMediaMicro/Fotolia, (CL) WavebreakmediaMicro/Fotolia; **166** (BR) Eskymaks/Fotolia, (TR) Marco mayer/Shutterstock; **167**: Onairjiw/Fotolia; **177**: RapidEye/iStock/Getty Images Plus/Getty Images; **179**: Marquisphoto/Shutterstock; **180** (Bkgrd) Macrovector/Fotolia, (BR) Zooropa/Fotolia; **183** (T) Wavebreakmedia/Shutterstock, (B) Connel/Shutterstock; **184** (T) Monkey Business Images/Shutterstock, (B) Sergey Lavrentev/Shutterstock; **185**: Voronin76/Shutterstock; **186**: Andersphoto/Fotolia; **187** (Bkgrd) 5second/Fotolia, (C) Imfotograf/Fotolia, (CR) Nikolaj Kondratenko/Fotolia, (TC) Gelpi/Fotolia, (TCL) Jon Barlow/Pearson Education Ltd., (TCR) Kues1/Fotolia; **191**: hagehige/Fotolia; **196**: letfluis/Fotolia; **204** (CL) Fototaras/Fotolia, (CR) Fototaras/Fotolia, **204** Giadophoto/Fotolia, **204** Weris7554/Fotolia; **215** (BR): Denyshutter/Fotolia; **219**: Tom Wang/Fotolia; **225**: Racorn/Shutterstock; **226**: yossarian6/Fotolia; **241**: Rafael Ben Ari/123RF; **243**: bloomua/Fotolia; **247**: Ron Nickel/Design Pics/Getty Images; **248**: Dani Simmonds/Fotolia; **251**: Erik Lam/Fotolia.